Fre...

A ROUGH GUIDE
PHRASEBOOK

P9-CAR-742

Compiled
by Lexus

Credits

Compiled by Lexus with Nadine Mongeard Morandi

Lexus Series Editor:	Sally Davies
Rough Guides Phrase Book Editor:	Jonathan Buckley
Rough Guides Series Editor:	Mark Ellingham

This first edition published in 1995 by Rough Guides Ltd, 1 Mercer Street, London WC2H 9QJ.

Distributed by the Penguin Group.

Penguin Books Ltd, 27 Wrights Lane, London W8 5TZ
Penguin Books USA Inc., 375 Hudson Street, New York 10014, USA
Penguin Books Australia Ltd, 487 Maroondah Highway, PO Box 257, Ringwood, Victoria 3134, Australia
Penguin Books Canada Ltd, Alcorn Avenue, Toronto, Ontario, Canada M4V 1E4
Penguin Book (NZ) Ltd, 182–190 Wairau Road, Auckland 10, New Zealand

Typeset in Rough Serif and Rough Sans to an original design by Henry Iles.
Printed by Cox & Wyman Ltd, Reading.

© Lexus Ltd 1995
240pp.

British Library Cataloguing in Publication Data
A catalogue for this book is available from the British Library.

ISBN 1-85828-144-X

CONTENTS

INTRODUCTION

The Rough Guide French phrasebook is a highly practical introduction to the contemporary language. Laid out in clear A-Z style, it uses key-word referencing to lead you straight to the words and phrases you want – so if you need to book a room, just look up 'room'. The Rough Guide gets straight to the point in every situation, in bars and shops, on trains and buses, and in hotels and banks.

The main part of the Rough Guide is a double dictionary: English-French then French-English. Before that, there's a page explaining the pronunciation system we've used, then a section called **The Basics**, which sets out the fundamental rules of the language, with plenty of practical examples. You'll also find here other essentials like numbers, dates and telling the time.

Forming the heart of the guide, the **English-French** section gives easy-to-use transliterations of the French words wherever pronunciation might be a problem, and to get you involved quickly in two-way communication, the Rough Guide includes dialogues featuring typical responses on key topics – such as renting a car and asking directions. Feature boxes fill you in on cultural pitfalls as well as the simple mechanics of how to make a phone call, what to do in an emergency, where to change money, and more. Throughout this section, cross-references enable you to pinpoint key facts and phrases, while asterisked words indicate where further information can be found in the Basics.

In the **French-English** dictionary, we've given not just the phrases you're likely to hear, but also all the signs, labels, instructions and other basic words you might come across in print or in public places.

Finally the Rough Guide rounds off with an extensive **Menu Reader**, giving a run-down of food and drink terms that you'll find indispensable whether you're eating out, stopping for a quick drink, or browsing through a local food market.

bon voyage!
have a good trip!

PRONUNCIATION

In this phrase book, the French has been written in a system of imitated pronunciation so that it can be read as though it were English. Bear in mind the notes on pronunciation given below:

AN	a French nasal sound; say the English word 'tan' clipping off the final 'n' and you are close
ay	as in m**ay**
e	as in g**e**t
g	always hard as in **g**oat
ī	as the 'i' sound in m**i**ght
j	like the 's' sound in plea**s**ure
ñ	like the final sound in lasa**gne**
ON	a French nasal sound; say the English word 'on' through your nose and cutting off the final 'n'
oo	like the 'ew' in f**ew** but without any 'y' sound
r	comes from the back of the throat
uh	like the 'e' in butt**e**r but a little longer
y	as in **y**es

The French often run together or elide a word ending with a consonant and a following word that starts with a vowel. This has been shown in the pronunciation as, for example: 'do you have ...?' **est-ce que vous avez ...?** [eskuh voo zavay]. The 'z' at the beginning of 'zavay' has been run on from the preceding word.

ABBREVIATIONS

adj	adjective	m	masculine
f	feminine	mpl	masculine plural
fpl	feminine plural	sing	singular

NOTES

In the English-French section, when two forms of the verb are given in phrases such as 'can you ...?' **est-ce tu peux/vous pouvez ...?**, the first is the familiar form and the second the polite form (see the entry for **you**).

An asterisk (*) next to a word means that you should refer to the Basics section for further information.

The Basics

the Basics

NOUNS

All French nouns have one of two genders – masculine (un / le) or feminine (une / la).

Plural Nouns

The most common way of forming the plural of a noun – of saying, for example, 'the passports' instead of 'the passport' – is by adding an -s to the singular:

le passeport	les passeports
luh pass-por	lay pass-por
the passport	the passports

le magasin	les magasins
luh magazAN	lay magazAN
the shop	the shops

This -s is not normally pronounced in French.

To make the plural of words ending in -au or -eu you add an -x:

un bureau	leurs bureaux
AN booro	lurr booro
an office	their offices

le lieu	les lieux
luh l-yuh	lay l-yuh
the place	the places

This -x is not normally pronounced in French.

To make the plural of words ending in -al change -al to -aux:

un cheval	deux chevaux
AN shuhval	duh shuhvo
a horse	two horses

One important irregular plural:

mon œil	mes yeux
mON uh-ee	may z-yuh
my eye	my eyes

ARTICLES

The words for articles ('the' and 'a') in French vary according to three elements:

the gender of the noun
the first letter of the noun
whether the noun is
   singular or plural

Singular Articles

The equivalents for saying 'the' are:

le luh	for masculine singular nouns
la	for feminine singular nouns

In front of a noun beginning with a vowel (or an 'h' that is not pronounced) le and la change to l'.

le marché	la gare
luh marshay	la gar
the market	the station

l'homme	l'actrice
lom	laktreess
the man	the actress

The equivalents for saying 'a' are:

un AN   for all masculine nouns
une OOn   for all feminine nouns

un marché	une gare
AN marshay	OOn gar
a market	a station

Plural Articles

les lay   for both masculine and feminine nouns

les marchés	les gares
lay marshay	lay gar
the markets	the stations

les hommes	les actrices
lay zom	lay zaktreess
the men	the actresses

The plural form of the indefinite article, translated in English as 'some', or often omitted, is des day:

des marchés
day marshay
(some) markets

des gares
day gar
(some) stations

PREPOSITIONS

When used with the prepositions de and à, the definite article may change its form:

If you are using le / les with de (of; from) make the following changes:

de + le = du   dOO
de + les = des day

With à (to; at) make these changes:

à + le = au   o
à + les = aux o

le nom du supermarché
luh NON dOO sOOpairmarshay
the name of the supermarket

il vient des Etats-Unis
eel v-yAN day zaytazOOnee
he comes from the United States

au supermarché
o sOOpairmarshay
at the supermarket

aux Etats-Unis
o zaytazOOnee
to the United States

If you are using la or l' the preposition does not change.

à la plage	à l'hôtel
a la plahj	a lotel
at the beach	at the hotel

ADJECTIVES AND ADVERBS

In French, adjectives have to 'agree' with the noun they are used with. This means that if a noun is feminine, then an adjective used with it must be in the feminine form too. If a noun is plural, then an adjective used with it must be in the plural form too, masculine or feminine. In the English into French section of this book, all adjectives are translated by the masculine form – the form used with nouns preceded by un or le.

For most adjectives, the feminine form is made by adding -e. The plural is formed in two ways: for those with masculine nouns, by adding -s; and for those with feminine nouns, by adding -es. Plurals for adjectives ending in -au are usually formed by adding -x, although the -s or -x is not pronounced.

Important exceptions are shown in the English into French section.

un journal allemand
AN joornal almON
a German newspaper

une famille allemande
OOn famee almOND
a German family

des journaux américains
day joorno zamaayreekAN
American newspapers

deux familles écossaises
duh famee zaykossez
two Scottish families

Most adjectives in French, as in these examples, are placed after the noun, not in front of it as in English.

Some common adjectives, however, are put in front of nouns:

beau	bo	beautiful
long	lON	long
bon	bON	good
joli	jolee	pretty
mauvais	movay	bad
gentil	jONtee	nice
nouveau	noovo	new
grand	grON	big
petit	puhtee	little
jeune	jurn	young
vieux	vyuh	old

Comparatives

To say that something is, for example, more expensive or faster than something else, you use the comparative form of the adjective (or adverb). In French these are all formed by using the word **plus** in front of the adjective or adverb:

grand	plus grand
groN	pl00 groN
big	bigger

intéressant	plus intéressant
ANtayressoN	pl00 zANtayressoN
interesting	more interesting

je voudrais une plus grande chambre
juh voodray z00n pl00 groNd shoNbr
I'd like a bigger room

c'est plus intéressant que le château
say pl00 zANtayressoN kuh luh shato
it's more interesting than the castle

cette plage est plus calme que l'autre
set plahj ay pl00 kalm kuh lohtr
this beach is quieter than the other one

pouvez-vous parler plus clairement, s'il vous plaît?
poovay-voo parlay pl00 klairmoN seel voo play
could you speak more clearly please?

'As ... as' is translated as follows:

ce restaurant est aussi cher que l'autre
suh restoroN ay tohsee shair kuh lohtr
this restaurant is as expensive as the other one

ce n'était pas aussi cher que je croyais
suh naytay pa zohsee shair kuh juh krwy-ay
it wasn't as expensive as I thought

aussi lentement que possible
ohsee loNtuhmoN kuh posseebl
as slowly as possible

Superlatives

To say that something is, for example, the most expensive or the fastest, you use the superlative form of the adjective (or adverb). This is formed by using the words **le plus** in front of the adjective for a masculine singular noun; **la plus** for a feminine singular noun; and **les plus** for a plural noun (see **ADJECTIVES**):

grand	le plus grand
grON	luh plOO grON
big	biggest

intéressant	le plus intéressant
ANtayressON	luh plOO zANtayressON
interesting	most interesting

le plus grand hôtel de la ville
luh plOO grON otel duh la veel
the biggest hotel in town

où est la poste la plus
  proche?
oo ay la posst la plOO prosh
where is the nearest post
  office?

le barman parle le plus
  clairement
luh barman parl luh plOO
  klairmON
the barman speaks the
  most clearly

Some forms are irregular:

bon	bON	good
meilleur	may-yurr	better
le meilleur	luh may-yurr	best

mauvais	mo-vay	bad
pire	peer	worse
le pire	luh peer	worst

Adverbs

Adverbs are formed by adding
-ment to the feminine form of
the adjective if it ends in a
consonant, and to the masculine form if it ends in a vowel:

vrai / vraie	vraiment
vray	vraymON
real	really

final / finale	finalement
feenal	feenalmON
final	finally

Adjectives which end in -ent
and -ant change to -emment
and -amment:

évident	évidemment
ayveedON	ayveedamON
obvious	obviously

constant	constamment
kONstON	kONstamON
constant	constantly

But not:

lent	lentement
lON	lONtuhmON
slow	slowly

Some forms are irregular:

bon	bien
bON	b-yAN
good	well

mauvais	mal
movay	mal
bad	badly

meilleur	mieux
may-yurr	m-yuh
better	better

Possessive Adjectives

If you want to say that something is 'your car' or 'his car' or 'her car' etc, then you use the following words in French. Notice that there are three forms: one for masculine words (given with le in the phrase book); one for feminine words (given with la); and one for plural words.

feminine	masculine	plural
my	mon	mON
ma	ma	mes
may		
your	ton	tON
ta	ta	tes
tay		
his / its	son	sON
sa	sa	ses
say		
her / its	son	sON
sa	sa	ses
say		
our	notre	notr
notre	notr	nos
no		
your	votre	votr
votre	votr	vos
vo		
their	leur	lurr
leur	lurr	leurs
lurr		

Some points to note:

The forms ton / ta / tes are used for people you are speaking to as tu. The forms votre / vos are used for people you are speaking to as vous (see PRONOUNS).

Whether you use son / sa or mon / ma depends on the gender of the thing / person 'possessed'. So for example:

> **ma chambre**
> ma shONbr
> my room

can be said by both a man and a woman. Likewise:

> **sa chambre**
> sa shONbr

can mean either 'his room' or 'her room'.

If this is confusing you can say:

> **sa chambre à lui**
> sa shONbr a lwee
> his room

> **sa chambre à elle**
> sa shONbr a el
> her room

Ma / ta / sa change to mon / ton / son in front of a vowel:

> **mon épouse**
> mON aypooz
> my wife

PRONOUNS

Subject Pronouns

If you are using a pronoun as the subject of a verb, saying 'he is' or 'we are' or 'can you?' etc, the words are:

je	juh	I
tu	too	you
il	eel	he / it
elle	el	she / it
nous	noo	we
vous	voo	you
ils	eel	they
elles	el	they

Points to note:

YOU: tu is used when speaking to someone who is a friend, or to someone of your own general age group with whom you want to establish a friendly atmosphere. **Vous** is used when speaking to several friends (ie it is the plural of tu) or when speaking to someone you don't know. In the vast majority of cases, as a foreigner in France you will use the **vous** form. Certainly, if you are in any doubt as to which form to use, choose the **vous** form.

IT: if you are using 'it' to refer to something like 'the car', 'the train' etc (as opposed to saying 'it is cold today' etc), you should use either il or elle depending on the gender of the thing you are talking about (see ARTICLES). For example, la voiture (the car) is elle (it) and le train (the train) is il (it).

Direct Object Pronouns

If you are using the pronoun as an object, saying 'Peter knows him' or 'Mary saw them' etc, you must use the following object pronouns, which will normally precede the verb:

me	muh	me
te	tuh	you
le	luh	him / it
la	la	her / it
nous	noo	us
vous	voo	you
les	lay	them

je le vois
juh luh vwa
I see him

il les a achetés
eel lay za ashtay
he bought them

vous me comprenez?
voo muh koNpruhnay
do you understand me?

Indirect Object Pronouns

If you are using a pronoun to say, for example, you sent something to her or that you spoke to him, then you must use the following indirect object pronouns:

me	muh	to me
te	tuh	to you
lui	lwee	to him / her / it
nous	noo	to us
vous	voo	to you
leur	lurr	to them

> **je lui ai écrit**
> juh lwee ay aykree
> I wrote to him

> **je le lui ai expliqué**
> juh luh lwee ay expleekay
> I explained it to him

Emphatic Pronouns

If you are using a pronoun to say 'it's me', 'with her', 'for them' etc, then you must use the following emphatic pronouns:

moi	mwa	me
toi	twa	you
lui	lwee	him
elle	el	her
nous	noo	us
vous	voo	you
eux	uh	them
elles	el	them

> **c'est eux**
> set uh
> it's them

> **venez avec moi**
> vuhnay avek mwa
> come with me

> **ces cafés sont pour nous**
> say kafay SON poor noo
> those coffees are for us

A useful word for 'it' or 'that' to refer to a specific thing, or a more general situation, is **ça** sa:

> **donne-moi ça!**
> don mwa sa
> give it / that to me!

> **tu as vu ça?**
> too a voo sa
> did you see that?

Reflexive Pronouns

These are used with reflexive verbs like **se laver** (to get washed, to wash oneself), where the subject and the object are the same.

me	muh	myself
te	tuh	yourself
se	suh	himself / herself / itself
nous	noo	ourselves
vous	voo	yourself / yourselves
se	suh	themselves

There are many more verbs used reflexively in French than in English. Some examples are:

> **je m'appelle Anna**
> juh mapel anna
> I am called Anna

> **nous nous levons toujours de bonne heure**
> noo noo luhvON toojoor duh bon urr
> we always get up early

> **ils se sont bien amusés**
> eel suh SON b-yAN amOOzay
> they enjoyed themselves very much

Possessive Pronouns

If you want to say that something is yours or his or hers etc, then you use the following possessive pronouns. Notice that there are four forms: masculine singular and plural, and feminine singular and plural:

	m sing	mpl	
mine	le mien	les miens	luh / lay m-yAN
yours	le tien	les tiens	luh / lay t-yAN
his / its	le sien	les siens	luh / lay s-yAN
hers / its	le sien	les siens	luh / lay s-yAN
ours	le nôtre	les nôtres	luh / lay nohtr
yours	le vôtre	les vôtres	luh / lay vohtr
theirs	le leur	les leurs	luh / lay lurr

	f sing	fpl	
mine	la mienne	les miennes	luh / lay m-yen
yours	la tienne	les tiennes	luh / lay t-yen
his / its	la sienne	les siennes	luh / lay s-yen
hers / its	la sienne	les siennes	luh / lay s-yen
ours	la nôtre	les nôtres	luh / lay nohtr
yours	la vôtre	les vôtres	luh / lay vohtr
theirs	la leur	les leurs	luh / lay lurr

Again, the use of 'le sien / la sienne' and 'le mien / la mienne' etc will depend on the gender of the thing(s) possessed:

cette voiture n'est pas la nôtre
set vwatOOr nay pa la nohtr
this car isn't ours

cette valise est la mienne, la tienne est là-bas
set valeez ay la m-yen, la t-yen ay la-ba
this suitcase is mine, yours is over there

After the verb être (to be), the possessive pronouns can be replaced by à + the appropriate emphatic pronoun (see **PRONOUNS**).

ce sac est à moi
suh sak ay ta mwa
this bag is mine

est-ce que cet appareil photo est à vous?
eskuh set aparay foto ay ta voo
is this camera yours?

VERBS

There are three main verb types, recognizable by their endings: -er, -ir, and -re.

Present Tense

The present tense of a verb corresponds to 'you are doing' or 'you do' or 'something happens' etc. To form the present tense for the three main types of verb, remove the endings and conjugate as follows:

donner (to give)

je donne [juh don]	I give
tu donnes [tOO don]	you give
il / elle donne [eel / el don]	he / she gives
nous donnons [noo donON]	we give
vous donnez [voo donay]	you give
ils / elles donnent [eel / el don]	they give

finir (to finish)

je finis [juh feenee]	I finish
tu finis [tOO feenee]	you finish
il / elle finit [eel / el feenee]	he / she finishes
nous finissons [noo feeneessON]	we finish
vous finissez [voo feeneessay]	you finish
ils / elles finissent [eel / el feeneess]	they finish

attendre (to wait)

j'attends [jatON]	I wait
tu attends [tOO atON]	you wait
il / elle attend [eel / el atON]	he / she waits
nous attendons [noo zatONdON]	we wait
vous attendez [voo zatONday]	you wait
ils / elles attendent [eel / el zatONd]	they wait

Remember that this tense also covers English forms like 'I am doing':

je lui parle
juh lwee parl
I talk to him OR I'm talking to him

Some common verbs have irregular forms in the present tense:

aller (to go)

je vais	juh vay
tu vas	tOO va
il / elle va	eel / el va
nous allons	noo zalON
vous allez	voo zalay
ils / elles vont	eel / el vON

boire (to drink)

je bois	bwa
tu bois	bwa
il / elle boit	bwa
nous buvons	bOOvON
vous buvez	bOOvay
ils / elles boivent	bwav

devoir (to have to, must)

je dois	dwa
tu dois	dwa
il / elle doit	dwa
nous devons	duhvON
vous devez	duhvay
ils / elles doivent	dwav

dire (to say)

je dis	dee
tu dis	dee
il / elle dit	dee
nous disons	deezON
vous dites	deet
ils / elles disent	deez

faire (to do, to make)

je fais	fay
tu fais	fay
il / elle fait	fay
nous faisons	fuhzON
vous faites	fet
ils / elles font	fON

partir (to leave, to go away)

je pars	par
tu pars	par
il / elle part	par
nous partons	partON
vous partez	partay
ils / elles partent	part

pouvoir (to be able to)

je peux	juh puh
tu peux	too puh
il / elle peut	eel / el puh
nous pouvons	noo poovON
vous pouvez	voo poovay
ils / elles peuvent	eel / el puhv

savoir (to know)

je sais	say
tu sais	say
il / elle sait	say
nous savons	savON
vous savez	savay
ils / elles savent	sav

sortir (to go out)

je sors	sor
tu sors	sor
il / elle sort	sor
nous sortons	sortON
vous sortez	sortay
ils / elles sortent	sort

venir (to come)

je viens	juh v-yAN
tu viens	too v-yAN
il / elle vient	eel / el v-yAN
nous venons	noo vuhnON
vous venez	voo vuhnay
ils / elles viennent	eel / el v-yen

vouloir (to want)

je veux	juh vuh
tu veux	too vuh
il / elle veut	eel / el vuh
nous voulons	noo voolON
vous voulez	voo voolay
ils / elles veulent	eel / el vurl

See also **PAST TENSES** for avoir (to have) and être (to be).

Past Tenses: Perfect Tense

To put something into the perfect tense – to say that 'you have done' or 'did do' something – you use the present tense of the verb avoir plus the past participle of the verb:

avoir (to have)

j'ai	jay
tu as	too a
il / elle a	eel / el a
nous avons	noo zavON
vous avez	voo zavay
ils / elles ont	eel / el zON

A basic rule for forming the past participle is: for verbs ending in -er, change -er to -é (pronunciation same: ay); for verbs ending in -ir, change -ir to -i; for verbs ending in -re, change -re to -u.

où est-ce que vous avez mangé hier soir?
oo eskuh voo zavay mONjay yair swahr
where did you eat last night?

GRAMMAR

nous avons visité la
  cathédrale cet après-midi
noo zavON veezeetay la kataydral
  set apray-meedee
we visited the cathedral
  this afternoon

vous avez fini de manger?
voo zavay feenee duh mONjay
have you finished eating?

je l'ai attendu toute la journée
juh lay atONdoo toot la joornay
I waited for him all day

For some verbs the perfect
tense is formed using être
instead of avoir.

être (literal sense: to be)

je suis	juh swee
tu es	too ay
il / elle est	eel / el ay
nous sommes	noo som
vous êtes	voo zet
ils / elles sont	eel / el sON

The most common and useful of these are:

aller	to go	je suis allé	juh swee alay
arriver	to arrive	arrivé	areevay
descendre	to go / come down	descendu	duhsONdoo
entrer	to go / come in	entré	ONtray
monter	to go / come up	monté	mONtay
naître	to be born	né	nay
partir	to leave / go away	parti	partee
passer	to pass	passé	passay
rentrer	to go / come back	rentré	rONtray
rester	to stay	resté	restay
retourner	to return	retourné	ruhtoornay
revenir	to come back	revenu	ruhvuhnoo
sortir	to go / come out	sorti	sortee
tomber	to fall	tombé	tONbay
venir	to come	venu	vuhnoo

il est parti
eel ay partee
he has left

nous sommes revenus samedi dernier
noo som ruhvuhnoo samdee dairn-yay
we came back last Saturday

elle est restée deux semaines
el ay restay duh suhmen
she stayed for two weeks

je suis rentré très tard hier soir
juh swee rONtray tray tar yair swahr
I got home very late last night

The following verbs have irregular past participles:

avoir	to have	eu	oo
comprendre	to understand	compris	kONpree
connaître	to know (person, place)	connu	konoo
croire	to believe	cru	kroo
devoir	to have to	dû	doo
dire	to say	dit	dee
disparaître	to disappear	disparu	deesparoo
être	to be	été	aytay
mourir*	to die	mort	mor
naître*	to be born	né	nay
offrir	to offer	offert	ofair
ouvrir	to open	ouvert	oovair
permettre	to allow	permis	pairmee
plaire	to please	plu	ploo
pouvoir	to be able to	pu	poo
prendre	to take	pris	pree
recevoir	to receive	reçu	ruhsoo
s'asseoir*	to sit down	assis	assee
savoir	to know	su	soo
venir*	to come	venu	vuhnoo
voir	to see	vu	voo
vouloir	to want	voulu	vooloo

* conjugated with être

Imperfect Tense

This is used to describe an action in the past which was repeated, habitual, or often taking place over a period of time. To put something into the imperfect tense – to say that you 'were doing', 'used to do', or 'did do' something – change the verb endings as follows:

donner (to give)

I was giving, I used to give, I gave etc

je donnais	juh donay
tu donnais	too donay
il / elle donnait	eel / el donay
nous donnions	noo donee-ON
vous donniez	voo donee-ay
ils / elles donnaient	eel / el donay

finir (to finish)

I was finishing, I used to finish, I finished etc

je finissais	juh feeneessay
tu finissais	too feeneessay
il / elle finissait	eel / el feeneessay
nous finissions	noo feeneessee-ON
vous finissiez	voo feeneessee-ay
ils / elles finissaient	eel / el feeneessay

attendre (to wait)

I was waiting, I used to wait, I waited etc

j'attendais	jatONday
tu attendais	too atONday
il / elle attendait	eel / el atONday
nous attendions	noo zatONdee-ON
vous attendiez	voo zatONdee-ay
ils / elles attendaient	eel / el zatONday

Three common verbs have irregular imperfect tenses:

être (to be)

j'étais	jaytay	I was
tu étais	too aytay	you were
il / elle était	eel / el aytay	he / she / it was
nous étions	noo zaytee-ON	we were
vous étiez	voo zaytee-ay	you were
ils / elles étaient	eel / el zaytay	they were

avoir (to have)

j'avais	javay	I had
tu avais	too avay	you had
il / elle avait	eel / el avay	he / she / it had
nous avions	noo zavee-ON	we had
vous aviez	voo zavee-ay	you had
ils / elles avaient	eel / el zavay	they had

faire (to do, to make)

je faisais	juh fuhzay	I did
tu faisais	too fuhzay	you did
il / elle faisait	eel / el fuhzay	he / she / it / did
nous faisions	noo fuhzee-ON	we did
vous faisiez	voo fuhzee-ay	you did
ils / elles faisaient	eel / el fuhzay	they did

Future Tense

To talk about what is going to happen in the future both French and English very often use the present tense (see Present), for example:

nous allons à la plage demain
noo zalON a la plahj duhmAN
we're going to the beach tomorrow

il rentre bientôt à Londres
eel rONtr b-yANto a lONdr
he's going back to London soon

French often uses the present tense where English uses the future:

j'arrive dans une minute
jareev dON zoon meenoot
I'll be there in a minute

The actual future tense in French, used to say 'I will, you will' etc, is formed by making the following changes:

donner (to give) - I etc will give

je donnerai	donuhray	nous donnerons	donuhrON
tu donneras	donuhra	vous donnerez	donuhray
il / elle donnera	donuhra	ils / elles donneront	donuhrON

finir (to finish) - I etc will finish

je finirai	feeneeray	nous finirons	feeneerON
tu finiras	feeneera	vous finirez	feeneeray
il / elle finira	feeneera	ils / elles finiront	feeneerON

attendre (to wait) - I etc will wait

j'attendrai	atONdray	nous attendrons	atONdrON
tu attendras	atONdra	vous attendrez	atONdray
il / elle attendra	atONdra	ils / elles attendront	atONdrON

Some common irregular verbs:

être (to be) - I etc will be

je serai	suhray	nous serons	suhrON
tu seras	suhra	vous serez	suhray
il / elle sera	suhra	ils / elles seront	suhrON

avoir (to have) - I etc will have

j'aurai	joray	nous aurons	orON
tu auras	ora	vous aurez	oray
il / elle aura	ora	ils / elles auront	orON

aller (to go) - I etc will go

j'irai	jeeray	nous irons	eerON
tu iras	eera	vous irez	eeray
il / elle ira	eera	ils / elles iront	eerON

venir (to come) - I etc will come

je viendrai	v-yANdray	nous viendrons	v-yANdrON
tu viendras	v-yANdra	vous viendrez	v-yANdray
il / elle viendra	v-yANdra	ils / elles viendront	v-yANdrON

Some examples:

mes enfants arriveront demain
may ZONfON areevuhrON duhmAN
my children will be arriving
tomorrow

**j'espère qu'il fera beau
demain**
jespair keel fuhra bo duhmAN
I hope it'll be fine
tomorrow

Negatives

To express a negative in
French – to say 'I don't
know', 'it's not here' etc –
you use the words ne ... pas
placed around the verb:

j'ai faim   je n'ai pas faim
jay fAN   juh nay pa fAN
I'm hungry   I'm not hungry

il aime la glace
eel em la glass
he likes ice cream

il n'aime pas la glace
eel nem pa la glass
he doesn't like ice cream

elle a une voiture
el a OOn vwatOOr
she has a car

elle n'a pas de voiture
el na pa duh vwatOOr
she doesn't have a car

If the verb is in the past tense
(see **Perfect Tense**) the ne ...
pas is used as follows:

je l'ai vu   je ne l'ai pas vu
juh lay vOO   juh nuh lay pa vOO
I saw him   I didn't see him

The following negatives work
in the same way as ne ... pas:

ne ... jamais
nuh ... jamay
never

ne ... plus
nuh ... plOO
no more

ne ... rien
nuh ... ree-AN
nothing

je n'y suis jamais allé
juh nee swee jamay alay
I've never been there

il ne boit plus de bière
eel nuh bwa plOO duh bee-air
he doesn't drink beer any
more

nous n'avons rien acheté
nOO navON ree-AN ashtay
we didn't buy anything

If there is no verb, just use
pas:

pas toi!
pa twa
not you!

comment vas-tu? – pas mal
komON va-tOO – pa mal
how are you? – not bad

In spoken French, the ne is
often left out:

c'est pas possible!
say pa posseebl
impossible!

To say 'no' with nouns (no sugar, no cigarettes) use **pas de**:

pas de vin pour moi, merci
pa duh VAN poor mwa mairsee
no wine for me thanks

il n'y a pas d'eau chaude
eel nya pa do shohd
there is no (isn't any) hot water

Imperative

To express commands in French, remove the endings -er, -ir or -re and then add the following endings.

	tu	vous
donner (to give)	donne don give	donnez donay
finir (to finish)	finis feenee finish	finissez feeneessay
attendre (to wait)	attends atON wait	attendez atONday

Some examples:

regardez!
ruhgarday
look!

allez-vous-en!
alay-voo zoN
go away!

dites-moi!
deet-mwa
tell me!

apporte-moi ça!
aport-mwa sa
bring me that!

To tell someone not to do something, to give a negative command, put the words **ne ... pas** around the forms as given above, for example:

n'attends pas   n'attendez pas
natON pa   natONday pa
don't wait

ne parlez pas si vite!
nuh parlay pa see veet
don't speak so quickly!

ne me regarde pas comme ça!
nuh muh ruhgard pa kom sa
don't look at me like that!

Some irregular forms:

ne sois / soyez pas en colère
nuh swa / swy-yay pa ON kolair
don't be angry

viens / venez avec moi!
v-yAN / vuhnay avek mwa
come with me!

On signs you might see the form:

ne pas toucher
nuh pa tooshay
do not touch

QUESTIONS

Often word order remains the same in a question, but the intonation changes – the voice should be raised at the end of the question.

vous parlez anglais?
voo parlay ONglay
do you speak English?

The word order can also be inverted to form a question. If the subject is a pronoun, subject and verb are inverted, and linked with a hyphen:

parlez-vous anglais?
parlay-voo ONglay
do you speak English?

If the subject is a noun, the verb is placed with the relevant pronoun after the subject, inserting -t- between verb and pronoun where the verb ends in a vowel:

le directeur parle-t-il anglais?
luh deerekturr parlteel ONglay
does the manager speak English?

Both the above types of question may be introduced by est-ce que? The word order then remains the same as that of a statement:

est-ce que vous parlez anglais?
eskuh voo parlay ONglay
do you speak English?

DATES

Use the numbers on pages 23-24 to express the date, except for the first, when le premier should be used:

le premier septembre
the first of September
luh pruhm-yay septONbr

le deux décembre
the second of December
luh duh daysONbr

le trois mars
the third of March
luh trwa marss

le vingt mai
the twentieth of May
luh vaN may

le vingt-et-un juin
the twenty-first of June
luh vaNtay-aN jwaN

TIME

a.m.	du matin
	doo mataN
p.m.	
(afternoon)	de l'après-midi
	duh lapray-meedee
(evening)	du soir
	doo swahr

what time is it? quelle heure est-il? [kel urr eteel]
one o'clock une heure [oon urr]
two o'clock deux heures [duh zur]
it's one o'clock il est une heure [eel ay oon urr]

it's two o'clock il est deux heures [eel ay duh zurr]

it's ten o'clock il est dix heures [eel ay dee zurr]

five past one une heure cinq [ᴏᴏn urr sᴀɴk]

ten past two deux heures dix [duh zurr deess]

quarter past one une heure et quart [ᴏᴏn urr ay kar]

quarter past two deux heures et quart [duh zurr ay kar]

half past ten dix heures et demie [dee zurr ay duhmee]

twenty to ten dix heures moins vingt [dee zurr mwᴀɴ vᴀɴ]

quarter to two deux heures moins le quart [duh zurr mwᴀɴ luh kar]

at half past four à quatre heures et demie [a katr urr ay duhmee]

at eight o'clock à huit heures [a weet urr]

14.00 quatorze heures [katorz urr]

17.30 dix-sept heures trente [deesset urr trᴏɴt]

2 a.m. deux heures du matin [duh zurr dᴏᴏ matᴀɴ]

2 p.m. deux heures de l'après-midi [duh zurr duh lapray-meedee]

6 a.m. six heures du matin [seez urr dᴏᴏ matᴀɴ]

6 p.m. six heures du soir [seez urr dᴏᴏ swahr]

noon midi [meedee]

midnight minuit [meenwee]

an hour une heure [ᴏᴏn urr]

a minute une minute [ᴏᴏn meenᴏᴏt]

two minutes deux minutes [duh meenᴏᴏt]

a second une seconde [ᴏᴏn suhgᴏɴd]

a quarter of an hour un quart d'heure [ᴀɴ kar durr]

half an hour une demi-heure [ᴏᴏn duhmee urr]

three quarters of an hour trois quarts d'heure [trwa kar durr]

NUMBERS

0	zéro [zayro]
1	un [ᴀɴ]
2	deux [duh]
3	trois [trwa]
4	quatre [katr]
5	cinq [sᴀɴk]
6	six [seess]
7	sept [set]
8	huit [weet]
9	neuf [nuhf]
10	dix [deess]
11	onze [ᴏɴz]
12	douze [dooz]
13	treize [trez]
14	quartorze [katorz]
15	quinze [kᴀɴz]
16	seize [sez]
17	dix-sept [deesset]
18	dix-huit [deez-weet]
19	dix-neuf [deez-nuhf]
20	vingt [vᴀɴ]
21	vingt-et-un [vᴀɴtay-ᴀɴ]
22	vingt-deux [vᴀɴ-duh]

23	vingt-trois [vAN-trwa]	6th	sixième [seez-yem]
30	trente [trONt]	7th	septième [set-yem]
31	trente-et-un	8th	huitième [weet-yem]
	[trONtay-AN]	9th	neuvième [nuhv-yem]
40	quarante [karONt]	10th	dixième [deez-yem]
50	cinquante [sANkONt]		
60	soixante [swassONt]		
70	soixante-dix		
	[swassONt-deess]		
80	quatre-vingts		
	[katr-vAN]		
90	quatre-vingt-dix		
	[katr-vAN-deess]		
100	cent [sON]		
110	cent dix [sON deess]		
200	deux cents [duh sON]		
1,000	mille [meel]		
2,000	deux mille		
	[duh meel]		
5,000	cinq mille [sANk meel]		
1,000,000	un million [AN meel-yON]		

In French, millions are
written with spaces instead of
commas, e.g. 1 500 000.
Thousands are written
without spaces or commas,
e.g. 2700. Decimals are
written with a comma, e.g.
3.5 would be 3,5 in French.

Ordinals

1st	premier [pruhm-yay]	
2nd	deuxième [duhz-yem]	
3rd	troisième [trwaz-yem]	
4th	quatrième [katree-yem]	
5th	cinquième [sANk-yem]	

CONVERSION TABLES

1 centimetre = 0.39 inches

1 metre = 39.37 inches =
  1.09 yards

1 kilometre = 0.62 miles =
  5/8 mile

1 inch = 2.54 cm

1 foot = 30.48 cm

1 yard = 0.91 m

1 mile = 1.61 km

km	1	2	3	4	5	10	20	30	40	50	100
miles	0.6	1.2	1.9	2.5	3.1	6.2	12.4	18.6	24.8	31.0	62.1

miles	1	2	3	4	5	10	20	30	40	50	100
km	1.6	3.2	4.8	6.4	8.0	16.1	32.2	48.3	64.4	80.5	161

1 gram = 0.035 ounces

g	100	250	500
oz	3.5	8.75	17.5

1 kilo = 1000 g = 2.2 pounds

1 oz = 28.35 g

1 lb = 0.45 kg

kg	0.5	1	2	3	4	5	6	7	8	9	10
lb	1.1	2.2	4.4	6.6	8.8	11.0	13.2	15.4	17.6	19.8	22.0

kg	20	30	40	50	60	70	80	90	100
lb	44	66	88	110	132	154	176	198	220

lb	0.5	1	2	3	4	5	6	7	8	9	10	20
kg	0.2	0.5	0.9	1.4	1.8	2.3	2.7	3.2	3.6	4.1	4.5	9.0

1 litre = 1.75 UK pints / 2.13 US pints

1 UK pint = 0.57 l

1 US pint = 0.47 l

1 UK gallon = 4.55 l

1 US gallon = 3.79 l

centigrade / Celsius

$C = (F - 32) \times 5/9$

C	-5	0	5	10	15	18	20	25	30	36.8	38
F	23	32	41	50	59	64	68	77	86	98.4	100.4

Fahrenheit

$F = (C \times 9/5) + 32$

F	23	32	40	50	60	65	70	80	85	98.4	101
C	-5	0	4	10	16	18	21	27	29	36.8	38.3

English-French

A

a, an* un, une [AN, ᴏᴏn]
about: about 20 environ vingt
[ᴏNveerᴏN]
  it's about 5 o'clock il est cinq
  heures environ
  a film about France un film
  sur la France [sᴏᴏr]
above au-dessus de [o-duh-sᴏᴏ
  duh]
abroad à l'étranger
  [a laytrᴏNjay]
absolutely (I agree) absolument
  [absolᴏᴏmᴏN]
accelerator l'accélérateur m
  [axaylayraturr]
accept accepter [axeptay]
accident l'accident m [axeedᴏN]
  there's been an accident il y a
  eu un accident [eelya ᴏᴏ]
accommodation le logement
  [lojmᴏN]
  see hotel and room
accurate précis [praysee]
ache la douleur [doolurr]
  my back aches j'ai mal au dos
  [jay]
across: across the road de
  l'autre côté de la route [duh
  lohtr kohtay duh]
adapter l'adaptateur m
  [adaptaturr]
  (plug) la prise multiple [preez
  mᴏᴏlteepl]
address l'adresse f [adress]
  what's your address? quelle
  est votre adresse? [kel ay votr]
address book le carnet

d'adresses [karnay dadress]
admission charge le droit
  d'entrée [drwa dᴏNtray]
adult l'adulte mf [adᴏᴏlt]
advance: in advance d'avance
  [davᴏNss]
aeroplane l'avion m [av-yᴏN]
after après [apray]
  after you après toi/vous [twa/
  voo]
afternoon l'après-midi m [apray-
  meedee]
  in the afternoon l'après-midi
  this afternoon cet après-midi
aftershave l'après-rasage m
  [apray-razahj]
aftersun cream la crème après-
  soleil [krem apray-solay]
afterwards ensuite [ᴏNsweet]
again de nouveau [duh noovo]
against contre [kᴏNtr]
age l'âge m [ahj]
ago: a week ago il y a une
  semaine [eelya]
  an hour ago il y a une heure
agree: I agree je suis d'accord
  [juh swee dakor]
AIDS le SIDA [seeda]
air l'air m
  by air en avion [ᴏN avyᴏN]
air-conditioning la climatisation
  [kleemateezass-yᴏN]
airmail: by airmail par avion
  [avyᴏN]
airmail envelope l'enveloppe
  par avion f [ᴏNvlop par avyᴏN]
airport l'aéroport m [a-airopor]
  to the airport, please à
  l'aéroport, s'il vous plaît

airport bus la navette de l'aéroport [navet]

aisle seat la place côté couloir [plass kohtay koolwahr]

alarm clock le réveil [rayvay]

alcohol l'alcool m [alkol]

alcoholic alcoolisé [alkoleezay]

Algeria l'Algérie f [aljayree]

Algerian (adj) algérien [aljayree-AN]

all: all the boys tous les garçons [too]

all the girls toutes les filles [toot]

all of it tout [too]

all of them tous [tooss]

that's all, thanks c'est tout, merci

allergic: I'm allergic to ... je suis allergique à ... [juh swee alairjeek]

allowed: is it allowed? est-ce que c'est permis? [eskuh say pairmee]

all right d'accord [dakor]

I'm all right ça va [sa]

are you all right? ça va?

almond l'amande f [amONd]

almost presque [presk]

alone seul [surl]

alphabet l'alphabet m [alfabay]

a ah	h ash	o o	v vay
b bay	i ee	p pay	w doobl-vay
c say	j jee	q koo	x eeks
d day	k ka	r air	y ee-grek
e uh	l el	s ess	z zed
f ef	m em	t tay	
g jay	n en	u oo	

Alps les Alpes fpl [alp]

already déjà [dayja]

also aussi [o-see]

although bien que [b-yAN kuh]

altogether en tout [ON too]

always toujours [toojoor]

am*: I am je suis [juh swee]

a.m.: at seven a.m. à sept heures du matin [urr doo matAN]

amazing (surprising) étonnant [aytonON]

(very good) remarquable [ruhmark-abl]

ambulance l'ambulance f [ONboolONss]

call an ambulance! appelez une ambulance! [aplay]

Call **Police Secours (17)** or the **Pompiers (18)** for an ambulance.

America l'Amérique f [amayreek]

American américain(e) [amayreekAN, -ken]

I'm American (man/woman) je suis américain/américaine

among parmi [parmee]

amount la quantité [kONteetay]

(money) la somme [som]

amp: a 13-amp fuse un fusible de 13 ampères [foozeebl ... ONpair]

amphitheatre l'amphithéâtre m [ONfeetay-ahtr]

and et [ay]

Andorra Andorre f [ONdor]

angry fâché [fashay]

animal l'animal m [aneemal]
ankle la cheville [shuhvee]
anniversary (wedding)
l'anniversaire de mariage m
[aneevairsair duh maree-ahj]
annoy: this man's annoying me
cet homme m'importune
[ANportOOn]
annoying ennuyeux [ONwee-uh]
another un autre [ohtr]
can we have another room?
est-ce que nous pouvons
avoir une autre chambre?
[eskuh noo poovON zavwa OOn
ohtr]
another beer, please encore
une bière, s'il vous plaît
[ONkor]
antibiotics les antibiotiques
[ONteebeeoteek]
antifreeze l'antigel m [ONteejel]
antihistamine
l'antihistaminique m [ONtee-
eestameeneek]
antique: is it an antique? est-ce
un objet d'époque? [ess AN
objay daypok]
antique shop l'antiquaire m
[ONteekair]
antiseptic le désinfectant
[dayzANfektON]
any: have you got any bread/
tomatoes? avez-vous du pain/
des tomates? [avay-voo dOO .../
day]
do you have any change?
avez-vous de la monnaie?
[duh]
sorry, I don't have any désolé,

je n'en ai pas [juh nON ay pa]
anybody quelqu'un [kelkAN]
does anybody speak English?
est-ce qu'il y a quelqu'un
qui parle anglais? [eskeel-ya
ONgleh]
there wasn't anybody there il
n'y avait personne [pairson]
anything n'importe quoi

•••••• DIALOGUES ••••••

anything else? désirez-vous autre
chose? [dayzeeray-voo ohtr shohz]
nothing else, thanks c'est tout,
merci [say too mairsee]

would you like anything to drink?
veux-tu/voulez-vous boire
quelque chose? [vuh-tOO/voolay-voo
bwahr kelkuh-shohz]
I don't want anything, thanks je ne
veux rien, merci [ree-AN]

apart from sauf [sohf]
apartment l'appartement m
[apartmON]
appendicitis l'appendicite f
[apONdeesseet]
aperitif l'apéritif m [apayreeteef]
apology les excuses [exkOOz]
appetizer l'entrée f [ONtray]
apple la pomme [pom]
appointment le rendez-vous

•••••• DIALOGUE ••••••

good afternoon, how can I help
you? bonjour monsieur/madame,
que puis-je faire pour vous? [kuh
pweej fair poor voo]
I'd like to make an appointment
j'aimerais prendre rendez-vous
[jemray prONdr]

what time would you like? quelle
heure vous conviendrait-elle?
[kel urr voo koNvee-ANdrayt-el]
three o'clock trois heures
I'm afraid that's not possible, is four
o'clock all right? cela ne va pas
être possible, est-ce que quatre
heures vous irait? [vooz eeray]
yes, that will be fine oui, cela ira
parfaitement [eera parfetmoN]
the name was ...? c'est monsieur/
madame ...? [say]

apricot l'abricot m [abreeko]
April avril [avreel]
are*: we are nous sommes [noo
som]
you are tu es/vous êtes [t∞
ay, voo zet]
they are ils sont [eel soN]
area la région [rayjee-oN]
area code l'indicatif m
[ANdeekateef]
arm le bras [bra]
arrange: will you arrange it for
us? pouvez-vous vous en
occuper? [poovay-voo voo zoN
ok∞pay]
arrival l'arrivée f [areevay]
arrive arriver [areevay]
when do we arrive? à quelle
heure arrivons-nous?
[areevoN-noo]
has my fax arrived yet? mon
fax est-il arrivé? [areevay]
we arrived today nous
sommes arrivés aujourd'hui
art l'art m [ar]
art gallery le musée d'art

[m∞zay]
artist l'artiste mf [arteest]
as: as big as aussi gros que
[ohsee gro kuh]
as soon as possible dès que
possible [day]
ashtray le cendrier [soNdreeay]
ask demander [duhmoNday]
I didn't ask for this ce n'est
pas ce que j'ai commandé
[suh nay pa suh kuy jay
komoNday]
could you ask him to ...?
peux-tu/pouvez-vous lui
demander de ...? [puh-t∞/
poovay-voo lwee ...]
asleep: she's asleep elle dort
[dor]
aspirin l'aspirine f [aspeereen]
asthma l'asthme m [as-muh]
astonishing étonnant [aytonoN]
at: at the hotel à l'hôtel [a]
at the station à la gare
at the café au café [o]
at six o'clock à six heures
at Paul's chez Paul [shay]
athletics l'athlétisme m
[atlayteess-muh]
Atlantic l'Atlantique m
[atloNteek]
attractive séduisant [saydweezoN]
aubergine l'aubergine f
August août [oo]
aunt la tante [toNt]
Australia l'Australie f [ostralee]
Australian australien(ne)
[ostralee-AN, -en]
I'm Australian (man/woman) je
suis australien/australienne

Austria l'Autriche f [otreesh]
automatic (car) la voiture automatique [vwatœr otomateek]
autumn l'automne m [oton]
  in the autumn en automne [ON]
avenue l'avenue f
average (not good) moyen [mwy-AN]
  on average en moyenne [ON mwy-en]
awake: is he awake? est-il réveillé? [rayvay-yay]
away: go away! allez-vous en! [alay-voo zON]
  is it far away? est-ce que c'est loin? [eskuh say lwAN]
awful affreux [afruh]
axle l'essieu m [ess-yuh]

B

baby le bébé [baybay]
baby food les aliments pour bébé [aleemON poor]
baby's bottle biberon m [beeberON]
baby-sitter le/la baby-sitter
back (of body) le dos [doh]
  (back part) l'arrière m [aree-air]
  at the back à l'arrière
  can I have my money back? est-ce que vous pouvez me rendre mon argent? [eskuh voo poovay muh rONdr]
  to come back revenir [ruh-veneer]
  to go back rentrer [rONtray]

backache le mal de reins [duh rAN]
bacon le lard [lar]
bad mauvais [movay]
  a bad headache un violent mal de tête [veeolON]
badly mal
bag le sac
  (handbag) le sac à main [mAN]
  (suitcase) la valise [valeez]
baggage les bagages mpl [bagahj]
baggage check la consigne [kONseeñ]
baggage claim le retrait des bagages [ruhtray]
bakery la boulangerie [boolONjree]
balcony le balcon [balkON]
  a room with a balcony une chambre avec balcon
bald chauve [shohv]
ball (large) le ballon [balON]
  (small) la balle [bal]
ballet le ballet
banana la banane [banan]
band (musical) l'orchestre m [orkestr]
bandage le pansement [pONsmON]
Bandaids® les pansements mpl [pONsmON]
bank (money) la banque [bONk]

Banks are generally open from Monday to Friday, usually from 9 a.m. to noon, then again from 2 p.m. to 4 or 4.30 p.m. →

Branches of the **Banque de France** close on Mondays. A passport is sometimes required for transactions. The best rates for exchanging money or travellers' cheques are to be found in banks or post offices in larger cities, rather than in bureaux de change. What's more, the **Banque de France** and the post offices don't take a commission.

bank account le compte en banque [kONt ON bONk]
bar le bar

Bars sell hot drinks, soft and alcoholic drinks, and also savoury snacks. It's almost always cheaper if you stand at the bar to drink. A **bar-tabac** will have a special counter where you can buy cigarettes, stamps and phonecards.
see **café**

a bar of chocolate une tablette de chocolat [tablet duh shokola]
barber's le coiffeur pour hommes [kwafurr poor om]
basket le panier [pan-yay]
bath le bain [bAN]
  can I have a bath? est-ce que je peux prendre un bain? [eskuh juh puh proNdr AN bAN]
bathroom la salle de bain [sal duh bAN]
  with a private bathroom avec salle de bain
bath towel la serviette de bain
battery la pile [peel]
  (for car) la batterie
bay la baie [bay]
be* être [etr]
beach la plage [plahj]
beach mat la natte [nat]
beach umbrella le parasol
beans les haricots [areeko]
  runner beans les haricots à rames [ram]
  broad beans les fèves [fev]
beard la barbe [barb]
beautiful beau, f belle [bo, bel]
because parce que [parss-kuh]
  because of ... à cause de ... [a kohz duh]
bed le lit [lee]
  I'm going to bed je vais me coucher [juh vay muh kooshay]
bed and breakfast la chambre avec petit déjeuner [shONbr avek puhtee dayjuhnay]

Prices of hotel rooms do not include breakfast.

bedroom la chambre à coucher [shONbr a kooshay]
beef le bœuf [burf]
beer la bière [bee-air]
  two beers, please deux bières, s'il vous plaît [bee-air]

Some beer terms are:
blonde amber-coloured, light beer
rousse darker, maltier beer
brune [broon] dark beer
un panaché [panashay] a shandy
en bouteille [ON bootay] bottled
pression [press-yON] draught
un demi approximately half an imperial pint (250 cl)

before avant [avON]
begin: when does it begin? à quelle heure est-ce que ça commence? [sa kom-mONss]
beginner le débutant, la débutante [dayboton, -tONt]
beginning: at the beginning au début [o dayboo]
behind derrière [dairyair]
    behind me derrière moi
beige beige [bej]
Belgian belge [belj]
    (man) le Belge
    (woman) la Belge
Belgium la Belgique [beljeek]
believe croire [krwahr]
below sous [soo]
belt la ceinture [SANtoor]
bend (in road) le virage [veerahj]
berth (on ship) la couchette [kooshet]
beside: beside the ... à côté du/de la ... [a kotay doo]
best le meilleur [may-yurr]
better mieux [m-yuh]

are you feeling better? est-ce que tu te sens/vous vous sentez mieux? [eskuh too tuh sON/voo voo sONtay]
between entre [ONtr]
beyond au delà [o duhla]
bicycle le vélo [vaylo]
big grand [grON]
    too big trop grand
    it's not big enough ce n'est pas assez grand [pa zassay]
bike le vélo [vaylo]
    (motorbike) la moto
bikini le bikini
bill l'addition f [adeess-yON]
    (US) le billet (de banque) [bee-yay duh bONk]
    could I have the bill, please? l'addition, s'il vous plaît

If you go out informally with a group, it is usual to share the bill equally. If someone intends to pay for everything, they will say 'c'est pour moi' or 'c'est moi qui paie'. If someone invites other people out, he or she is expected to pay.

bin la poubelle [poo-bel]
bin liners les sacs poubelle mpl
binding (ski) la fixation [feexass-yON]
bird l'oiseau m [wazo]
biro® le stylo-bille [steelo-bee]
birthday l'anniversaire m [aneevairsair]
    happy birthday! bon anniversaire!

biscuit le biscuit [beeskwee]
bit: a little bit un peu [AN puh]
  a big bit un gros morceau
  [gro morso]
  a bit of ... un morceau de ...
  a bit expensive un peu cher
bite (by insect) la piqûre
  [peekOOr]
  (by dog) la morsure [morsOOr]
bitter (taste etc) amer [amair]
black noir [nwahr]
blanket la couverture
  [koovairtOOr]
bleach (for toilet) l'eau de Javel f
  [ohd javel]
bless you! santé! [sONtay]
blind aveugle [avurgl]
blind (on window) le store [stor]
blister l'ampoule f [ONpool]
blocked (road, pipe, sink) bouché
  [booshay]
block of flats l'immeuble m
  [eemurbl]
blond(e) blond [blON]
blood le sang [sON]
  high blood pressure
  l'hypertension f [eepairtONs-
  yON]
blouse le chemisier [shuhmeez-
  yay]
blow-dry le brushing
  I'd like a cut and blow-dry je
  voudrais une coupe et un
  brushing
blue bleu [bluh]
blusher le rouge à joues [rooj a
  joo]
boarding house la pension
  [pONs-yON]

boarding pass la carte
  d'embarquement [dONbarkuh-
  mON]
boat le bateau [bato]
body le corps [kor]
boil (water) faire bouillir [fair
  booyeer]
  (potatoes etc) faire cuire à
  l'eau [kweer a lo]
boiled egg l'œuf à la coque m
  [urf ala kok]
bone l'os m [oss]
bonnet (of car) le capot [kapo]
book le livre [leevr]
  (verb) réserver [rayzairvay]
  can I book a seat? est-ce que
  je peux réserver une place?

•••••• DIALOGUE ••••••

I'd like to book a table for two
j'aimerais réserver une table
pour deux [jemray rayzairvay]
what time would you like it booked
for? pour quelle heure voudriez-
vous réserver? [poor kel urr
voodree-ay-ay-voo]
half past seven sept heures et
demi
that's fine très bien
and your name? votre nom?

bookshop la librairie
  [leebrairee]
bookstore la librairie
boot (footwear) la botte [bot]
  (of car) le coffre [kofr]
border (of country) la frontière
  [frONt-yair]
bored: I'm bored je m'ennuie
  [juh mON-nwee]

boring ennuyeux [ON-nwee-yuh]

born: I was born in Manchester
je suis né à Manchester [juh
swee nay]
I was born in 1960 je suis né
en 1960 [ON]

borrow emprunter [ONprANtay]
may I borrow ...? puis-je
emprunter ...?

both les deux [lay duh]

bother: sorry to bother you je
suis désolé de vous
déranger [juh swee dayzolay
duh voo dayrON-jay]

bottle la bouteille [bootay]
a bottle of house red une
bouteille de rouge maison
[mezzON]

bottle-opener l'ouvre-bouteille
m [oovr-bootay]

bottom (of person) le derrière
[dairyair]
at the bottom of ... (hill etc) en
bas de ... [ON ba duh]

box la boîte [bwat]

box office le guichet [geeshay]

boy le garçon [garsON]

boyfriend le petit ami [puhtee
tami]

bra le soutien-gorge [soot-yAN-
gorj]

bracelet le bracelet [braslay]

brake le frein [frAN]

brandy le cognac

bread le pain [pAN]
white bread du pain blanc
[blON]
brown bread du pain noir
[nwar]

wholemeal bread du pain
complet [kONplay]

break casser [kassay]
I've broken the ... j'ai cassé
le ... [jay kassay]
I think I've broken my wrist je
crois que je me suis cassé le
poignet [juh muh swee]

breakdown la panne [pan]
I've had a breakdown je suis
tombé en panne [juh swee
tONbay ON]

> If you are taking a car with you
> make sure that you take out
> breakdown insurance cover
> before you go.

breakdown service le service de
dépannage [sairveess duh
daypanahj]

breakfast le petit déjeuner [ptee
day-juhnay]
English/full breakfast le petit
déjeuner anglais [ONglay]

break-in: I've had a break-in il y
a eu un cambriolage [eel ya
∞ AN kONbreeolahj]

breast le sein [SAN]

breathe respirer [respeeray]

breeze la brise [breez]

bridge (over river) le pont [pON]

brief court [koor]

briefcase la serviette

bright (light etc) clair
bright red rouge vif [veef]

brilliant (idea, person) génial
[jayn-yal]

bring apporter [aportay]

I'll bring it back later je le rapporterai plus tard [raportuhray]

Britain la Grande-Bretagne [groND-bruhtañ]

British britannique [breetaneek]

Brittany la Bretagne [bruhtañ]

brochure le prospectus [prospektooss]

broken cassé [kassay]

bronchitis la bronchite [broNsheet]

brooch la broche [brosh]

broom le balai [balay]

brother le frère [frair]

brother-in-law le beau-frère [bo-frair]

brown marron [maroN]

(hair) brun [brAN]

bruise le bleu [bluh]

brush (for hair) la brosse [bross]

(artist's) le pinceau [pAN-so]

(for cleaning) le balai [balay]

Brussels Bruxelles [brOOssel]

bucket le seau [so]

buffet car le wagon-restaurant [vagoN-restoroN]

buggy (for child) le landau [loNdo]

building le bâtiment [bateemoN]

bulb l'ampoule f [oNpool]

I need a new bulb j'ai besoin d'une nouvelle ampoule

bumper le pare-chocs [par-shok]

bunk la couchette [kooshet]

bureau de change le bureau de change

see **bank**

burglary le cambriolage [koNbreeolahj]

burn la brûlure [brOOloor]

(verb) brûler [brOOlay]

burnt: this is burnt c'est brûlé [brOOlay]

burst: a burst pipe un tuyau crevé [twee-o kruhvay]

bus le bus [booss]

what number bus is it to ...? quel bus va à ...? [kel]

when is the next bus to ...? à quelle heure part le prochain bus pour ...? [a kel urr par luh proshAN]

what time is the last bus? à quelle heure passe le dernier bus? [dairn-yay]

could you let me know when we get there? est-ce que vous pourrez me dire quand on y sera? [eskuh voo pooray muh deer koN toN ee suhra]

In Paris, bus tickets are cheaper if bought in advance from news-stands, tobacconists or under-ground stations in a book of ten (**un carnet de tickets**) – they can also be bought on boarding the bus, but will be more expensive. Tickets have to be validated in the ticket-stamping machine on the bus. If travelling for more than two sections in Paris and some larger towns – as indicated on the route chart – you have to validate two →

ENGLISH ◆ FRENCH

Br

tickets. Special day-tickets are also available which give you un-limited travel on the bus (and underground) for one day. In Paris, bus tickets can also be used in the underground.

• • • • • • DIALOGUE • • • • • •

does this bus go to ...? est-ce que ce bus va à ...?

no, you need a number ... non, vous devez prendre le ... [pron.dr]

where does it leave from? où est-ce que je le prends? [weskuh juh luh pron]

business les affaires fpl [lay zafair]

bus station la gare routière [gar root-yair]

bus stop l'arrêt d'autobus m [aray dotobooss]

bust la poitrine [pwatreen]

busy (person) occupé [okoopay]
the restaurant is very busy il y a beaucoup de monde dans le restaurant [eel ya bohkoo duh mond]
I'm busy tomorrow demain, je suis pris(e) [duhman juh swee pree/preez]

but mais [may]

butcher's la boucherie [booshree]

butter le beurre [burr]

button le bouton [booton]

buy acheter [ashtay]
where can I buy ...? où puis-je acheter ...? [oo pweej]

by: by bus/car en bus/voiture [on]
written by ... écrit par ...
by the window près de la fenêtre [pray duh]
by the sea au bord de la mer [o bor]
by Thursday pour jeudi [poor]

bye au revoir [o ruh-vwa]

C

cabbage le chou [shoo]

cabin (on ship) la cabine [kabeen]

cable car le téléférique [taylayfayreek]

café le café

Every bar or café has to display its full price list (usually with-out the fifteen per cent service charge added). In addition to coffee, tea etc, cafés also serve alcoholic drinks and usually snacks or even simple dishes; they have waiter service, al-though drinks are cheaper at the bar (**comptoir**) than at a table (**en salle**) or outside (**en terrasse**). You normally pay just before you leave, rather than on ordering.

cagoule le K-way [ka-way]

cake le gâteau [gato]

cake shop la pâtisserie

call appeler [aplay]
(to phone) téléphoner

[taylayfonay]
what's it called? comment ça s'appelle? [komON sa sa-pel]
he/she is called ... il/elle s'appelle ...
please call the doctor appelez le docteur, s'il vous plaît [aplay]
please give me a call at 7.30 a.m. tomorrow pouvez-vous me réveiller à sept heures trente demain matin? [poovay-voo muh rayvayay]
please ask him to call me pouvez-vous lui demander de m'appeler?
call back: I'll call back later je reviendrai plus tard [ruhveeANdray]
(phone back) je rappelerai plus tard [rapelray]
call round: I'll call round tomorrow je passerai demain [passuhray]
camcorder le caméscope [kamayskop]
camera (for stills) l'appareil-photo m [aparay-]
camera shop le photographe [fotograf]
camp camper [kONpay]
can we camp here? est-ce qu'on peut camper ici? [eskON puh]
camping gas le butagaz

Camping gas canisters can be bought either from a →

quincaillerie (hardware store) or from campsite shops; you can't carry canisters on aeroplanes.

campsite le terrain de camping [terrAN duh kONpeeng]

In France, campsites are classified in four categories, ranging from 1 to 4 stars according to the facilities they offer. Never camp rough on anyone's land without first asking permission of the landowner – farmers have been known to shoot before asking questions. In many parts of France, camping rough on public land is not tolerated at all, although Brittany is a notable exception.

can (tin) la boîte [bwat]
a can of beer une bière en boîte [bee-air ON]
can*: can you ...? peux-tu/pouvez-vous ...? [puh-too/poovay-voo]
can I have ...? est-ce que je peux avoir ...? [eskuh juh puh avwahr]
I can't ... je ne peux pas ... [juh nuh puh pa]
Canada le Canada
Canadian canadien(ne) [kanadee-AN, -ee-en]
I'm Canadian (man/woman) je suis canadien/canadienne

canal le canal

cancel annuler [anɔɔlay]

candies les bonbons, les sucreries [sɔɔkruhree]

candle la bougie [boo-jee]

canoe le canoë [kano-ay]

canoeing le canoë

can-opener l'ouvre-boîte m [oovr-bwat]

cap (hat) la casquette [kasket] (of bottle) la capsule

car la voiture [vwatɔɔr]
  by car en voiture

carafe une carafe
  a carafe of house white, please une carafe de blanc maison, s'il vous plaît [mezzON]

caravan la caravane

caravan site le terrain de camping pour caravanes [terrAN duh kONpeeng poor]

carburettor le carburateur [karbɔɔraturr]

card (birthday etc) la carte [kart]
  here's my (business) card voici ma carte [vwa-see]

cardigan le gilet [jeelay]

cardphone le téléphone à carte [taylayfon a kart]

careful prudent [prɔɔdON]
  be careful! faites attention! [fet zatONs-yON]

caretaker le/la concierge

car ferry le ferry

car hire la location de voitures [lokass-yON duh vwatɔɔr]
  see rent

car park le parking [parkeeng]

carpet la moquette [moket]

carriage (of train) le wagon [vagON]

carrier bag le sac en plastique [ON plasteek]

carrot la carotte [karrot]

carry porter [portay]

carry-cot le porte-bébé [port-baybay]

carton (of orange juice etc) le carton [kartON]

carwash (place) le lave-auto [lav-oto]

case (suitcase) la valise [valeez]

cash l'argent liquide m [arjON leekeed]
  (verb) encaisser
  will you cash this for me? est-ce que vous pouvez encaisser cela pour moi? [eskuh voo poovay]

cash desk la caisse [kess]

cash dispenser le distributeur automatique de billets de banque [deestreebɔɔturr otomateek duh bee-yay duh bONk]

cashier (cash desk) la caisse [kess]

cassette la cassette

cassette recorder le magnétophone à cassettes [man-yetofon]

castle le château [shato]

casualty department le service des urgences [sairveess day zoorjONss]

cat le chat [sha]

catch attraper [atrapay]
  where do we catch the bus to ...? où est-ce qu'on peut

prendre le bus pour ...?
[weskON puh proNdr luh bOOss]

cathedral la cathédrale [kataydral]

Catholic (adj) catholique [katoleek]

cauliflower le chou-fleur [shooflurr]

cave la grotte [grot]

ceiling le plafond [plafON]

celery le céleri en branche [saylree ON broNsh]

cellar (for wine) la cave [kahv]

cemetery le cimetière [seemteeair]

Centigrade* centigrade [sONteegrad]

centimetre* le centimètre [sONteemetr]

central central [soN-tral]

central heating le chauffage central [shofahj soN-tral]

centre le centre [sONtr]

how do we get to the city centre? comment va-t-on au centre-ville? [komON vatON o sONtr-veel]

it's in the city centre c'est dans le centre-ville

cereal les céréales [sayray-al]

certainly certainement [sairtenmON]

certainly not certainement pas [pa]

chair la chaise [shez]

champagne le champagne [shONpañ]

change (money) la monnaie [monay]

(verb) **changer** [shONjay]

can I change this for ...?
j'aimerais échanger ceci contre ... [jemray ayshONjay suhsee]

I don't have any change je n'ai pas de monnaie [juh nay pa duh]

can you give me change for a 200 francs note? pouvez-vous me faire la monnaie sur un billet de deux cents francs? [muh fair]

•••••• DIALOGUE ••••••

do we have to change (trains)? est-ce qu'il faut changer? [eskeel fo]

yes, change at Bordeaux oui, il faut changer à Bordeaux

no, it's direct non, c'est direct [deerekt]

changed: to get changed se changer [shONjay]

Channel la Manche [moNsh]

Channel Islands les îles Anglo-Normandes [eel ONglo-normONd]

Channel Tunnel le tunnel sous la Manche [tOOnel soo la moNsh]

chapel la chapelle [shapel]

charge (verb) faire payer

cheap bon marché [bON marshay]

do you have anything cheaper? avez-vous quelque chose de meilleur marché? [avay-voo kelkuh shohz duh may-yurr marshay]

check (US) le chèque [shek]
  see **cheque**
  (US: bill) l'addition f [adeess-yON]
  see **bill**
  (verb) vérifier [vayreef-yay]
  **could you check the ...,
  please?** pouvez-vous
  vérifier ..., s'il vous plaît?
checkbook le chéquier
  [shaykee-ay]
check-in l'enregistrement des
  bagages m [ONrejeestruh-mON
  day bagahj]
check in (at airport) se faire
  enregistrer [suh fair
  ONrejeestray]
  where do we have to check in?
  où est l'enregistrement?
checkout (in shop) la caisse
  [kess]
cheek (on face) la joue [joo]
cheerio! (bye-bye) au revoir!
  [o ruh-vwa]
cheers! (toast) santé! [sONtay]
  (thanks) merci [mairsee]
cheese le fromage [fromahj]

In France there are over 250
officially recognized types of
cheeses, with each region
having its own speciality.
Cheese is served at nearly every
meal, after or along with the
green salad and before dessert.

chemist's (shop) la pharmacie
  [farmassee]

Chemist's are identified by a
green cross sign. They are well-
qualified to give you advice on
minor ailments. There's an
all-night chemist's in bigger
towns and cities and they work
on a rota system. You generally
find the address of the one
currently open on the door of
any chemist's.

cheque le chèque [shek]
  do you take cheques? est-ce
  que vous acceptez les
  chèques? [eskuh voo zaxeptay]
cheque book le chéquier
  [shaykee-ay]
cheque card la carte d'identité
  bancaire [kart deedONteetay
  bONkair]
cherry la cerise [suhreez]
chess les échecs [lay zayshek]
chest (body) la poitrine
  [pwatreen]
chewing gum le chewing-gum
  [shween-gom]
chicken la poule [pool]
  (meat) le poulet [poolay]
chickenpox la varicelle
  [vareessel]
child l'enfant mf [ON-fON]
  children les enfants
child minder le/la gardien(ne)
  d'enfants [gardee-AN, -ee-en]
children's pool la piscine pour
  enfants [peesseen]
children's portion la portion
  pour enfants [pors-yON]

chin le menton [monton]

china la porcelaine

Chinese chinois [sheenwa]

chips les frites [freet]

chocolate le chocolat [shokola]

  milk chocolate le chocolat au lait [o lay]

  plain chocolate le chocolat à croquer [a krokay]

  a hot chocolate un chocolat chaud [sho]

choose choisir [shwazeer]

Christian name le prénom [praynON]

Christmas Noël [no-el]

  Christmas Eve la veille de Noël [vay duh]

  merry Christmas! joyeux Noël! [jwy-uh]

church l'église f [aygleez]

cider le cidre [seedr]

cigar le cigare [see-gar]

cigarette la cigarette [see-]

Cigarettes can be bought from the bureaux de tabac (tobacconists) which can be identified by a red diamond-shaped sign with Tabac written on it

cigarette lighter le briquet [breekay]

cinema le cinéma [seenayma]

circle le cercle [sairkl]

  (in theatre) le balcon [balkON]

city la ville [veel]

city centre le centre-ville [sONtr-veel]

clean (adj) propre [propr]

can you clean these for me? pouvez-vous me nettoyer ça? [poovay-voo muh net-wy-ay sa]

cleaning solution (for contact lenses) la solution de nettoyage [solOOss-yON duh net-wy-ahj]

cleansing lotion (cosmetic) la crème démaquillante [krem daymakeeyONt]

clear clair [klair]

clever intelligent [ANtayleejON]

cliff la falaise [falez]

climbing l'escalade f

cling film le cellophane [selofan]

clinic la clinique [kleeneek]

cloakroom (for coats) le vestiaire [vestee-air]

clock l'horloge f [orloj]

close fermer [fairmay]

•••••• DIALOGUE ••••••

what time do you close? à quelle heure est-ce que vous fermez? [a kel urr eskuh voo fairmay]

we close at 8 pm on weekdays and 6 pm on Saturdays nous fermons à huit heures pendant la semaine et à six heures le samedi [noo fairmON]

do you close for lunch? est-ce que vous fermez pour déjeuner?

yes, between 1 and 3.30 pm oui, entre une heure et trois heures et demi

closed fermé [fairmay]

cloth (fabric) le tissu [teessOO]

  (for cleaning etc) le chiffon

[sheefON]

clothes les vêtements [vetmON]

clothes line la corde à linge [kord a lANj]

clothes peg la pince à linge [pANss]

cloud le nuage [nOO-ahj]

cloudy nuageux [nOO-ahjuh]

clutch l'embrayage m [ONbray-ahj]

coach (bus) le car
(on train) le wagon [vagON]

coach station la gare routière [gar rootee-air]

coach trip l'excursion en autocar f [exkOOrss-yON ON otokar]

coast la côte [koht]
on the coast sur la côte

coat (long coat) le manteau [mONto]
(jacket) la veste [vest]

coathanger le cintre [sANtr]

cockroach le cafard [kafar]

cocoa le cacao [kakow]

coconut la noix de coco [nwa duh]

code (when dialling) l'indicatif m [ANdeekateef]
what's the (dialling) code for outside Paris? quel est l'indicatif pour la province? [kel ay lANdeekateef poor]

coffee le café
two coffees, please deux cafés, s'il vous plaît [kafay]

If you ask for **un café** you will be given an **express** (strong black coffee); you can also ask for one of the following:

un (café) crème [krem] coffee with cream or milk
un (café) décaféiné [day-kafeenay] decaffeinated coffee
un café serré [serray] strong express

coin la pièce [p-yess]

Coke® le coca-cola

cold (weather, food etc) froid [frwa]
I'm cold j'ai froid [jay]
I have a cold je me suis enrhumé [juh muh swee zONrOOmay]

collapse: he's collapsed il s'est effondré [eel set ayfONdray]

collar le col

collect: I've come to collect ... je suis venu chercher ... [juh swee vuhnOO shairshay]

collect call une communication en PCV [-kass-yON ON pay-say-vay]

college l'université f [OOneevairseetay]

colour la couleur [koolurr]
do you have this in other colours? l'avez-vous en d'autres teintes? [lavay voo ON dohtr tANt]

colour film la pellicule couleur [pelikOOl]

comb le peigne [peñ]

come venir [vuhneer]

•••••• DIALOGUES ••••••

where do you come from? d'où es-tu/êtes-vous? [doo ay-tᴏᴏ/et-voo]

I come from Edinburgh je suis d'Édimbourg [juh swee]

come back revenir

I'll come back tomorrow je reviens demain [juh ruhv-yAN]

come in entrer [ONtray]

comfortable confortable [kONfort-abl]

compact disc le disque compact

company (business) la société [sos-yay-tay]

compartment (on train) le compartiment [kONparteemON]

compass la boussole [boossol]

complain se plaindre [suh plANdr]

complaint la réclamation [rayklamass-yON]

I have a complaint j'ai une réclamation à faire

completely complètement [kONpletmON]

computer l'ordinateur m [ordeenaturr]

concert le concert [kONsair]

concussion la commotion cérébrale [komoss-yON sayray-bral]

conditioner (for hair) l'après-shampoing m [apray -shONpwAN]

condom le préservatif [prayzairvateef]

conference la conférence [kONfay-rONss]

confirm confirmer [kONfeermay]

congratulations! félicitations! [fayleesseetass-yON]

connecting flight le vol qui assure la correspondance [kee assᴏᴏr la korespONdONss]

connection (in travelling) la correspondance

conscious conscient [kONs-yON]

constipation la constipation [kONsteepass-yON]

consulate le consulat [kONsᴏᴏ-la]

contact contacter [kONtaktay]

contact lenses les lentilles de contact fpl [lONtee]

contraceptive le contraceptif [kONtrasepteef]

convenient (location) pratique [prateek]

(time) qui convient [kee kONvee-AN]

that's not convenient cela ne me convient pas

cook le cuisinier, la cuisinière [kweezeenee-ay, -yair]

not cooked (is underdone) pas cuit [pa kwee]

cooker la cuisinière [kweezeenyair]

cookie le biscuit [beeskwee]

cooking utensils les ustensiles de cuisine [ᴏᴏstONseel duh kweezeen]

cool (day, weather) frais, f fraîche [fray, fresh]

cork (in bottle) le bouchon [booshON]

corkscrew le tire-bouchon [teer-booshON]

corner: on the corner (of street)
au coin de la rue [kwAN duh la
rOO]
in the corner dans le coin
cornflakes les cornflakes
correct (adj) correct, exact
corridor le couloir [koolwahr]
Corsica la Corse [korss]
Corsican (adj) corse
cosmetics les produits de
beauté [prodwee duh bohtay]
cost coûter [kootay]
how much does it cost?
combien ça coûte? [kONb-yAN
sa koot]
cot (for baby) le lit d'enfant [lee
dONfON]
cotton le coton [kotON]
cotton wool le coton
hydrophile [kotON eedrofeel]
couch (sofa) le canapé [kanapay]
couchette la couchette
cough la toux [too]
cough medicine le sirop contre
la toux [seero kONtr]
could: could you ...? pourriez-
vous ...? [pooree-ay-voo]
could I have ...? j'aimerais ...
[jemray]
I couldn't ... je ne pouvais
pas ... [juh nuh poovay pa]
country (nation) le pays [payee]
(countryside) la campagne
[kONpañ]
countryside la campagne
couple (man and woman) le
couple [koopl]
a couple of ... quelques ...

[kelkuh]

courier le/la guide [geed]
course (of meal) le plat [pla]
of course bien sûr [b-yAN sOOr]
of course not bien sûr que
non [kuh nON]
cousin le cousin, la cousine
[koozAN, koozeen]
cow la vache [vash]
crab le crabe [krab]
cracker (biscuit) le biscuit salé
[beeskwee salay]
craft shop la boutique
d'artisanat [arteezana]
crash la collision [koleez-yON]
I've had a crash j'ai eu un
accident [jay OO AN axeedON]
crazy fou, f folle [foo, fol]
cream (on milk, in cake, lotion) la
crème [krem]
(colour) crème
creche (for babies) la crèche
credit card la carte de crédit
[kart duh kraydee]

Credit cards are widely
accepted; just look out for the
window stickers. Visa/
Barclaycard — known as the
Carte Bleue — is almost
universally recognized. Access
(Eurocard/Mastercard in
France) ranks considerably
lower — only the Crédit Agricole
and the Crédit Mutuel banks
provide facilities for the latter.
Cash advances can be had at all
banks — you should ask for a PIN
number before you go.

•••••• DIALOGUE ••••••

can I pay by credit card? est-ce que
je peux payer par carte de
crédit? [eskuh juh puh pay-ay]
which card do you want to use?
avec quelle carte désirez-vous
payer?
yes, sir oui monsieur
what's the number? quel est le
numéro? [noomayro]
and the expiry date? et la date
d'expiration?

crisps les chips fpl [cheeps]
crockery la vaisselle [vess-el]
crossing (by sea) la traversée
[travairsay]
crossroads le carrefour [karfoor]
crowd la foule [fool]
crowded (streets, bars) bondé
[bONday]
crown (on tooth) la couronne
[kooron]
cruise (by ship) la croisière
[krwaz-yair]
crutches les béquilles fpl
[baykee]
cry pleurer [plurray]
cucumber le concombre
[kONkONbr]
cup la tasse [tass]
a cup of ..., please une tasse
de ..., s'il vous plaît
cupboard l'armoire f [armwahr]
curly (hair) frisé
current le courant [kooroN]
curtains les rideaux mpl [reedo]
cushion le coussin [koossAN]
custom la coutume [kootoom]

Customs la douane [dwan]
cut la coupure [koopoor]
(hair) la coupe [koop]
(verb) couper [koopay]
I've cut myself je me suis
coupé [juh muh swee koopay]
cutlery les couverts [kouvair]
cycling le cyclisme [seekleess-
muh]
cyclist le/la cycliste [seekleest]

D

dad le papa
daily: they run daily il y en a
tous les jours [eel yON a too lay
joor]
a daily paper un (journal)
quotidien [joornal koteedee-AN]
damage endommager [ONdoma-
jay]
damaged abîmé [abeemay]
I'm sorry, I've damaged this je
suis désolé, j'ai abimé ça [jay
abeemay]
damn! zut! [zoot]
damp (adj) humide [oo-meed]
dance la danse [dONss]
(verb) danser [dONsay]
would you like to dance?
veux-tu/voulez-vous danser
avec moi? [vuh-too/voolay-voo –
avek mwa]
dangerous dangereux [dONj-ruh]
Danish danois [danwa]
dark (adj: colour) foncé [fONsay]
(hair) brun [brAN]
it's getting dark il commence
à faire sombre [eel komoNss a

fair sONbr]

date*: what's the date today?
quel jour sommes-nous? [kel
joor som-noo]
**let's make a date for next
Monday** prenons rendez-
vous pour lundi prochain
[pruhnON]
dates (fruit) les dattes fpl [dat]
daughter la fille [fee]
daughter-in-law la belle-fille
[bel-fee]
dawn l'aurore f [oror]
at dawn au lever du jour [o
luhvay doo joor]
day le jour [joor]
the day after le lendemain
[lONdmAN]
the day after tomorrow après-
demain [apray-duhmAN]
the day before la veille [vay]
the day before yesterday
avant-hier [avON-tee-air]
every day chaque jour
are you open all day? est-ce
que vous êtes ouverts toute
la journée? [toot la joornay]
in two days' time dans deux
jours
have a nice day bonne
journée [bon joornay]
day trip l'excursion d'une
journée f [exkoors-yON doon
joornay]
dead mort [mor]
deaf sourd [soor]
deal (business) l'affaire f
it's a deal d'accord! [dakor]
death la mort [mor]

decaffeinated coffee le café
décaféiné [daykafeenay]
December décembre [daysONbr]
decide décider [dayseeday]
we haven't decided yet nous
n'avons pas encore décidé
[noo navON pa zONkor dayseeday]
decision la décision [dayseez-
yON]
deck (on ship) le pont [pON]
deckchair la chaise longue [shez
lON-g]
deduct déduire [daydweer]
deep profond [profON]
definitely certainement [sairten-
mON]
definitely not certainement
pas [pa]
degree (qualification) le diplôme
[deeplohm]
delay le retard [ruhtar]
deliberately exprès [expray]
delicatessen l'épicerie fine f
[aypeesree feen]
delicious délicieux [dayleess-yuh]
deliver livrer [leevray]
delivery (of mail) la distribution
[deestreebooss-yON]
Denmark le Danemark
[danmark]
dental floss le fil dentaire [feel
dONtair]
dentist le/la dentiste [dON-teest]
see **doctor**

••••• DIALOGUE •••••

it's this one here c'est celle-là [say
sel-la]
this one? celle-ci? [sel-see]
no that one non, celle-là

here? ici? [ee-see]
yes oui [wee]

dentures le dentier [dONt-yay]
deodorant le déodorant
[dayodoroN]
department le service [sairveess]
department store le grand
magasin [groN magazAN]
departure le départ [daypar]
departure lounge le hall de
départ [al duh]
depend: it depends ça dépend
[sa daypON]
it depends on ... ça dépend
de ...
deposit (as security) la caution
[kohs-yON]
(as part payment) l'acompte m
[akONt]
description la description
[deskreeps-yON]
dessert le dessert [desair]
destination la destination
[desteenass-yON]
develop développer [dayv-lopay]

When leaving your films to be
developed, you will be asked if
you want your photos **en mat ou
brillant** (matt or glossy finish).
If you don't specify, you're likely
to get the matt finish.

•••••• DIALOGUE ••••••

could you develop these films?
pouvez-vous développer ces
pellicules? [poovay-voo ... say
peleekool]

---

when will they be ready? quand
est-ce que ça sera prêt? [koN
teskuh sa suhra pray]
tomorrow afternoon demain
après-midi
how much is the four-hour service?
combien coûte le service de
développement en quatre
heures?

diabetic le/la diabétique [dee-
abayteek]
diabetic foods les aliments
pour diabétiques [aleemON]
dial composer [kONpohzay]
dialling code l'indicatif m
[ANdeekateef]

For direct international calls
from France, dial 19, then the
country code (given below), the
area code (minus the first 0),
and finally the subscriber
number. After dialling 19, pause
a second and wait for the
continuous tone.
UK: 19 44   Australia: 19 61
Ireland: 19 353
New Zealand: 19 64
US & Canada: 19 1

To call other locations in France
from Paris, dial 16 before the
number. To call Paris from elsewhere in France, dial 16 1 and
the number.

---

diamond le diamant [dee-amON]
diaper la couche [koosh]
diarrhoea la diarrhée [dee-aray]

diary (business etc) l'agenda m
[ajANda]
(for personal experiences) le
journal [joornal]

dictionary le dictionnaire [deex-
yonair]

didn't*
see not

die mourir [mooreer]

diesel (fuel) le gas-oil

diet le régime [ray-jeem]
I'm on a diet je suis au
régime [juh swee zo]
I have to follow a special diet
je dois suivre un régime
spécial [dwa sweevr]

difference la différence
[deefayrONss]
what's the difference? quelle
est la différence? [kel ay]

different différent [deefayrON]
this one is different celui-ci
est différent [suhlwee-see]
a different table une autre
table [ohtr]

difficult difficile [deefeesseel]

difficulty la difficulté
[deefeekOOltay]

dinghy (rubber) le canot
pneumatique [kano
p-nuhmateek]
(sailing) le dériveur
[dayreevurr]

dining room la salle à manger
[sal a mONjay]

dinner (evening meal) le dîner
[deenay]
to have dinner dîner

direct (adj) direct [deerekt]

is there a direct train? est-ce
qu'il y a un train direct?
[eskeel ya]

direction le sens [sONss]
which direction is it? dans
quelle direction est-ce? [dON
kel deereex-yON ess]
is it in this direction? est-ce
par là?

directory enquiries les
renseignements [rONsen-
yuhmON]

The number for directory enquiries is 11. For international
directory enquiries dial 11 19
followed by the appropriate
country code. Most post offices
also have **Minitel** terminals at
the disposal of the public, which
give you the telephone number
and the address of the person
you want to phone – all you need
to use this is their name and the
city or **département** they live in.

dirt la saleté [sal-tay]

dirty sale [sal]

disabled handicapé
[ONdeekapay]
is there access for the
disabled? est-ce que c'est
aménagé pour les
handicapés? [eskuh say
amaynah-jay]

disappear disparaître
[deesparetr]
it's disappeared (I've lost it) il/
elle a disparu [deesparOO]

disappointed déçu [daysOO]

disappointing décevant [day-svON]

disaster le désastre [day-zastr]

disco la discothèque

discount le rabais [rabay]

disease la maladie [maladee]

disgusting dégoûtant [daygootON]

dish (meal, bowl) le plat [pla]

dishcloth le torchon à vaisselle [torshON a vess-el]

disinfectant le désinfectant [dayzANfek-tON]

disk (for computer) la disquette

disposable diapers les couches jetables fpl [koosh juhtahbl]

disposable nappies les couches jetables fpl

distance la distance [deestONss]
in the distance au loin [o lwAN]

distilled water l'eau distillée f [o deesteelay]

district le quartier [kart-yay]

disturb déranger [dayrONjay]

diversion (detour) la déviation [dayvee-ass-yON]

diving board le plongeoir [plON-jwahr]

divorced divorcé [deevorsay]

dizzy: I feel dizzy j'ai la tête qui tourne [jay la tet kee toorn]

do faire [fair]
what shall we do? qu'est-ce qu'on fait? [keskON fay]
how do you do it? comment est-ce qu'on fait? [komON eskON fay]

will you do it for me? est-ce que tu peux/vous pouvez le faire pour moi? [eskuh tOO puh/voo poovay]

•••••• DIALOGUES ••••••

how do you do? comment vas-tu/allez-vous? [va-tOO/alay-voo]

nice to meet you enchanté [ONshONtay]

what do you do? (work) qu'est-ce que tu fais/vous faites dans la vie? [kes kuh tOO fay/voo fet dON la vee]

I'm a teacher, and you? je suis enseignant(e), et toi/vous? [twa]

I'm a student je suis étudiant(e)

what are you doing this evening? qu'est-ce que tu fais/vous faites ce soir? [suh swahr]

we're going out for a drink, do you want to join us? nous allons prendre un verre, veux-tu te/voulez-vous vous joindre à nous? [vuh-tOO tuh/voolay-voo voo jwANdr]

do you want cream? voulez-vous de la crème?

I do, but she doesn't moi oui, mais pas elle [mwa]

doctor le médecin [maydsAN]
we need a doctor nous avons besoin d'un médecin
please call a doctor appelez un médecin s'il vous plaît [aplay]

Citizens of all EC countries are entitled to take advantage of each others' health services under the same terms as the residents of the country, if they have the correct documentation. British citizens need form E111 (obtainable from post offices in the UK) – this will enable you to get subsidized treatment and pay for prescriptions at the local rate. Non-EC citizens should take out health insurance. In France, every hospital visit, doctor's consultation and prescribed medicine is charged for. Although all employed French people are entitled to a refund of 75-80 per cent of their medical expenses, this can still leave a hefty shortfall. To find a doctor, stop at any **pharmacie** and ask for an address. The doctor should give you a **Feuille de soins** (Statement of Treatment) for later documentation of insurance claims. The medicines you buy will have **vignettes** (stickers) attached to them which you must remove and attach to your **Feuille de soins**, together with the prescription itself.

•••••• DIALOGUE ••••••

where does it hurt? où est-ce que ça fait mal? [weskuh sa fay]
right here ici [ee-see]

does that hurt now? est-ce que ça fait mal là?
yes oui [wee]
take this to the chemist emmenez ça chez le pharmacien [ONmuhnay sa shay luh farmass-yAN]

document le document [dokOOmON]
dog le chien [shee-AN]
doll la poupée [poopay]
domestic flight le vol intérieur [ANtayree-urr]
don't!* non! [nON] see **not**
   don't do that! ne faites pas ça! [nuh fet pa sa]
door (of room) la porte [port]
   (of train, car) la portière [port-yair]
doorman le portier [port-yay]
double double [doobl]
double bed le grand lit [grON lee]
double room la chambre pour deux personnes [shONbr poor duh pairson]
doughnut le beignet [benyay]
down sous [soo]
   put it down over there posez-le là [pohzay-luh]
   it's down there on the right c'est par là sur la droite
   it's further down the road c'est plus loin sur cette route [plOO lwAN sOOr set root]
downhill skiing le ski de descente [duh duhsONt]
downmarket (restaurant etc) simple [sANpl]

downstairs en bas [ON ba]

dozen la douzaine [doozen]
   half a dozen une demi-
   douzaine [duhmee-]

drain le tuyau d'écoulement
   [twee-yo day-koolmON]

draught beer la bière pression
   [bee-air press-yON]

draughty: it's draughty il y a un
   courant d'air [eelya AN koorON
   dair]

drawer le tiroir [teer-wa]

drawing le dessin [duh-SAN]

dreadful épouvantable
   [aypoovONtabl]

dream le rêve [rev]

dress la robe [rob]

dressed: to get dressed
   s'habiller [sabeeyay]

dressing (for cut) le pansement
   [pONsmON]
   (for salad) la vinaigrette

dressing gown la robe de
   chambre [rob duh shONbr]

drink la boisson [bwassON]
   (verb) boire [bwahr]
   a cold drink une boisson
   fraîche [fresh]
   can I get you a drink? tu
   prends/vous prenez un
   verre? [too prON/voo pruhnay
   ZAN vair]
   what would you like (to drink)?
   qu'est-ce que tu veux/vous
   voulez boire? [keskuh]
   no thanks, I don't drink non
   merci, je ne bois pas [juh nuh
   bwa pa]
   I'll just have a drink of water

un verre d'eau, c'est tout
   [vair do say too]

drinking water l'eau potable f
   [o pot-abl]
   is this drinking water? est-ce
   que cette eau est potable?
   [eskuh]

Public water supplies are safe,
although in some cities tap
water (**l'eau du robinet**)
doesn't taste wonderful and you
might prefer to drink mineral
water (**de l'eau minérale**).

---

drive conduire [kONdweer]
   we drove here nous sommes
   venus en voiture [noo som
   vuhnoo en vwatoor]
   I'll drive you home je vais te/
   vous reconduire [juh vay tuh/
   voo ruhkONdweer]

EC and US driving licences are
valid, though an International
Driver's Licence makes life
easier if you get a policeman
unwilling to peruse a document
in English. The vehicle
registration documents and the
insurance papers must be
carried with you. If your car is
right-hand drive, you are
required by law to fit headlight
or beam converters (available
from car accessory shops) to
redirect the beams to the right.
A rule of the road to remember
                                →

in France is that you must often give way to traffic coming from a minor road on the right – the law of **priorité à droite**. Look out along the roadside for the yellow diamond on a white background that gives you right of way – until you see the same sign crossed out which indicates that vehicles emerging from the right have priority. Speed limits are: 130km/hr (80mph) on the tolled motorways; 110km/hr (68mph) on two-lane highways; 90km/hr (56mph) on other roads; and 60km/hr (37mph) or less in towns.

---

driver (of car) le conducteur [kONdookturr]
  (of bus) le chauffeur
driving licence le permis de conduire [pairmee duh kONdweer]
drop: just a drop, please (of drink) une petite goutte, s'il vous plaît [oon puhteet goot]
drug (medical) le médicament [maydeekamON]
drugs (narcotics) la drogue [drog]
drunk (adj) ivre [eevr]
drunken driving la conduite en état d'ivresse [kONdweet ON ayta deevress]

The legal limit for alcohol in the blood for drivers is 0.7%. Don't drink and drive. If you are found
→

---

to be over the limit, you are liable to a term of imprisonment of between one month and a year, and/or a fine of 8,000 to 15,000 francs.

---

drunkenness l'ivresse f [eevress]
dry (adj) sec, f sèche [sek, sesh]
dry-cleaner le teinturier [tANtooree-ay]
duck le canard [kanar]
due: he was due to arrive yesterday il devait arriver hier [eel duhvay]
  when is the train due? quand est-ce que le train doit arriver? [dwa]
dull (pain) sourd [soor]
  (weather) sombre [sONbr]
dummy (baby's) la tétine [tayteen]
during pendant [pONdON]
dust la poussière [pooss-yair]
dusty poussiéreux [pooss-yayruh]
dustbin la poubelle [poo-bel]
Dutch hollandais [olONday]
duty-free hors taxes [or tax]
duty-free shop la boutique hors taxes
duvet la couette [kwet]

E

each (every) chaque [shak]
  how much are they each? combien est-ce qu'ils sont la pièce? [kONb-yAN eskeel sON la

p-yess]

ear l'oreille f [oray]

earache: I have earache j'ai mal
à l'oreille [jay mal a loray]

early tôt [toh]

early in the morning tôt le
matin

I called by earlier je suis passé
tout à l'heure [toot a lurr]

earring la boucle d'oreille
[bookl doray]

east l'est m [est]

in the east à l'est

Easter Pâques [pak]

easy facile [fasseel]

eat manger [mONjay]

we've already eaten, thanks
nous avons déjà mangé,
merci [noo zavON dayja mONjay]

---

eating habits
The French usually have three
meals a day: a light breakfast,
consisting of **café** or **café au lait**
and bread/**croissants**, butter
and jam; a substantial lunch,
with a first course of **charcuterie**
or salad, a second course of
meat or fish and vegetables
(vegetarianism still hasn't made
a great impact on France),
followed by cheese and/or
dessert, then coffee (the
majority of people still have a
substantial lunch-time meal,
although in cities, snacks and
sandwiches are popular among
office workers); the evening →

---

meal (similar courses to lunch)
is normally quite substantial as
well. It is quite common to have
an **apéritif** (drink and snack)
before lunch and dinner.

---

eau de toilette l'eau de
toilette f

EC CE f [say uh]

economy class la classe
économique [klass
aykonomeek]

egg l'œuf m [urf]

eggplant l'aubergine f
[obairjeen]

either: either ... or ... soit ...
soit ... [swa]

either of them soit l'un soit
l'autre

elastic l'élastique m [aylasteek]

elastic band l'élastique m

elbow le coude [kood]

electric électrique [aylektreek]

electrical appliances les
appareils électriques mpl
[aparay]

electric fire le radiateur
électrique [rad-yaturr]

electrician l'électricien m
[aylektreess-yAN]

electricity l'électricité f
[aylektreesseetay]
see **voltage**

elevator l'ascenseur m
[asONsurr]

else: something else autre
chose [ohtr shohz]

somewhere else ailleurs
[ī-yurr]

•••••• D I A L O G U E ••••••

would you like anything else?
désirez-vous autre chose?
no, nothing else, thanks non, c'est
tout, merci [say too]

embassy l'ambassade f
[ONbasad]

emergency l'urgence f [ꝏrjONss]
this is an emergency! c'est
une urgence! [sayt ꝏn]

emergency exit la sortie de
secours [sortee duh suhkoor]

empty vide [veed]

end la fin [fAN]
(verb) finir [feeneer]
at the end of the street au
bout de la rue [o boo duh la
rꝏ]
when does it end? quand est-
ce que ça finit? [kONteskuh sa
feenee]

engaged (toilet, telephone)
occupé [okꝏpay]
(to be married) fiancé [f-yONsay]

engine (car) le moteur [moturr]

England l'Angleterre f
[ONgluhtair]

English anglais [ONglay]
I'm English (man/woman) je
suis anglais/anglaise [-ez]
do you speak English? parlez-
vous l'anglais? [parlay voo]

enjoy: to enjoy oneself
s'amuser [samꝏzay]

•••••• D I A L O G U E ••••••

how did you like the film?
comment as-tu trouvé le film?
[komON atꝏ troovay]

I enjoyed it very much j'ai
beaucoup aimé [jay bo-koo paymay]

enjoyable très agréable [tray
zagrayabl]

enlargement (of photo)
l'agrandissement m
[agrONdeesmON]

enormous énorme [aynorm]

enough assez [assay]
there's not enough il n'y a pas
assez [eel nya pa]
it's not big enough ce n'est
pas assez grand
that's enough ça suffit [sa
sꝏfee]

entrance l'entrée f [ONtray]

envelope l'enveloppe f [ONvlop]

epileptic épileptique
[aypeelepteek]

equipment (for climbing etc)
l'équipement m [aykeepmON]

error l'erreur f [air-rurr]

especially spécialement [spays-
yalmON]

essential essentiel [aysONs-yel]
it is essential that ... il est
essentiel que ...

EU (European Union) l'Union
Européenne f [ꝏn-yON
urropay-en]

Eurocheque l'Eurochèque m
[urroshek]

Eurocheque card la carte
Eurochèque [kart]

Europe l'Europe f [urrop]

European européen(ne)
[urropay-AN, -en]

even même [mem]

even if ... même si ...
evening le soir [swahr]
  this evening ce soir
  in the evening le soir
evening meal le repas du soir [ruhpa]
eventually finalement [feenalmON]
ever jamais [jamay]

•••••• DIALOGUE ••••••

have you ever been to Cannes? est-ce que vous êtes déjà allé à Cannes? [eskuh voo zet dayja alay a]
yes, I was there two years ago oui, j'y suis allé il y a deux ans

every chaque [shak]
  every day chaque jour
everyone tout le monde [too luh mONd]
everything tout [too]
everywhere partout [partoo]
exactly! exactement! [exaktuhmON]
exam l'examen m [examAN]
example l'exemple m [exONpl]
  for example par exemple
excellent excellent [exsaylON]
  excellent! parfait! [parfay]
except sauf [sohf]
excess baggage l'excédent de bagages m [exsaydON duh bagahj]
exchange rate le cours du change [koor dOO shONj]
exciting passionnant [pass-yonON]
excuse me (to get past, to get attention) pardon [par-dON]

(to say sorry) excusez-moi, pardon
exhaust (pipe) le tuyau d'échappement [twee-o dayshapmON]
exhausted (tired) épuisé [aypweezay]
exhibition l'exposition f [expozeess-yON]
exit la sortie [sortee]
  where's the nearest exit? où se trouve la sortie la plus proche?
expect attendre [atONdr]
expensive cher [shair]
experienced expérimenté [expayreemONtay]
explain expliquer [expleekay]
  can you explain that? pouvez-vous expliquer cela? [poovay-voo]
express (mail) par exprès [express]
  (train) express
extension le poste [posst]
  extension 21, please poste vingt-et-un, s'il vous plaît
extension lead la rallonge [ralONj]
extra: can we have an extra one? pouvons-nous en avoir un/une supplémentaire? [poovON-noo zON avwahr AN/OOn sOOplaymONtair]
  do you charge extra for that? est-ce qu'il faut payer un supplément pour ça? [eskeel fo pay-ay AN sOOplaymON poor sa]
extraordinary (strange)

extraordinaire

extremely extrêmement [extrem-mON]

eye l'œil m [uh-ee]

  will you keep an eye on my suitcase for me? est-ce que vous pouvez surveiller ma valise? [eskuh voo poovay sOOrvay-ay]

eyebrow pencil le crayon à sourcils [soorsee]

eye drops les gouttes pour les yeux [goot poor lay z-juh]

eyeglasses les lunettes [lOOnet]

eyeliner l'eye-liner m

eye make-up remover le démaquillant pour les yeux [daymalee-yON]

eye shadow l'ombre à paupière f [ONbr a pohp-yair]

F

face le visage [veezahj]

factory l'usine f [OOzeen]

Fahrenheit* fahrenheit [faren-ī-t]

faint s'évanouir [sayvanweer]

  she's fainted elle s'est évanouie [el set ayvanwee]

  I feel faint je me sens mal [juh muh sON]

fair la foire [fwahr]

  (adj) juste [jOOst]

fairly (quite) assez [assay]

fake le faux [fo]

fall l'automne m [oton]

  see **autumn**

fall (verb) tomber [tONbay]

she's had a fall elle est tombée [eel ay tONbay]

false faux, f fausse [fo, fohss]

family la famille [famee]

famous célèbre [saylebr]

fan (electrical) le ventilateur [vONteelaturr]

  (hand held) l'éventail m [ayvONt-ī]

  (sports) le/la fan [fan]

fan belt la courroie du ventilateur [koorwa dOO]

fantastic fantastique [fONtasteek]

far loin [lwAN]

•••••• DIALOGUE ••••••

is it far from here? c'est loin d'ici? [say lwAN dee-see]

no, not very far non, pas très loin

it's about 20 kilometres c'est à vingt kilomètres environ [ONveerON]

fare le prix (du billet) [pree (dOO beeyay)]

farm la ferme [fairm]

fashionable à la mode [mod]

fast rapide [rapeed]

fat (person) gros, f grosse [gro, gross]

  (on meat) le gras [gra]

father le père [pair]

father-in-law le beau-père [bo-pair]

faucet le robinet [robeenay]

fault le défaut [dayfo]

  sorry, it was my fault désolé, c'est de ma faute [say duh ma foht]

  it's not my fault ce n'est pas

de ma faute

faulty (equipment) défectueux [dayfektoo-uh]

favourite préféré [prayfay-ray]

fax le fax

(verb) (person) envoyer un fax à [ONvwy-ay]

(document) faxer [faxay]

February février [fayvree-ay]

feel sentir [sONteer]

I feel hot j'ai chaud [jay sho]

I feel unwell je ne me sens pas bien [juh nuh muh sON pa b-yAN]

I feel like going for a walk j'ai envie d'aller me promener [jay ONvee]

how are you feeling? comment te sens-tu/vous sentez-vous? [komON tuh sON-too/voo sONtay-voo]

I'm feeling better je me sens mieux [juh muh sON m-yuh]

felt-tip pen le stylo-feutre [steelo-furtr]

fence la barrière [baree-air]

fender le pare-chocs [par-shok]

ferry le ferry

festival le festival [festeeval]

fetch aller chercher [alay shairshay]

I'll fetch him j'irai le chercher [jeeray]

will you come and fetch me later? est-ce que tu peux/vous pouvez venir me chercher plus tard? [eskuh too puh/voo poovay vuh-neer muh]

feverish fiévreux [fee-evruh]

few: a few quelques-uns, quelques-unes [kelkuh-zAN, kelkuh-zoon]

a few days quelques jours

fiancé le fiancé [fee-ONsay]

fiancée la fiancée [fee-ONsay]

field le champ [shON]

fight la bagarre [bagar]

fill remplir [rONpleer]

fill in remplir [rONpleer]

do I have to fill this in? est-ce que je dois remplir ceci? [eskuh juh dwa]

fill up remplir [rONpleer]

fill it up, please le plein, s'il vous plaît [luh plAN]

filling (in cake, sandwich) la garniture

(in tooth) le plombage [plONbahj]

film (movie) le film [feelm]

(for camera) la pellicule [peleekool]

do you have this kind of film? avez-vous ce genre de pellicule? [avay-voo]

yes, how many exposures? oui, avec combien de poses? [kONb-yAN duh pohz]

36 trente-six

film processing le développement de la pellicule [dayv-lopmON]

filter coffee le café filtre [feeltr]

filter papers les filtres mpl

filthy crasseux [krassuh]

find trouver [troovay]
  I can't find it je n'arrive pas à
  le retrouver [juh nareev pa a
  luh ruh-]
  I've found it je l'ai trouvé [lay
  troovay]
find out découvrir [daykoovreer]
  could you find out for me?
  pourriez-vous vous
  renseigner pour moi?
  [pooree-ay-voo voo rONsen-yay
  poor mwa]
fine (weather) beau [bo]
  (punishment) l'amende f
  [amONd]

•••••• DIALOGUES ••••••

how are you? comment vas-tu/
allez-vous? [komON vatoo/alay-voo]
I'm fine thanks bien, merci [b-yAN]
and you? et toi/vous? [twa]

is that OK? est-ce que ça ira?
[eskuh sa eera]
that's fine thanks ça ira très bien
comme cela, merci [tray b-yAN kom
suhla]

finger le doigt [dwa]
finish terminer [tairmeenay]
  I haven't finished yet je n'ai
  pas encore terminé [juh nay
  pa zONkor tairmeenay]
  when does it finish? à quelle
  heure est-ce que ça finit? [a
  kel urr eskuh sa feenee]
fire le feu [fuh]
  can we light a fire here?
  pouvons-nous faire du feu
  ici? [poovON-noo fair doo]

  it's on fire il a pris feu [eel a
  pree]
fire alarm l'avertisseur
  d'incendie m [avairteessurr
  dANSONdee]
fire brigade les pompiers
  [pONp-yay]

In the event of a fire, phone 18.

fire escape la sortie de secours
  [sortee duh suhkoor]
fire extinguisher l'extincteur m
  [extANkturr]
first premier [pruhm-yay]
  I was first je suis arrivé avant
  vous [juh sweez areevay avON
  voo]
  at first tout d'abord [too
  dabor]
  the first time la première fois
  [pruhm-yair fwa]
  first on the left la première à
  gauche
first aid les premiers secours
  [pruhm-yay suhkoor]
first aid kit la trousse de
  premiers secours [trooss duh]
first class (compartment etc) de
  première (classe) [duh
  pruhm-yair klass]
first floor le premier [pruhm-yay]
  US le rez-de-chaussée [rayd-
  shoh-say]
first name le prénom [praynON]
fish le poisson [pwassON]
fishing village le village de
  pêcheurs [veelahj duh peshurr]
fishmonger's la poissonnerie

ENGLISH ◆ FRENCH Fi

[pwassonnuh-ree]

fit (attack) l'attaque f [atak]
(verb) it doesn't fit me ce n'est
pas la bonne taille [suh
nay pa la bon tī]

fitting room la cabine
d'essayage [kabeen dessay-ahj]

fix réparer [rayparay]
can you fix this? pouvez-vous
réparer ceci? [poovay-voo]

fizzy gazeux [gazuh]

flag le drapeau [drapo]

flannel le gant de toilette [goN
duh twalet]

flash (for camera) le flash

flat (apartment) l'appartement m
[apartmoN]
(adj) plat [pla]
I've got a flat tyre j'ai un pneu
à plat [jay un pnuh]

flavour l'arôme m [arohm]

flea la puce [pʊss]

flight le vol

flight number le numéro de vol
[nʊmay-ro]

flippers les palmes fpl [pal-m]

flood l'inondation f [eenoNdass-
yoN]

floor (of room) le plancher
[ploNshay]
(storey) l'étage m [aytahj]
on the floor par terre [tair]

florist le/la fleuriste [flurreest]

flour la farine [fareen]

flower la fleur [flurr]

flu la grippe [greep]

fluent: he speaks fluent French il
parle couramment le
français [kooramoN]

fly la mouche [moosh]
(verb) voler [volay]

fly in arriver en avion [arrevay
en av-yoN]

fly out partir en avion [parteer]

fog le brouillard [broo-yar]

foggy: it's foggy il y a du
brouillard [eelya dʊ broo-yar]

folk dancing les danses
folkloriques [doNss]

folk music la musique
folklorique [mʊzeek]

follow suivre [sweevr]
follow me suivez-moi
[sweevay-mwa]

food la nourriture [nooreetʊr]

food poisoning l'intoxication
alimentaire f [ANtoxeekass-yoN
aleemoNtair]

food shop/store le magasin
d'alimentation [magazaN
daleemoNtass-yoN]

foot* le pied [p-yay]
on foot à pied

football (game) le football
(ball) le ballon de football
[baloN]

football match le match de
football

for pour [poor]
do you have something for ...?
(headache/diarrhoea etc) avez-
vous quelque chose
contre ...? [avay-voo kelkuh-
shohz koNtr]

•••••• DIALOGUES ••••••

who's the chocolate mousse for? la
mousse au chocolat, c'est pour

qui?

that's for me c'est pour moi [mwa]

and this one? et l'autre?

that's for her c'est pour elle

where do I get the bus for Gare de
l'Est? où dois-je prendre le bus
pour aller à la gare de l'Est? [oo
dwaj pRONdr luh bOOss poor alay]

the bus for Gare de l'Est leaves
from rue de Rivoli le bus qui va à
la gare de l'Est part de la rue de
Rivoli

how long have you been here for?
ça fait combien de temps que
vous êtes ici? [sa fay kONb-yAN duh
tON kuh voo zet ee-see]

I've been here for two days, how
about you? je suis ici depuis deux
jours, et vous? [juh swee zee-see
duhpwee]

I've been here for a week je suis
ici depuis une semaine

forehead le front [frON]

foreign étranger [aytrONjay]

foreigner l'étranger m,
l'étrangère f [aytrONjay, -jair]

forest la forêt [foray]

forget oublier [ooblee-ay]

I forget, I've forgotten j'ai
oublié [jay ooblee-ay]

fork (for eating) la fourchette
[foorshet]
(in road) l'embranchement m
[ONbrONshmON]

form (document) le formulaire

formal dress la tenue de soirée
[tuhnoo duh swahray]

fortnight la quinzaine [kANzen]

fortunately heureusement
[urrurzmON]

forward: could you forward my
mail? est-ce que vous pouvez
faire suivre mon courrier?
[eskuh voo' poovay fair sweevr
mON koor-yay]

forwarding address l'adresse
pour faire suivre le
courrier f

foundation cream le fond de
teint [fON duh tAN]

fountain la fontaine [fONten]

foyer (of hotel) le hall [awl]
(of theatre) le foyer

fracture la fracture [fraktOOr]

France la France [frONss]

free libre [leebr]
(no charge) gratuit [gratwee]

is it free (of charge)? est-ce
que c'est gratuit? [eskuh say]

freeway l'autoroute f [otoroot]

freezer le congélateur
[kONjaylaturr]

French français, f française
[frONsay, -ez]

French fries les frites fpl [freet]

Frenchman le Français [frONsay]

Frenchwoman la Française
[frONsez]

frequent fréquent [fraykON]

how frequent is the bus to
Marseilles? à quels intervalles
y a-t-il un bus pour
Marseille? [a kel ANtairval
yateel]

fresh frais, f fraîche [fray, fresh]

fresh orange l'orange pressée f

[orONj pressay]

Friday vendredi [vONdruhdee]
fridge le frigo [freego]
fried frit [free]
fried egg l'œuf sur le plat m
[urf soor luh pla]
friend l'ami m, l'amie f [amee]
friendly amical [ameekal]
from de [duh]

when does the next train from
Lyons arrive? à quelle heure
arrive le prochain train en
provenance de Lyon? [ON
provuhnONss]
from Monday to Friday du
lundi au vendredi [doo ... o]
from next Thursday à partir de
jeudi prochain [a parteer]

•••••• DIALOGUE ••••••

where are you from? d'où es-tu/
êtes-vous? [doo ay-too/et-voo]
I'm from Slough je suis de Slough
[juh swee]

front l'avant m [avON]
in front devant [duhvON]
in front of the hotel devant
l'hôtel
at the front à l'avant
frost le gel [jel]
frozen gelé [juhlay]
frozen food les aliments
surgelés [aleemON soorjuhlay]
fruit les fruits mpl [frwee]
fruit juice le jus de fruit [joo duh
frwee]
fry frire [freer]
frying pan la poêle [pwal]
full plein [plAN]

it's full of ... c'est plein de ...
I'm full j'ai trop mangé [jay tro
mONjay]
full board la pension complète
[pONs-yON kONplet]
fun: it was fun on s'est bien
amusé [ON say b-yAN amoozay]
funny (strange, amusing) drôle
furniture les meubles mpl
[murbl]
further plus loin [ploo lwAN]
it's further down the road c'est
plus loin sur cette route
[root]

•••••• DIALOGUE ••••••

how much further is it to Figeac? il
y a encore combien de
kilomètres pour arriver à
Figeac? [eelya ONkor kONb-yAN duh
keelometr]
about 5 kilometres environ cinq
kilomètres [ONveerON]

fuse le fusible [foozeebl]
the lights have fused les
plombs ont sauté [lay plON ON
sohtay]
fuse box la boîte à fusibles
[bwat]
fuse wire le fusible
future le futur [footoor]
in future à l'avenir [a lavneer]

G

gallon* le gallon [galON]
game (cards etc) le jeu [juh]
(match) la partie [partee]
(meat) le gibier [jeeb-yay]

garage (for fuel) la station
d'essence [stass-yON dessONss]
(for repairs, parking) le garage
[garahj]

Although motorway and big city
garages are open 24 hours seven
days a week, those situated on
smaller roads and in small
towns usually close all day
Sunday and at 7.30-8 p.m. on
other days. Nowadays, most
garages are self-service – only in
smaller garages will the pump
assistant fill the tank for you or
clean the windscreen and check
the water, oil and tyres.

---

garden le jardin [jardAN]
garlic l'ail m [ī]
gas l'essence f [essONss]
gas cylinder (camping gas) la
bouteille de gaz [bootay]
gasoline (US) l'essence f
[essONss]
see **petrol**
gas permeable lenses les
lentilles semi-rigides fpl
[lontee suhmee-reejeed]
gas station la station-service
[stass-yON-sairveess]
gate le portail [port-ī]
(at airport) la porte [port]
gay homosexuel
gay bar le bar d'homosexuels
gears les vitesses fpl [veetess]
gearbox la boîte de vitesses
[bwat]
gear lever le levier de vitesses

[luhv-yay]
general (adj) général [jaynay-ral]
Geneva Genève [juhnev]
gents (toilet) les toilettes pour
hommes [twalet poor om]
genuine (antique etc)
authentique [otONteek]
German allemand [almON]
German measles la rubéole
[rOObay-ol]
Germany l'Allemagne f [almañ]
get (fetch) obtenir [obtuhneer]
will you get me another one,
please? est-ce que vous
pouvez m'en apporter un
autre, s'il vous plaît? [eskuh
voo poovay mON aportay AN ohtr]
how do I get to ...? pouvez-
vous m'indiquer comment
aller à ...? [poovay-voo
mANdeekay komON talay]
do you know where I can get
them? est-ce que vous savez
où je peux en trouver?
[eskuh voo savay oo juh puh zON
troovay]

•••••• DIALOGUE ••••••

can I get you a drink? puis-je
t'offrir/vous offrir un verre?
[pweej tofreer ...]
no, I'll get this one, what would
you like? non, celui-là c'est pour
moi, que voudrais-tu/voudriez-
vous? [suhlwee-la say poor mwa]
a glass of red wine un verre de
vin rouge

get back (return) rentrer
[rONtray]

get in (arrive) arriver [areevay]

get off descendre [duhsONdr]
  where do I get off? où dois-je
  descendre? [oo dwaj]

get on (to train etc) monter
  [mONtay]

get out (of car etc) descendre
  [duhsONdr]

get up (in the morning, stand up) se
  lever [suh luhvay]

gift le cadeau [kado]

gift shop la boutique de
  cadeaux

gin le gin [djeen]
  a gin and tonic, please un
  gin-tonic, s'il vous plaît

girl la fille [fee]

girlfriend la petite amie [puhteet
  amee]

give donner [donay]
  can you give me some
  change? pouvez-vous me
  donner de la monnaie?
  [poovay-voo] ~
  I gave it to him je le lui ai
  donné [juh luh lwee ay donay]
  will you give this to ...?
  pouvez-vous donner ceci
  à ...?

•••••• DIALOGUE ••••••

how much do you want for this?
combien en voulez-vous? [kONb-
yAN ON voolay-voo]
100 francs cent francs
I'll give you 90 francs je vous en
donne 90 francs [juh voo zON don]

give back rendre [rONdr]

glad content [kONtON]

glass le verre [vair]
  a glass of wine un verre de
  vin

glasses (spectacles) les lunettes
  [loonet]

gloves les gants mpl [gON]

glue la colle [kol]

go aller [alay]
  we'd like to go to the cathedral
  nous aimerions aller à la
  cathédrale [noo zemree-ON
  alay a]
  where are you going? où vas-
  tu/allez-vous? [oo vatoo/alay
  voo]
  where does this bus go? où va
  ce bus?
  let's go! allons-y! [alONzee]
  she's gone (left) elle est
  partie [partee]
  where has he gone? où est-il
  allé? [alay]
  I went there last week j'y suis
  allé la semaine dernière

hamburger to go hamburger à
  emporter [ONportay]

go away partir [parteer]
  go away! va t'en!/allez-vous-
  en! [vatON/alay-voo-zON]

go back (return) retourner
  [ruhtoornay]

go down descendre [duhsONdr]
  (price) baisser [bessay]

go in entrer [ONtray]

go out (in the evening) sortir
  [sorteer]
  do you want to go out tonight?
  veux-tu/voulez-vous sortir
  ce soir? [vuh-too/voolay-voo]

go through traverser [travairsay]

go up monter [mONtay]

goat la chèvre [shevr]

goat's cheese le fromage de chèvre [fromahj]

God Dieu [d-yuh]

goggles (ski) les lunettes de ski [lōōnet]

gold l'or m

golf le golf

golf course le terrain de golf [terrAN]

good bon, f bonne [bON, bon]
   good! bien! [b-yAN]
   it's no good ça ne va pas [sa nuh va pa]

goodbye au revoir [o ruh-vwa]

good evening bonsoir [bON-swa]

Good Friday le Vendredi Saint [vONdruhdee sAN]

good morning bonjour [bON-joor]

good night bonne nuit [bon nwee]

goose l'oie f [wa]

got: we've got to leave il faut que nous partions [eel fo kuh]
   I've got to ... il faut que je ...
   have you got any ...? est-ce que tu as/vous avez des/du ...? [eskuh tōō a/voo zavay ...]

government le gouvernement [goovairnuhmON]

gradually peu à peu [puh a puh]

grammar la grammaire

gram(me) le gramme

granddaughter la petite-fille [puhteet-fee]

grandfather le grand-père [grON-pair]

grandmother la grand-mère [grON-mair]

grandson le petit-fils [puhtee-feess]

grapefruit le pamplemousse [pONpluh-mooss]

grapefruit juice le jus de pamplemousse [jōō]

grapes le raisin [rez-AN]

grass l'herbe f [airb]

grateful reconnaissant [ruhkonessON]

gravy la sauce au jus de viande [sohss o joo duh vee-ONd]

great (excellent) fantastique [fONtasteek]
   that's great! c'est formidable! [say formee-dabl]
   a great success un grand succès [grON sōōk-say]

Great Britain la Grande-Bretagne [grOND-bruhtañ]

Greece la Grèce [gress]

greedy gourmand [goormON]

Greek grec

green vert [vair]

green card (car insurance) la carte verte [kart vairt]

greengrocer's le marchand de légumes [marshON duh laygōōm]

grey gris [gree]

grill le grill

grilled grillé [gree-yay]

grocer's l'épicerie f [aypeesree]

ground le sol
   on the ground par terre [tair]

ground floor le rez-de-chaussée

[rayd-shoh-say]

group le groupe [groop]

guarantee la garantie [garONtee]
is it guaranteed? y a-t-il une garantie? [yateel]

guest l'invité(e) [ANveetay]

guesthouse la pension [pONs-yON]
see **hotel**

guide le guide [geed]

guidebook le guide

guided tour la visite guidée [veezeet geeday]

guitar la guitare [geetar]

gum (in mouth) la gencive [jONseev]

gun le fusil [fOOzee]

gym le gymnase [jeemnaz]

H

hair les cheveux mpl [shuhvuh]

hairbrush la brosse à cheveux [bross]

haircut la coupe de cheveux [koop]

hairdresser le coiffeur [kwafurr]

hairdryer le sèche-cheveux [sesh-shuhvuh]

hair gel le gel (pour les cheveux) [jel]

hairgrips les pinces à cheveux fpl [pANss]

hair spray la laque [lak]

half* la moitié [mwatee-ay]
half an hour une demi-heure [duhmee-urr]
half a litre un demi-litre
about half that la moitié

half board la demi-pension [duhmee-pONs-yON]

half-bottle la demi bouteille [bootay]

half fare le demi-tarif [tareef]

half price moitié prix [mwatee-ay pree]

ham le jambon [jONbON]

hamburger le hamburger [ONboorgair]

hammer le marteau [marto]

hand la main [mAN]

handbag le sac à main

handbrake le frein à main [frAN]

handkerchief le mouchoir [mooshwahr]

handle la poignée [pwAN-yay]

hand luggage les bagages à main mpl [bagahj]

hang-gliding le deltaplane [-plahn]

hangover la gueule de bois [gurl duh bwa]
I've got a hangover j'ai la gueule de bois

happen arriver [areevay]
what's happening? qu'est-ce qui se passe? [kes-kee suh pass]
what has happened? qu'est-ce qui s'est passé? [say passay]

happy heureux [ur-ruh]
I'm not happy about this ça ne me plaît pas [sa nuh muh play pa]

harbour le port [por]

hard dur [dOOr]
(difficult) difficile [deefeesseel]

hard-boiled egg l'œuf dur m
[urf]

hard lenses les lentilles dures
fpl [lONtee dOOr]

hardly à peine [a pen]
    hardly ever presque jamais
    [presk jamay]

hardware shop la quincaillerie
[kAN-ky-ree]

hat le chapeau [shapo]

hate détester [daytestay]

have* avoir [avwahr]
    can I have a ...? j'aimerais ...
    [jemray]
    do you have ...? as-tu/avez-
    vous ...? [atOO/avay-voo]
    what'll you have? qu'est-ce
    que tu prends/vous prenez?
    [keskuh tOO prON/voo pruhnay]
    I have to leave now je dois
    partir maintenant [juh dwa]
    do I have to ...? est-ce que je
    dois ...? [eskuh]
    can we have some ...? est-ce
    que nous pouvons avoir
    du ...?
    we don't have any left nous
    n'en avons plus [noo nON avON
    plOO]

hayfever le rhume des foins
[rOOm day fwAN]

hazelnuts les noisettes fpl
[nwazet]

he* il [eel]

head la tête [tet]

headache le mal de tête

headlights les phares mpl [far]

headphones les écouteurs mpl
[aykooturr]

health food shop le magasin de
produits diététiques m
[magazAN duh prodwee dee-
aytayteek]

healthy (food, climate) bon pour
la santé [sONtay]
    (person) bien portant [b-yAN
    portON]

hear entendre [ONtONdr]

•••••• DIALOGUE ••••••

    can you hear me? m'entendez-
    vous? [mONtONday-voo]
    I can't hear you, could you repeat
    that? je ne vous entends pas,
    pouvez-vous répéter? [juh nuh voo
    zONtON pa poovay-voo raypaytay]

hearing aid l'audiophone m
[odeeo-fon]

heart le cœur [kurr]

heart attack la crise cardiaque
[kreez kard-yak]

heat la chaleur [shalurr]

heater (in room) le radiateur
[rad-yaturr]
    (in car) le chauffage [shohfahj]

heating le chauffage

heavy lourd [loor]

heel le talon [talON]
    could you heel these? pouvez-
    vous refaire les talons?
    [poovay-voo ruhfair]

heelbar le talon-minute [talON-
meenOOt]

height (of person) la taille [tī]
    (of mountain) l'altitude f

helicopter l'hélicoptère m
[ayleekoptair]

hello bonjour [bONjoor]

(answer on phone) **allô**

helmet (for motorcycle) **le casque** [kask]

help **l'aide** f [ed]
(verb) **aider** [ayday]
help! au secours! [o suhkoor]
can you help me? est-ce que vous pouvez m'aider? [eskuh voo poovay]
thank you very much for your help merci de votre aide

helpful (person) **serviable** [sairvee-abl]
(objects) **utile** [ooteel]

hepatitis l'hépatite f [aypateet]

her*: I haven't seen her je ne l'ai pas vue
to her à elle [el]
with her avec elle
for her pour elle
that's her c'est elle
that's her towel c'est sa serviette

herbal tea la tisane [teezahn]

herbs les fines herbes fpl [feen zairb]

here ici [ee-see]
here is/are ... voici ... [vwa-see]
here you are (offering) **voilà** [vwala]

hers*: that's hers c'est à elle [set a el]

hey! hé! [hay]

hi! (hello) **salut!**

hide cacher [kashay]

high haut [o]

highchair la chaise haute [shez oht]

highway l'autoroute f [otoroot]

hill la colline [koleen]

him*: I haven't seen him je ne l'ai pas vu
to him à lui [lwee]
with him avec lui
for him pour lui
that's him c'est lui

hip la hanche [ONsh]

hire: for hire à louer [loo-ay]
(verb) **louer**
where can I hire a bike? où y a-t-il des vélos à louer? [oo yateel]
see also **rent**

his*: it's his car c'est sa voiture
it's his bike c'est son vélo [sON]
that's his c'est à lui [set a lwee]

hit frapper [frapay]

hitch-hike faire de l'autostop [fair duh lotostop]

hobby le hobby [obbee]

hockey le hockey [ockee]

hold tenir [tuhneer]

hole le trou [troo]

holiday les vacances fpl [vakONss]
on holiday en vacances [ON]

Holland la Hollande [ollONd]

home la maison [mezzON]
at home (in my house etc) **chez moi** [shay mwa]
(in my country) **dans mon pays** [dON mON payee]
we go home tomorrow nous rentrons demain [rONtrON duhmAN]

honest honnête [onnet]
honey le miel [mee-el]
honeymoon la lune de miel
  [l∞n]
hood (US) le capot [kapo]
hope espérer [espayray]
  I hope so j'espère que oui
  [jespair kuh wee]
  I hope not j'espère que non
hopefully: hopefully he'll arrive
  soon espérons qu'il arrive
  bientôt [espairON]
horn (of car) le klaxon
horrible horrible [oreebl]
horse le cheval [shuhval]
horse riding l'équitation f
  [aykeetass-yON]
hospital l'hôpital m [opee-tal]
hospitality l'hospitalité f [-eetay]
  thank you for your hospitality
  merci de votre hospitalité

If you are invited to someone's
home, you can take a bunch of
flowers (but not chrysan-
themums which are used in
cemeteries) or a plant, or a box
of chocolates. Unlike in the UK,
it is not very common to take a
bottle of wine as a present when
invited for a meal. If you are
staying at someone's house, you
may want to take presents such
as whisky, tea, etc.

hot chaud [sho]
  (spicy) épicé [aypeessay]
  I'm hot j'ai chaud [jay]
  it's hot today il fait chaud

aujourd'hui [eel fay]
hotel l'hôtel m [otel]

Most French hotels are graded
from zero to five stars. The price
more or less corresponds to the
number of stars, although the
system is a little haphazard.
Ungraded and single-star hotels
are often very good. Remember
that the price displayed is the
price for the room only,
excluding breakfast. In rural
areas, you'll also find chambres
d'hôte – bed and breakfast
accommodation in someone's
house or farm. These vary in
standard but are rarely an
inexpensive option. If you are
planning to stay a week or more
in any one place it might be
worth considering renting
accommodation (gîte). You can
do this by checking adverts in
British Sunday newspapers or
trying one of the numerous
holiday firms that market
accommodation/travel
packages. It's easier, however,
to use the London office of the
official French government
service Gîtes de France.

hotel room: in my hotel room
  dans ma chambre d'hôtel
  [shONbr]
hour l'heure f [urr]
house la maison [mezzON]
house wine le vin maison [vaN]

In most restaurants, **le vin maison** will be a good value quality wine. You can ask for **une carafe** (4-5 glasses) or **une demi-carafe** (2-3 glasses).

hovercraft l'aéroglisseur m [a-ayro-gleessurr]

how comment [komON]

how many? combien? [kONb-yAN]

how do you do? enchanté! [ONshONtay]

•••••• DIALOGUE ••••••

how are you? comment vas-tu/allez-vous? [komON va-tœ/alay-voo]

fine, thanks, and you? bien, merci, et toi/vous? [twa]

how much is it? c'est combien? **... francs** ... francs **I'll take it** je le prends [juh luh prON]

humid humide [œmeed]

humour l'humour m [œmoor]

hungry: I'm hungry j'ai faim [jay fAN]

are you hungry? est-ce que tu as/vous avez faim? [eskuh tœ a/voo zavay]

hurry se dépêcher [suh daypeshay]

I'm in a hurry je suis pressé [juh swee pressay]

there's no hurry ce n'est pas pressé [suh nay pa]

hurry up! dépêche-toi!/dépêchez-vous! [daypesh-twa/

daypeshay-voo]

hurt faire mal

it really hurts ça fait vraiment mal [sa fay vraymON]

husband le mari [maree]

hydrofoil l'hydrofoil m [eedro-]

hypermarket l'hypermarché m [eepairmarshay]

I

I je [juh]

ice la glace [glass]

with ice avec des glaçons [glassON]

no ice, thanks pas de glaçons, merci

ice cream la glace [glass]

ice-cream cone le cornet de glace [kornay]

iced coffee le café glacé [glassay]

ice lolly l'esquimau m [eskeemo]

ice rink la patinoire [pateenwahr]

ice skates les patins à glace mpl [patAN a glass]

idea l'idée f [eeday]

idiot l'idiot m [eedee-o]

if si [see]

ignition l'allumage m [alœmahj]

ill malade [malad]

I feel ill je ne me sens pas bien [juh nuh muh sON pa b-yAN]

illness la maladie [maladee]

imitation (leather etc) l'imitation f [eemeetass-yON]

immediately immédiatement [eemaydee-atmON], tout de

suite [toot sweet]

important important [ANportON]
it's very important c'est très
important [say tray]
it's not important ça ne fait
rien [sa nuh fay ree-AN]

impossible impossible [ANposs-
eebl]

impressive impressionnant
[ANpress-yonON]

improve améliorer [amayleeoray]
I want to improve my French je
veux améliorer mon
français [juh vuh]

in: it's in the centre c'est au
centre [o sONtr]
in my car dans ma voiture
[dON]
in Dijon à Dijon
in two days from now d'ici
deux jours
in May en mai [ON]
in English en anglais
in French en français
is he in? il est là? [eel ay la]
in five minutes dans cinq
minutes

inch* le pouce [pooss]

include inclure [ANkloor]
does that include meals? est-
ce que les repas sont
compris? [ekuh lay ruhpa sON
kONpree]
is that included? est-ce que
c'est compris?

inconvenient inopportun
[eenoportAN]

incredible (very good, amazing)
incroyable [ANkrwy-abl]

Indian indien, f indienne
[ANdee-AN, -en]

indicator (on car) le clignotant
[kleen-yotON]

indigestion l'indigestion f
[ANdeejest-yON]

indoor pool la piscine couverte
[peesseen koovairt]

indoors à l'intérieur [lANtay-ree-
urr]

inexpensive bon marché [bON
marshay]

infection l'infection f [ANfex-yON]

infectious contagieux [kONtahj-
yuh]

inflammation l'inflammation f
[ANflamass-yON]

informal simple [SAN-pl]

information le renseignement
[rONsen-yuhmON]
do you have any information
about ...? est-ce que vous
avez des renseignements
sur ...? [eskuh voo zavay]

information desk les
renseignements [rONsen-
yuhmON]

injection la piqûre [pee-koor]

injured blessé [blessay]
she's been injured elle est
blessée

in-laws les beaux-parents
[bo-parON]

inner tube la chambre à air
[shONbr]

innocent innocent [eenosON]

insect l'insecte m [ANsekt]

insect bite la piqûre d'insecte
[peekoor]

do you have anything for insect bites? est-ce que vous avez quelque chose contre les piqûres d'insecte? [eskuh voo zavay kelkuh shohz]

insect repellent la crème anti-insecte [krem ONtee-ANsekt]

inside à l'intérieur [lANtayree-urr]

inside the hotel dans l'hôtel [dON]

let's sit inside allons nous asseoir à l'intérieur

insist insister [ANseestay]

I insist j'insiste [jANseest]

insomnia l'insomnie f [ANsomnee]

instant coffee le café soluble [solꝏbl]

instead à la place [plass]

give me that one instead donnez-moi celui-ci à la place [donay-mwa suhlwee-see]

instead of ... au lieu de ... [o l-yuh duh]

insulin l'insuline f [ANsꝏleen]

insurance l'assurance f [assꝏroNss]

intelligent intelligent [ANtayleejON]

interested: I'm interested in ... je m'intéresse à ... [mANtay-ress]

interesting intéressant [ANtayressON]

that's very interesting c'est très intéressant

international international [ANtairnass-yonal]

interpret faire l'interprète [fair

lANtairpret]

interpreter l'interprète mf [ANtairpret]

intersection le carrefour [karfoor]

interval (at theatre) l'entracte m [ONtrakt]

into dans [dON]

I'm not into ... je n'aime pas ... [juh nem pa]

introduce présenter [prayzONtay]

may I introduce ...? puis-je vous présenter ...? [pweej voo]

invitation l'invitation f [ANveetass-yON]

invite inviter [ANveetay]

Ireland l'Irlande f [eerlOND]

Irish irlandais [eerlONday]

I'm Irish (man/woman) je suis irlandais/irlandaise [-ez]

iron (for ironing) le fer à repasser [fair a ruh-passay]

can you iron these for me? pouvez-vous me repasser ces vêtements? [vetmON]

is* est [ay]

island l'île f [eel]

it* ça [sa]; il [eel]; elle [el]

it is ... c'est ... [say]

is it ...? est-ce ...? [ess]

where is it? où est-ce que c'est? [weskuh say]

it's him c'est lui

it was ... c'était ... [saytay]

Italian italien [eetalyAN]

Italy l'Italie f [eetalee]

itch: it itches ça me démange [sa muh daymONj]

J

jack (for car) le cric [kreek]
jacket la veste [vest]
jar le pot [po]
jam la confiture [kONfeetoor]
jammed: it's jammed c'est
    coincé [say kwANsay]
January janvier [joNvee-ay]
jaw la mâchoire [mashwahr]
jazz le jazz
jealous jaloux [jaloo]
jeans le jean
jellyfish la méduse [maydooz]
jersey le tricot [treeko]
jetty la jetée [juhtay]
Jewish juif, f juive [jweef, jweev]
jeweller's la bijouterie
    [beejootuhree]
jewellery les bijoux [beejoo]
job le travail [trav-ī]
jogging le jogging
    to go jogging faire du jogging
    [fair]
joke la plaisanterie [plezzONtree]
journey le voyage [vwy-ahj]
    have a good journey! bon
    voyage!
jug le pot [po]
    a jug of water une carafe
    d'eau [do]
juice le jus [joo]
July juillet [jwee-yay]
jump sauter [sohtay]
jumper le pull [pool]
jump leads les câbles de
    démarrage [kahbl duh
    daymarahj]
junction le croisement

[krwazmON]
June juin [jwAN]
just (only) seul [surl]
    just two seulement deux
    [surlmON]
    just for me seulement pour
    moi [poor mwa]
    just here juste ici [joost ee-see]
    not just now pas maintenant
    [pa]
    we've just arrived nous
    venons d'arriver [noo vuhnON
    dareevay]

K

keep garder [garday]
    keep the change gardez la
    monnaie [garday la monay]
    can I keep it? est-ce que je
    peux le garder? [eskuh juh
    puh]
    please keep it gardez-le
ketchup le ketchup
kettle la bouilloire [boo-ee-wahr]
key la clé [klay]
    the key for room 201, please
    la clé de la chambre deux
    cent un, s'il vous plaît
key ring le porte-clé [port-klay]
kidneys (in body) les reins mpl
    [rAN]
    (food) les rognons mpl [roN-
    yON]
kill tuer [too-ay]
kilo* le kilo
kilometre* le kilomètre [keelo-
    metr]
    how many kilometres is it

to ...? combien y a-t-il de kilomètres pour aller à ...? [KONb-yAN yateel]

kind aimable [em-abl]
that's very kind c'est très aimable

•••••• DIALOGUE ••••••

which kind do you want? de quel type voulez-vous?
I want this/that kind c'est de ce type que je veux

king le roi [rwa]
kiosk le kiosque
kiss le baiser [bezzay]
(verb) embrasser [ONbrassay]

It is customary to greet friends and relatives by kissing them on both cheeks. The exception to this is when men greet each other, when they generally shake hands instead. The number of kisses can be two or four depending on which region you are in.

kitchen la cuisine [kweezeen]
kitchenette le coin-cuisine [kwAN-kweezeen]
Kleenex® les kleenex mpl®
knee le genou [juh-noo]
knickers le slip [sleep]
knife le couteau [kooto]
knitwear les tricots [treeko]
knock frapper [frapay]
knock down renverser [rONvairsay]
he's been knocked down il

s'est fait renverser [eel say fay]
knock over renverser [rONvairsay]
know (somebody, a place) connaître [konetr]
(something) savoir [savwahr]
I don't know je ne sais pas [juh nuh say pa]
I didn't know that je ne savais pas [savay]
do you know where I can find ...? savez-vous où je peux trouver ...? [savay-voo]

L

label l'étiquette f [ayteeket]
ladies' (toilets) les toilettes (pour dames) [twalet poor dam]
ladies' wear les vêtements pour femmes [vetmON poor fam]
lady la dame [dam]
lager la bière [bee-air]
see beer
lake le lac
lamb l'agneau m [an-yo]
lamp la lampe [lONp]
lane (on motorway) la voie [vwa]
(small road) le chemin [shuhmAN]
language la langue [lONg]
language course le cours de langue [koor duh lONg]
large grand [grON]
last dernier [dairn-yay]
last week la semaine

dernière [suhmen dairn-yair]
last Friday vendredi dernier
last night hier soir [yair swahr]
what time is the last train to Nancy? à quelle heure part le dernier train pour Nancy? [kel urr par]
late tard [tar]
sorry I'm late je suis désolé d'être en retard [juh swee dayzolay detr ON ruhtar]
the train was late le train avait du retard [avay dOO]
we'll be late nous allons arriver en retard [noo zalON areevay]
it's getting late il se fait tard [eel suh fay]
later plus tard [plOO tar]
I'll come back later je reviendrai plus tard [juh ruhvee-ANdray]
see you later à tout à l'heure [a toota lurr]
later on plus tard
latest dernier [dairn-yay]
by Wednesday at the latest d'ici mercredi au plus tard [o plOO tar]
laugh rire [reer]
launderette la laverie automatique [lavree otomateek]
laundromat la laverie automatique
laundry (clothes) le linge sale [lANj sal]
(place) la blanchisserie [blONsheesree]

lavatory les toilettes [twalet]
law la loi [lwa]
lawn la pelouse [puhlooz]
lawyer l'avocat m [avoka]
laxative le laxatif [laxateef]
lazy paresseux [paressuh]
lead (electrical) le fil
(électrique) [feel aylektreek]
(verb) mener à [muhnay]
where does this lead to? où cette route mène-t-elle? [oo set root mentel]
leaf la feuille [fuh-ee]
leaflet le dépliant [daypleeON]
leak la fuite [fweet]
(verb) fuir [fweer]
the roof leaks il y a une fuite dans le toit [eelya ... eelya]
learn apprendre [aprONdr]
least: not in the least pas du tout [pa dOO too]
at least au moins [o mwAN]
leather le cuir [kweer]
leave (go away) partir [parteer]
I am leaving tomorrow je m'en vais demain [juh mON vay]
he left yesterday il est parti hier [eel ay partee]
when does the bus for Avignon leave? à quelle heure part le bus pour Avignon? [par]
may I leave this here? puis-je laisser ceci ici? [pweej lessay suhsee ee-see]
I left my coat in the bar j'ai oublié ma veste au bar [jay ooblee-ay]
leeks les poireaux mpl [pwahro]
left la gauche [gohsh]

on the left à gauche
to the left sur la gauche [soor]
turn left tournez à gauche
there's none left il n'y en a
plus [eel n-yON a ploo]
left-handed gaucher [gohshay]
left luggage (office) la consigne
[kONseeñ]
leg la jambe [jONb]
lemon le citron [seetrON]
lemonade la limonade
[leemonad]
lemon tea le thé citron [tay
seetrON]
lend prêter [pretay]
will you lend me your ...?
pourrais-tu/pourriez-vous
me prêter ton/votre ...?
[pooray-too/pooree-ay-voo muh]
lens (of camera) l'objectif m
[objekteef]
lesbian la lesbienne
less moins [mwAN]
less than moins que
less expensive moins cher
lesson la leçon [luhsON]
let laisser [lessay]
will you let me know? pouvez-
vous me le faire savoir?
[poovay-voo muh luh fair
savwahr]
I'll let you know je te/vous
préviendrai [juh tuh/voo
prayvee-ANdray]
let's go for something to eat
allons manger un morceau
[alON mONjay]
let off laisser descendre [lessay
duhsONdr]

will you let me off at ...?
pouvez-vous me laisser
descendre à ..., s'il vous
plaît? [poovay-voo]
letter la lettre [letr]
do you have any letters for
me? est-ce qu'il y a du
courrier pour moi? [eskeel ya
doo kooree-ay poor mwa]
letterbox la boite à lettres [bwat
a letr]

Letterboxes in France are
yellow. They usually have one
slot for mail within the city
or **département** you're in,
and another one for **autres
destinations** (for mail going
everywhere else).

lettuce la laitue [letoo]
lever le levier [luhv-yay]
library la bibliothèque [beeblee-
otek]
licence le permis [pairmee]
lid le couvercle [koovairkl]
lie (tell untruth) mentir [mONteer]
lie down s'étendre [saytONdr]
life la vie [vee]
lifebelt la bouée de sauvetage
[boo-ay duh sohvtahj]
lifeguard le maître nageur [metr
nahjurr]
life jacket le gilet de sauvetage
[jeelay duh sohvtahj]
lift (in building) l'ascenseur m
[asONsurr]
could you give me a lift?
pouvez-vous m'emmener?

[poovay-voo mONmuhnay]

would you like a lift? est-ce
que je peux vous déposer
quelque part? [eskuh juh puh
voo daypohzay kelkuh par]

lift pass le forfait de remonte-
pente [forfay duh ruhmONt-pONt]

a daily/weekly lift pass un
forfait de remonte-pente
d'une journée/d'une
semaine

light la lumière [lOOm-yair]
(not heavy) léger [lay-jay]
do you have a light? avez-
vous du feu? [avay-voo dOO fuh]
light green vert clair

light bulb l'ampoule f [ONpool]

lighter (cigarette) le briquet
[breekay]

lightning les éclairs [ayklair]

like aimer [aymay]
I like it ça me plaît [sah muh
play]
I like going for walks j'aime
bien aller me promener [jem
b-yAN]
I like you tu me plais [tOO muh
play]
I don't like it ça ne me plaît
pas
do you like ...? est-ce que tu
aimes/vous aimez ...? [tOO
em/voo zaymay]
I'd like a beer je voudrais une
bière [juh voodray]
I'd like to go swimming
j'aimerais nager [jemray]
would you like a drink? veux-
tu/voulez-vous boire

quelque chose? [vuh-tOO/
voolay-voo]
**would you like to go for a
walk?** veux-tu/voulez-vous
aller faire une promenade?
what's it like? comment est-
ce? [komON ess]
one like this un comme ça
[kom]

lime le citron vert [seetrON vair]

lime cordial le jus de citron
vert [jOO]

line la ligne [leeñ]
**could you give me an outside
line?** pouvez-vous me donner
une ligne extérieure?
[poovay-voo]

lip la lèvre [levr]

lip salve la pommade pour les
lèvres [pomahd]

lipstick le rouge à lèvres
[rooj]

liqueur la liqueur [leekurr]

listen écouter [aykootay]

litre* le litre [leetr]
a litre of white wine un litre
de vin blanc

little peu [puh]
just a little, thanks un tout
petit peu, s'il vous plaît [an
too puhtee puh]
a little milk un peu de lait
a little bit more un petit peu
plus [plOOss]

live vivre [veevr]
we live together nous vivons
ensemble [noo veevON
zONsONbl]

• • • • • DIALOGUE • • • • •

where do you live? où est-ce que
tu habites/vous habitez? [weskuh
t∞ abeet/voo zabeetay]
I live in London je vis à Londres
[vee]

lively vivant [veevON]
liver le foie [fwa]
loaf le pain [pAN]
lobby (in hotel) le hall [al]
lobster la langouste [lONgoost]
local local
  a local wine/restaurant un vin
  de la région/un restaurant
  dans le quartier [duh la
  rayjON/... dON luh kart-yay]
lock la serrure [sair-r∞r]
  (verb) fermer à clé [fairmay a
  klay]
  it's locked c'est fermé à clé
  [fairmay]
lock in enfermer à clé
  [ONfairmay]
lock out enfermer dehors
  [duh-or]
  I've locked myself out je me
  suis enfermé dehors [juh muh
  swee zONfairmay]
locker (for luggage etc) le casier
  [kaz-yay]
lollipop la sucette [s∞sset]
London Londres [lONdr]
long long, f longue [lON, lON-g]
  how long will it take to fix it?
  combien de temps est-ce
  que ça prendra pour le
  réparer? [kONb-yAN duh tON]
  how long does it take?

combien de temps est-ce
que ça prend? [eskuh sa prON]
a long time longtemps
[lONtON]
one day/two days longer un
jour/deux jours en plus [ON
pl∞ss]
long distance call l'appel
longue-distance m
loo les toilettes [twalet]
look regarder [ruhgarday]
  I'm just looking, thanks je ne
  fais que regarder, merci [juh
  nuh fay kuh]
  you don't look well tu n'as
  pas l'air dans ton assiette
  [t∞ na pa lair dON tON ass-yet]
  look out! attention! [atONs-yON]
  can I have a look? puis-je
  regarder? [pweej]
look after garder [garday]
look at regarder [ruhgarday]
look for chercher [shairshay]
  I'm looking for ... je
  cherche ... [juh shairsh]
look forward to: I'm looking
  forward to it je m'en réjouis à
  l'avance [juh mON rayjwee a
  lavONss]
loose (handle etc) lâche [lahsh]
lorry le camion [kam-yON]
lose perdre [pairdr]
  I've lost my way je suis perdu
  [juh swee paird∞]
  I'm lost, I want to get to ... je
  suis perdu, je voudrais
  aller à ...
  I've lost my (hand)bag j'ai
  perdu mon sac à main [jay]

lost property (office) les objets
trouvés [objay troovay]

lot: a lot, lots beaucoup [bo-koo]
not a lot pas beaucoup [pa]
a lot of people beaucoup de
monde
a lot bigger beaucoup plus
gros
I like it a lot ça me plaît
beaucoup

lotion la lotion [lohss-yON]

loud fort [for]

lounge le salon
(in airport) la salle
d'embarquement [sal
dONbarkmON]

love l'amour m [amoor]
(verb) aimer [aymay]
I love Corsica j'aime la Corse
[jem]

lovely (view, present etc) ravissant
[ravee-sON]
(meal) délicieux [dayleess-yuh]
(weather) magnifique [mAN-
yeefeek]

low bas [ba]

luck la chance [shONss]
good luck! bonne chance!
[bon]

luggage les bagages mpl
[bagahj]

luggage trolley le chariot à
bagages [sharee-o]

lump (on body) la grosseur
[grossurr]

lunch le déjeuner [dayjuhnay]

lungs les poumons mpl
[poomON]

Luxembourg le Luxembourg

[lOOxONboor]

luxurious luxueux [lOOxOO-uh]

luxury le luxe [lOOx]

M

machine la machine

mad (insane) fou, f folle [foo, fol]
(angry) furieux [fooree-uh]

magazine le magazine

maid (in hotel) la femme de
chambre [fam duh shONbr]

maiden name le nom de jeune
fille [NON duh jurn fee]

mail le courrier [kooree-ay]
(verb) poster [postay]
is there any mail for me? est-
ce qu'il y a du courrier pour
moi? [eskeel ya doo]
see post

mailbox la boîte à lettres [bwat
a letr]
see letterbox

main principal [prANseepal]

main course le plat principal
[pla]

main post office la poste
principale [posst]

main road (in town) la rue
principale [rOO]
(in country) la grande route
[grOND root]

mains switch le disjoncteur
[deesjONkturr]

make (brand name) la marque
[mark]
(verb) faire [fair]
I make it 500 francs d'après
mes calculs, ça fait cinq

cents francs [dapray may kalkool sa fay]

what is it made of? en quoi est-ce? [ON kwa ess]

make-up le maquillage [makee-ahj]

man l'homme m [om]

manager le patron [pa-trON]
can I see the manager? puis-je parler au patron? [pweej parlay o]

manageress la directrice [deerektreess]

manual (car) la voiture à embrayage manuel [vwatoor a ONbrī-ahj mONooel]

many beaucoup [bo-koo]
not many pas beaucoup [pa]

map (of city) le plan [plON]
(road map, geographical) la carte [kart]

March mars [marss]

margarine la margarine [marghareen]

market le marché [marshay]

marmalade la confiture d'oranges [kONfeetoor dorONj]

married: I'm married je suis marié [juh swee maree-ay]
are you married? êtes-vous marié? [et-voo]

mascara le mascara

match (football etc) le match

matches les allumettes fpl [aloomet]

material (fabric) le tissu [teessoo]

matter: it doesn't matter ça ne fait rien [sa nuh fay ree-AN]
what's the matter? qu'est-ce

qu'il y a? [keskeel ya]

mattress le matelas [matla]

May mai [may]

may: may I have another one? puis-je en avoir un autre? [pweej]
may I come in? puis-je entrer?
may I see it? puis-je le/la voir?
may I sit here? est-ce que je peux m'asseoir ici? [eskuh juh puh masswahr]

maybe peut-être [puht-etr]

mayonnaise la mayonnaise

me* moi [mwa]
that's for me c'est pour moi
send it to me envoyez-le moi
me too moi aussi [o-see]

meal le repas [ruhpa]

•••••• DIALOGUE ••••••

did you enjoy your meal? est-ce que vous avez fait un bon repas? [eskuh voo zavay fay tAN bON]
it was excellent, thank you c'était excellent, merci [saytay]

mean signifier [seen-yeefee-ay]
what do you mean? qu'est-ce que vous voulez dire? [keskuh-voo voolay deer]

•••••• DIALOGUE ••••••

what does this word mean? que signifie ce mot? [kuh seen-yeefee suh mo]
it means ... in English ça veut dire ... en anglais [sa vuh deer]

measles la rougeole [roojol]

meat la viande [veeONd]

mechanic le mécanicien [maykaneess-yAN]

medicine le médicament [maydeekamON]

Mediterranean la Méditerranée [maydeetairanay]

medium (size) moyen [mwy-AN]

medium-dry (wine) demi-sec [duhmee-sek]

medium-rare (steak) à point [pwAN]

medium-sized moyen [mwy-AN]

meet rencontrer [rONkONtray]

nice to meet you enchanté [ONshONtay]

where shall I meet you? où nous retrouverons-nous? [oo noo ruhtroovuhrON-noo]

meeting la réunion [rayOOn-yON]

meeting place le point de rendez-vous [pwAN duh]

melon le melon [muhlON]

men les hommes [om]

mend réparer [rayparay]

could you mend this for me? pouvez-vous me réparer ça? [poovay-voo]

menswear les vêtements pour hommes [vetmON poor om]

mention mentionner [mONs-yONay]

don't mention it je vous en prie [juh voo zON pree]

menu la carte [kart]

may I see the menu, please? puis-je voir la carte, s'il vous plaît? [pweej wwahr]

see **Menu Reader** page 209

message le message [messahj]

are there any messages for me? est-ce que quelqu'un a laissé un message pour moi? [eskuh kelkAN a lessay]

I want to leave a message for ... je voudrais laisser un message pour ... [juh voodray]

metal le métal [may-tal]

metre* le mètre [metr]

microwave le micro-ondes [meekro-ONd]

midday midi [meedee]

at midday à midi

middle: in the middle au milieu [o meel-yuh]

in the middle of the night au milieu de la nuit

the middle one celui du milieu

midnight minuit [meenwee]

at midnight à minuit

might: I might want to stay another day il est possible que je reste encore un jour [eel ay posseebl kuh]

I might not leave tomorrow il est possible que je ne parte pas demain

migraine la migraine [meegren]

mild (taste, weather) doux, f douce [doo, dooss]

mile* le mille [meel]

milk le lait [lay]

milkshake le milk-shake

millimetre* le millimètre [meelee-metr]

minced meat la viande hachée [veeONd ashay]

mind: never mind tant pis [tON
pee]

I've changed my mind j'ai
changé d'avis [jay shONjay
davee]

•••••• DIALOGUE ••••••

do you mind if I open the window?
ça vous dérange si j'ouvre la
fenêtre? [sa voo dayrONj see]

no, I don't mind non, ça ne me
dérange pas [sa nuh muh]

mine*: it's mine c'est à moi [set
a mwa]

mineral water l'eau minérale f
[o meenayral]

mint-flavoured à la menthe
[mONt]

mint cordial la menthe à l'eau
[a lo]

mints (sweets) les bonbons à la
menthe mpl

minute la minute [meenOOt]

in a minute dans un instant
[dON ZAN ANstON]

just a minute un instant

mirror le mirroir [meer-wahr]

Miss Mademoiselle [mad-
mwazel]

miss rater

I missed the bus j'ai raté le
bus [jay ratay]

missing: to be missing manquer
[mONkay]

one of my ... is missing il me
manque un de mes ... [eel
muh mONk]

there's a suitcase missing il
manque une valise

mist la brume [brOOm]

mistake l'erreur f [air-rurr]

I think there's a mistake je
crois qu'il y a une erreur
[juh krwa keelya]

sorry, I've made a mistake
désolé, j'ai fait une erreur

misunderstanding le
malentendu [malONtONdOO]

mix-up: sorry, there's been a
mix-up désolé, il y a une
erreur [dayzolay eelya OOn air-
rurr]

modern moderne [modairn]

modern art gallery la galerie
d'art moderne [dar]

moisturizer la crème
hydratante [krem eedratONt]

moment: I'll be back in a
moment je reviens dans un
instant [juh ruhv-yan dON ZAN
ANstON]

Monday lundi [lANdee]

money l'argent m [arjON]

month le mois [mwa]

monument le monument
[monOOmON]

moon la lune [lOOn]

moped la mobylette [mobeelet]

more* plus [plOOss]

can I have some more water,
please? est-ce que je peux
avoir encore un peu d'eau,
s'il vous plaît? [eksuh juh puh
avwahr ONkor]

more expensive/interesting
plus cher/intéressant [plOO
shair]

more than 50 plus de

cinquante
more than that plus que ça
[plooss kuh sa]
a lot more beaucoup plus
[bo-koo]

•••••• DIALOGUE ••••••

would you like some more? est-ce
que vous en voulez encore?
[eskuh voo zON voolay]
no, no more for me, thanks non,
pas pour moi, merci
how about you? et vous?
I don't want any more, thanks je
n'en veux plus, merci

morning le matin [matAN]
this morning ce matin
in the morning le matin
Moroccan marocain [marokAN]
Morocco le Maroc
mosquito le moustique
[moosteek]
mosquito repellent le produit
anti-moustiques [prodwee
ONtee-]
most: I like that most of all c'est
ce que je préfère [say suh kuh
juh prayfair]
most of the time la plupart du
temps [ploopar]
most tourists la plupart des
touristes
mostly principalement
[prANseepal-mON]
mother la mère [mair]
motorbike la moto
motorboat le hors-bord [or-bor]
motorway l'autoroute f [otoroot]
mountain la montagne [mONtañ]

in the mountains à la
montagne
mountaineering l'alpinisme m
[alpeeneess-muh]
mouse la souris [sooree]
moustache la moustache
[mooss-tash]
mouth la bouche [boosh]
mouth ulcer l'aphte m [afft]
move bouger [boojay]
he's moved to another room il
a changé de chambre [eel a
shONjay duh shONbr]
could you move your car? est-
ce que vous pouvez
déplacer votre voiture?
[eskuh voo poovay dayplassay
votr vwatoor]
could you move up a little?
est-ce que vous pouvez vous
pousser un peu? [poossay]
where has it moved to? où se
trouve-t-il maintenant? [oo
suh troovteel mANtuhnON]
movie le film [feelm]
movie theater le cinéma
[seenayma]
Mr Monsieur [muhss-yuh]
Mrs Madame [ma-dam]
Ms Madame; Mademoiselle
[ma-dam, mad-mwazel]
much beaucoup [bo-koo]
much better/worse beaucoup
mieux/bien pire
much hotter beaucoup plus
chaud
not much pas beaucoup [pa]
not very much pas tellement
[telmON]

I don't want very much je n'en veux pas beaucoup [juh nON vuh pa]

mud la boue [boo]

mug (for drinking) la tasse [tass]

I've been mugged j'ai été dévalisé [jay aytay dayvaleezay]

mum la maman [ma-mON]

mumps les oreillons [oray-ON]

museum le musée [moozay]

Museums are not very generous with their hours, tending to open at around 10 a.m., close for lunch at noon until 2 p.m. or 3 p.m., and then run through only until 5 or 6 p.m. The usual closing day for museums and galleries is Monday, although some close on Tuesday.

mushrooms les champignons mpl [shONpeen-yON]

music la musique [moozeek]

musician le musicien, la musicienne [moozeess-yAN, -yen]

Muslim musulman [moozoolmON]

mussels les moules fpl [mool]

must*: I must je dois [juh dwa]

I mustn't drink alcohol il ne faut pas que je boive d'alcool [eel nuh fo pa juh d'alcool]

mustard la moutarde [mootard]

my*: my room ma chambre

my passport mon passeport [mON]

my parents mes parents [may]

myself: I'll do it myself je le ferai

moi-même [mwa-mem]

by myself tout seul [too surl]

N

nail (finger) l'ongle m [ONgl] (metal) le clou [kloo]

nail varnish le vernis à ongles [vairnee]

name le nom [nON]

First names are only used in informal relationships, between friends and relatives, or in semi-formal relationships (e.g. to shopkeepers, bar staff etc) provided you use the polite **vous** form of address. In formal situations **monsieur, madame** ou **mademoiselle** (Mr, Mrs or Ms) + surname are used.
see **you**

my name's John je m'appelle John [juh ma-pel]

what's your name? comment tu t'appelles/vous appelez-vous? [komON too ta-pel/voo zaplay-voo]

what is the name of this street? comment s'appelle cette rue? [sa-pel]

napkin la serviette [sairv-yet]

nappy la couche [koosh]

narrow (street) étroit [aytrwa]

nasty (person, taste) désagréable [dayzagray-abl]

(weather, accident) mauvais
[mo-vay]

national national [nass-yonal]

nationality la nationalité [nass-yonaleetay]

natural naturel [natoo-rel]

nausea la nausée [no-zay]

navy (blue) (bleu) marine [bluh mareen]

near près [pray]

  is it near the city centre? est-ce que c'est près du centre? [eskuh say]

  do you go near the harbour? est-ce que vous allez vers le port? [vair]

  where is the nearest ...? où est le/la ... le/la plus proche? [ploo prosh]

nearby tout près [too pray]

nearly presque [presk]

necessary nécessaire [naysessair]

neck le cou [koo]

necklace le collier [kol-yay]

necktie la cravate

need: I need ... j'ai besoin de ... [jay buhzwaN duh]

  do I need to pay? est-ce que je dois payer? [eskuh juh dwa]

needle l'aiguille f [aygwee]

negative (film) le négatif [naygateef]

neither: neither (one) of them ni l'un ni l'autre [nee laN nee lohtr]

  neither ... nor ... ni ... ni ...

nephew le neveu [nuhvuh]

net (in sport) le filet [feelay]

Netherlands les Pays-Bas [payee-ba]

network map le plan du réseau [ploN doo rayzo]

never jamais [jamay]

•••••• DIALOGUE ••••••

  have you ever been to Monaco?
  êtes-vous déjà allé à Monaco?
  [et-voo dayja alay]

  no, never, I've never been there
  non, jamais, je n'y suis jamais
  allé [juh nee swee]

new nouveau, f nouvelle [noovo, noovel]

news (radio, TV etc) les informations [ANformass-yoN]

newsagent's le marchand de journaux [marshoN duh joorno]

newspaper le journal [joor-nal]

newspaper kiosk le kiosque à journaux [keeosk]

New Year le Nouvel An [noovel oN]

New Year often involves a more elaborate celebration than Christmas. The French normally celebrate New Year with friends, either by organizing a party at somebody's house or by going out to a dance or dinner-dance. It is customary to wish people **bonne année** and **bonne santé**. People spend the next day visiting all the friends and relatives who weren't celebrating with them the night before.

Happy New Year! bonne année! [bon anay]

New Year's Eve la Saint-Sylvestre [SAN seelvestr]

New Zealand la Nouvelle-Zélande [noovel zaylONd]

New Zealander: I'm a New Zealander je suis Néo-Zélandais [nayozaylONday]

next prochain [proshAN]

the next on the left la prochaine à gauche [proshen a gohsh]

at the next stop au prochain arrêt

next week la semaine prochaine

next to à côté de [a kotay duh]

nice (food) bon [bON]

(looks, view etc) joli [jolee]

(person) sympathique, gentil [SANpateek, jONtee]

niece la nièce [nee-ess]

night la nuit [nwee]

at night la nuit

good night bonne nuit [bon]

•••••• DIALOGUE ••••••

do you have a single room for one night? est-ce que vous avez une chambre pour une personne pour une nuit? [eskuh voo zavay OOn shONbr poor OOn pairson]

yes, madam oui Madame

how much is it per night? combien est-ce par nuit? [kONb-yAN ess]

it's 300 francs for one night c'est trois cents francs la nuit

thank you, I'll take it d'accord, je la prends [juh la prON]

nightclub la boîte de nuit [bwat duh nwee]

nightdress la chemise de nuit [shuhmeez]

night porter le gardien de nuit [gardee-AN]

no non [nON]

I've no change je n'ai pas de monnaie [juh nay pa duh]

there's no ... left il n'y a plus de ... [eel nya plOO]

no way! pas question! [pa kest-yON]

oh no! (upset) ce n'est pas possible! [suh nay pa posseebl]

nobody personne [pairson]

there's nobody there il n'y a personne [eel nya]

noise le bruit [brwee]

noisy: it's too noisy c'est trop bruyant [say tro brwee-yON]

non-alcoholic sans alcool [sON zalkol]

none aucun [o-kAN]

nonsmoking compartment le compartiment

non-fumeurs [kONparteemON nON-fOOmurr]

noon midi [meedee]

no-one personne [pairson]

nor: nor do I moi non plus [mwa nON plOO]

normal normal [nor-mal]

north le nord [nor]

in the north dans le nord

north of Paris au nord de Paris [o]

northeast le nord-est [nor-est]

northern du nord [dOO]

northwest le nord-ouest [nor-west]

Northern Ireland l'Irlande du Nord f [eerlOND]

Norway la Norvège [norvej]

Norwegian (adj) norvégien [nor-vayj-yAN]

nose le nez [nay]

nosebleed le saignement de nez [senjuh-mON]

not** pas [pa]

  no, I'm not hungry non, je n'ai pas faim [juh nay pa]

  I don't want any, thank you je n'en veux pas, merci [nON vuh]

  it's not necessary ce n'est pas nécessaire

  I didn't know that je ne savais pas

  not that one – this one pas celui-là – celui-ci [suhlwee-la suhlwee-see]

note (banknote) le billet (de banque) [bee-yay (duh bONk)]

notebook le cahier [ky-yay]

notepaper (for letters) le papier à lettres [pap-yay a letr]

nothing rien [ree-AN]

  nothing for me, thanks pour moi rien, merci [poor mwa]

  nothing else rien d'autre [dohtr]

novel le roman [romON]

November novembre [no-vONbr]

now maintenant [mANtnON]

number le numéro [nOOmayro]

  I've got the wrong number j'ai fait un mauvais numéro [jay fay AN]

what is your phone number? quel est votre numéro de téléphone? [kel ay votr]

number plate la plaque minéralogique [plak meenay-ralojeek]

nurse (female) l'infirmière f [ANfeerm-yair]

  (male) l'infirmier m [ANfeerm-yay]

nursery slope la piste pour débutants [peest poor daybOOtON]

nut (for bolt) l'écrou m [aykroo]

nuts les noisettes fpl [nwazet]

O

o'clock*: it's 10 o'clock il est dix heures [urr]

occupied (toilet) occupé [okOOpay]

October octobre [oktobr]

odd (strange) étrange [aytrONj]

of* de [duh]

off (lights) éteint [aytAN]

  it's just off the Champs Elysées ... c'est tout près des Champs Elysées [too pray day]

  we're off tomorrow (leaving) nous partons demain [noo partON]

offensive (language, behaviour) choquant [shokON]

office le bureau [bOOro]

officer (said to policeman) monsieur l'agent [muhss-yuh lajON]

often souvent [soovoN]
 not often pas souvent [pa]
 how often are the buses? à
 quel intervalle les bus
 passent-ils? [kel ANtairval]
oil l'huile f [weel]
ointment la pommade [pomahd]
OK d'accord [dakor]
 are you OK? ça va? [sa va]
 is that OK with you? est-ce
 que ça te/vous va? [eskuh sa
 tuh/voo]
 is it OK to …? est-ce qu'on
 peut …? [puh]
 that's OK thanks (it doesn't
 matter) merci, ça va [mairsee]
 I'm OK (nothing for me, I've got
 enough) ça va comme ça
 (I feel OK) ça va
 is this train OK for …? ce train
 va bien à …? [b-yAN]
 I said I'm sorry, OK? j'ai dit
 pardon, ça ne suffit pas? [sa
 nuh soofee pa]
old vieux, f vieille [v-yuh, v-yay]

•••••• DIALOGUE ••••••

 how old are you? quel âge as-tu/
 avez-vous? [kel ahj atoo/avay-voo]
 I'm twenty-five j'ai vingt-cinq ans
 [jay]
 and you? et vous?

old-fashioned démodé
 [daymoday]
old town (old part of town) la
 vieille ville [v-yay veel]
 in the old town dans la vieille
 ville
olive oil l'huile d'olive f [weel

 doleev]
olives les olives fpl [oleev]
 black/green olives les olives
 noires/vertes
omelette l'omelette f
on* sur [soor]
 on the street/beach dans la
 rue/à la plage [doN]
 is it on this road? est-ce que
 c'est sur cette route?
 on the plane dans l'avion
 on Saturday samedi
 on television à la télévision
 I haven't got it on me je ne l'ai
 pas sur moi [juh nuh lay pa
 soor mwa]
 this one's on me (drink) c'est
 ma tournée [say ma toornay]
 the light wasn't on la lumière
 n'était pas allumée [aloomay]
 what's on tonight? qu'est-ce
 qu'il y a ce soir? [keskeel-ya
 suh swahr]
once une fois [oon fwa]
 at once (immediately) tout de
 suite [toot sweet]
one* un, une [AN, oon]
 the white one le blanc, la
 blanche
**one-way ticket: a one-way ticket
 to …** un aller simple pour …
 [alay sANpl poor]
onion l'oignon m [on-yoN]
only seulement [surlmoN]
 only one seulement un(e)
 only just à peine [pen]
 it's only 6 o'clock il n'est que
 six heures [eel nay kuh]
 I've only just got here je viens

h v-yAN dareevay]
l'interrupteur de
êt m [ANtairOOpturr
ray]

open (adj) ouvert [oovair]
(verb) ouvrir [oovreer]
when do you open? à quelle
heure est-ce que vous
ouvrez? [a kel urr eskuh voo
zoovray]
I can't get it open je n'arrive
pas à l'ouvrir [juh nareev pa]
in the open air en plein air
[ON plAN air]

opening times les heures
d'ouverture [urr doovairtOOr]

open ticket le billet open
[bee-yay]

opera l'opéra m [opayra]

operation l'opération f
[opayrass-yON]

operator (telephone) le/la
standardiste [stONdardeest]

opposite: the opposite direction
le sens inverse [anvairss]
opposite my hotel en face de
mon hôtel [ON fass duh]
the bar opposite le bar d'en
face

optician l'opticien m [opteess-
yAN]

or ou [oo]

orange (fruit) l'orange f [orONj]
(colour) orange

orange juice le jus d'orange
[jOO]

orchestra l'orchestre m [orkestr]

order: can we order now? est-
ce que nous pouvons

commander? [eskuh noo
poovON komONday]
I've already ordered, thanks j'ai
déjà commandé, merci [jay
dayja komONday]
I didn't order this ce n'est pas
ce que j'ai commandé [suh
nay pa suh kuh]
out of order hors service [or
sairveess]

ordinary ordinaire [ordeenair]

other autre [ohtr]
the other one l'autre
the other day (recently) l'autre
jour
I'm waiting for the others
j'attends les autres [lay zohtr]
do you have any others? est-
ce que vous en avez
d'autres? [eskuh voo zON avay
dohtr]

otherwise sinon [seenON]

our* notre, pl nos

ours* le/la nôtre [nohtr]

out: he's out il est sorti [eel ay
sortee]
three kilometres out of town à
trois kilomètres de la ville

outdoors en plein air [ON plAN
air]

outside (preposition) à
l'extérieur de [extayree-urr
duh]
can we sit outside? est-ce que
nous pouvons nous mettre
dehors? [eskuh noo poovON noo
metr duh-or]

oven le four [foor]

over: over here par ici [ee-see]

over there là-bas [laba]

over 500 plus de cinq cents [plOO duh]

it's over (finished) c'est fini [say feenee]

overcharge: you've overcharged me il y a une erreur dans la note [eelya OOn air-rurr dON la not]

overcoat le pardessus [parduhsOO]

overnight (travel) de nuit [duh nwee]

overtake doubler [dooblay]

owe: how much do I owe you? qu'est-ce que je vous dois? [keskuh juh voo dwa]

own: my own ... mon propre ... [propr]

are you on your own? êtes-vous seul? [et-voo surl]

I'm on my own je suis seul

owner le/la propriétaire [propree-aytair]

P

pack: a pack of ... un paquet de ... [pakay duh]

(verb) faire ses bagages [fair say bagahj]

package (at post office) le colis [kolee]

package holiday les vacances organisées [vakONss organeezay]

packed lunch le casse-croûte [kass-kroot]

packet: a packet of cigarettes un paquet de cigarettes [pak...]

padlock le cadenas [kadna]

page (of book) la page [pahj]

could you page Mr ...? pouvez-vous faire appeler M. ...? [poovay-voo fair aplay]

pain la douleur [doolurr]

I have a pain here j'ai mal ici [jay mal ee-see]

painful douloureux [doolooruh]

painkillers les analgésiques mpl [an-aljayzeek]

paint la peinture [pANtOOr]

painting (picture) le tableau [tablo]

pair: a pair of ... une paire de ... [pair duh]

Pakistani pakistanais [-ay]

palace le palais [palay]

pale pâle [pahl]

pale blue bleu clair

pan la poêle [pwal]

panties le slip [sleep]

pants (underwear) le slip

(US) le pantalon [pONtalON]

pantyhose le collant [kollON]

paper le papier [papyay]

(newspaper) le journal [joor-nal]

a piece of paper un bout de papier [boo]

paper handkerchiefs les kleenex® mpl

parcel le colis [kolee]

pardon? (didn't understand) pardon? [par-dON]

parents: my parents mes parents [parON]

parents-in-law les beaux-parents [bo-]

park le parc
 (verb) se garer [suh garay]
 can I park here? est-ce que je
 peux me garer ici?
parking lot le parking [parkeeng]
part une partie [partee]
partner (boyfriend, girlfriend) le/la
 partenaire [partuhnair]
party (group) le groupe
 (celebration) la fête [fet]
pass (in mountains) le col
passenger le passager, la
 passagère [passahjay, -jair]
passport le passeport [pass-por]
past*: in the past autrefois
 [ohtruh-fwa]
 just past the information office
 tout de suite après le centre
 d'information [toot sweet
 apray]
path le sentier [sONt-yay]
pattern le motif [moteef]
pavement le trottoir [trotwahr]
 on the pavement sur le
 trottoir
pavement café le café en
 terrasse [ON tairass]
pay (verb) payer [pay-ay]
 can I pay, please? l'addition,
 s'il vous plaît [ladeess-yON]
 it's already paid for ça a déjà
 été réglé [sa a day-ja aytay
 rayglay]

•••••• DIALOGUE ••••••

who's paying? qui est-ce qui paie?
 [kee eskee pay]
I'll pay c'est moi qui paie [say
 mwa]

no, you paid last time, I'll pay non,
 tu as payé la dernière fois, cette
 fois c'est mon tour [tOO a pay-ay la
 dairn-yair fwa set fwa say mON toor]

pay phone la cabine
 téléphonique [kabeen
 taylayfoneek]
peaceful paisible [pezzeebl]
peach la pêche [pesh]
peanuts les cacahuètes fpl
 [kaka-wet]
pear la poire [pwahr]
peas les petits pois mpl [puhtee
 pwa]
peculiar (taste, custom) bizarre
pedestrian crossing le passage
 pour piétons [passahj poor
 p-yaytON]
pedestrian precinct la zone
 piétonne [zohn p-yaytON]
peg (for washing) la pince à linge
 [pANss a lANj]
 (for tent) le piquet [peekay]
pen le stylo [steelo]
pencil le crayon [kray-ON]
penfriend le correspondant
 [-dON], la correspondante
 [-dONt]
penicillin la pénicilline
 [payneesseeleen]
penknife le canif [kaneef]
pensioner le retraité, la
 retraitée [ruhtraytay]
people les gens [jON]
 the other people les autres
 [lay zohtr]
 too many people trop de
 monde [tro duh mONd]

pepper (spice) le poivre [pwahvr]
(vegetable) le poivron
[pwahvrON]

peppermint (sweet) le bonbon à
la menthe [mONt]

per: per night par nuit
how much per day? quel est
le prix par jour? [kel ay]
per cent pour cent [poor sON]

perfect parfait [parfay]

perfume le parfum [parfAN]

perhaps peut-être [puht-etr]
perhaps not peut-être que
non [kuh nON]

period (of time) la période
[payree-od]
(menstruation) les règles [regl]

perm la permanente
[pairmanONt]

permit l'autorisation f
[otoreezass-yON]

person la personne [pairson]

personal stereo le baladeur
[baladurr]

petrol l'essence f [essONss]

Petrol is substantially more
expensive on the motorway, so
make sure you fill up your tank
beforehand. The best prices are
normally to be found in
supermarket petrol stations.
The following are available:
super (4-star), **ordinaire** (2-
star), **sans plomb** (unleaded)
et **gas-oil** (diesel).

petrol can le bidon d'essence
[beedON dessONss]

petrol station la station-service
[stass-yON-sairveess]

pharmacy la pharmacie
[farmasee]
see **chemist's**

phone le téléphone [taylay-]
(verb) téléphoner
could you phone the police?
pourriez-vous téléphoner à
la police? [pooree-ay-voo]

You can make domestic and
international calls from any box
(or **cabine**) and receive calls
where there's a blue logo of a
ringing bell. Most call boxes only
take phonecards (**télécarte**),
obtainable from post offices,
train stations and some
tobacconists (**tabac**). In central
Paris a phonecard is
indispensable. The least
expensive is 40F. Coin-only
payphones are still common in
cafés, bars and in rural areas.
They take 50 centimes, 1F, 5F
and 10F coins. International
calls are cheaper between
10 p.m. and 8 a.m. and on
Saturday after 1 p.m. and all day
Sunday.
see **speak**

phone box la cabine
téléphonique [kabeen
taylayfoneek]

phonecard la télécarte [taylay-
kart]

phone directory l'annuaire du

téléphone m [an∞air d∞
taylayfon]

phone number le numéro de
téléphone [n∞mayro]

photo la photographie [foto-
grafee]

**excuse me, could you take a
photo of us?** pourriez-vous
nous prendre en photo?
[pooree-ay-voo noo prONdr ON]

phrase book le manuel de
conversation [man∞el duh
kONvairsass-yON]

piano le piano

pickpocket le/la pickpocket

**pick up: will you be there to pick
me up?** est-ce que vous
viendrez me chercher?
[eskuh voo vee-ANdray muh
shairshay]

picnic le pique-nique [peek-
neek]

picture l'image f [eemahj]

pie (meat) le pâté en croûte
[patay ON kroot]
(fruit) la tarte

piece le morceau [morso]
a piece of ... un morceau
de ...

pill la pilule [peel∞l]
I'm on the pill je prends la
pilule [juh prON]

pillow l'oreiller m [oray-yay]

pillow case la taie d'oreiller
[tay]

pin l'épingle f [aypANgl]

pineapple l'ananas m [anana]

pineapple juice le jus d'ananas
[j∞]

pink rose [roz]

pipe (for smoking) la pipe [peep]
(for water) le tuyau [twee-o]

pipe cleaners les cure-pipes
mpl [k∞r-peep]

pity: it's a pity c'est dommage
[say domahj]

pizza la pizza

place l'endroit m [ONdrwa]
is this place taken? est-ce que
cette place est prise? [eskuh
set plass ay preez]
at your place chez toi/vous
[shay twa/voo]
at his place chez lui [lwee]

plain (not patterned) uni [∞nee]

plane l'avion m [av-yON]
by plane en avion

plant la plante [plONt]

plaster cast le plâtre [plahtr]

plasters les pansements mpl
[pONsmON]

plastic le plastique [plass-teek]
(credit cards) les cartes de
crédit [kart duh kray-dee]

plastic bag le sac en plastique
[ON plass-teek]

plate l'assiette f [ass-yet]

platform le quai [kay]
which platform is it for Paris?
c'est quelle voie pour Paris?
[say kel vwa]

ENGLISH ◆ FRENCH | **Pl**

In French stations a **quai** will
have two **voies**, the **voie** being
the side of the **quai** where a
train comes in.

play (verb) jouer [joo-ay]

(in theatre) la pièce de théâtre [p-yess duh tay-atr]

playground (for children) le terrain de jeux [terrAN duh juh]

pleasant agréable [agray-abl]

please s'il vous plaît [seel voo play]

(if using 'tu' form) s'il te plaît [seel tuh]

yes please oui, merci [wee mairsee]

could you please ...? pourriez-vous ..., s'il vous plaît? [pooree-ay-voo]

please don't wait for me ce n'est pas la peine de m'attendre [suh nay pa la pen]

pleased to meet you enchanté [ONshONtay]

pleasure le plaisir [plezzeer]

my pleasure tout le plaisir est pour moi [too luh ... ay poor mwa]

plenty: plenty of ... beaucoup de ... [bo-koo duh]

we've plenty of time nous avons largement le temps [noo zavON larj-mON luh tON]

that's plenty, thanks merci, ça suffit [sa soofee]

pliers la pince [pANss]

plug (electrical) la prise [preez]

(for car) la bougie [boojee]

(in sink) le bouchon [booshON]

plumber le plombier [plONb-yay]

p.m.* de l'après-midi [duh lapray-meedee]

poached egg l'œuf poché m [urf poshay]

pocket la poche [posh]

point: two point five deux virgule cinq [... veergool ...]

there's no point ça ne sert à rien [sa nuh sair a ree-AN]

points (in car) les vis platinées [veess plateenay]

poisonous toxique

police la police

call the police! appelez la police! [aplay]

There are two types of French police (popularly know as **les flics**): the **Police Nationale** and the **Gendarmerie Nationale**. For all practical purposes they are indistinguishable; if you need to report a theft or other incident you can go to either. The phone number for the police is 17.

---

policeman l'agent de police m [ajON]

police station le commissariat [komeessaree-a]

policewoman la femme agent [fam ajON]

polish le cirage [seerahj]

polite poli [polee]

polluted pollué [polOO-ay]

pony le poney [ponay]

pool (for swimming) la piscine [peesseen]

poor (not rich) pauvre [pohvr]

(quality) médiocre

[maydeeokr]
pop music la musique pop
[mœzeek]
pop singer le chanteur/la
chanteuse de musique pop
[shONturr/shONturz duh]
population la population
[popœlass-yON]
pork le porc [por]
port (for boats) le port [por]
(drink) le porto
porter (in hotel) le portier [port-
yay]
portrait le portrait [portray]
Portugal le Portugal
Portuguese (adj) portugais
[portœgay]
posh (restaurant, people) chic
[sheek]
possible possible [posseebl]
is it possible to ...? est-ce
qu'on peut ...? [eskON puh]
as ... as possible aussi ... que
possible [o-see]
post (mail) le courrier
[kooree-ay]
(verb) poster [postay]
could you post this for me?
pourriez-vous me poster
cette lettre? [pooree-ay-voo
muh postay set letr]
postbox la boîte aux lettres
[bwat o letr]
see **letterbox**
postcard la carte postale [kart
pos-tal]
poster l'affiche f [afeesh]
post office la poste [posst]

Post offices are generally open
from Monday to Friday from
9 a.m. to noon and from 2 to 5-
6 p.m.; on Saturdays they are
only open in the morning.
However, in larger towns main
post offices often don't close for
lunch, while in villages, lunch
hours and closing times can vary
enormously. To register a letter
send it **en recommandé**, and
send your urgent letters or
parcels **en urgent**. Post offices
also sell phonecards (**télécarte**)
and cardboard boxes for your
parcels. Major post offices
change money, generally at a
good rate and without charging
a commission.

poste restante la poste restante
potato la pomme de terre [pom
duh tair]
potato chips les chips fpl
[cheeps]
pots and pans les casseroles
[kassuhrohl]
pottery (objects) la poterie
[potree]
pound (money) la livre
(sterling) [leevr (stairleeng)]
(weight)* la livre
power cut la coupure de
courant [koopœr duh koorON]
power point la prise (de
courant) [preez]
**practise: I want to practise my
French** je veux m'exercer à

parler français [juh vuh mexairsay a parlay]

prawns les crevettes fpl [kruhvet]

prefer: I prefer ... je préfère ... [juh prayfair]

pregnant enceinte [ONSANt]

prescription (for chemist) l'ordonnance f [ordonONss]

present (gift) le cadeau [kado]

president le président [prayzeedON]

pretty joli [jolee]

it's pretty expensive c'est plutôt cher [say plOOto shair]

price le prix [pree]

priest le prêtre [pretr]

prime minister le Premier ministre [pruhm-yay meeneeestr]

printed matter l'imprimé m [ANpreemay]

priority (in driving) la priorité [preeoreetay]

prison la prison [preezON]

private privé [preevay]

private bathroom la salle de bain particulière [sal duh bAN parteekOOl-yair]

probably probablement [prob-abluhmON]

problem le problème [prob-lem]

no problem! pas de problème! [pa duh prob-lem]

program(me) le programme [prog-ram]

promise: I promise je te/vous le promets [juh tuh/voo luh promay]

pronounce: how is this

pronounced? comment est-ce que ça se prononce? [komON teskuh sa suh pronONss]

properly (repaired, locked etc) bien [b-yAN]

protection factor l'indice de protection m [ANdeess duh protex-yON]

Protestant protestant [-tON]

public convenience les toilettes publiques [twalet pOObleek]

public holiday le jour férié [joor fayree-ay]

pudding (dessert) le dessert [dessair]

pull tirer [teeray]

pullover le pull [pOOl]

puncture la crevaison [kruhvezzON]

purple violet [veeolay]

purse (for money) le porte-monnaie [port-monay]
(US) le sac à main [mAN]

push pousser [poossay]

pushchair la poussette [poosset]

put mettre [metr]

where can I put ...? où est-ce que je peux mettre ...? [weskuh juh puh]

could you put us up for the night? pourriez-vous nous héberger pour la nuit? [pooree-ay-voo noo zaybairjay poor la nwee]

pyjamas le pyjama [peejama]

Pyrenees les Pyrénées [peeraynay]

Q

quality la qualité [kaleetay]
quarantine la quarantaine
  [karoNten]
quarter le quart [kar]
quayside: on the quayside sur
  les quais [soor lay kay]
question la question [kest-yoN]
queue la queue [kuh]
quick rapide [rapeed]
  that was quick tu as/vous
  avez fait vite [too a/voo zavay
  fay veet]
  what's the quickest way there?
  quel est le chemin le plus
  court? [kel ay luh shuhmaN luh
  ploo koor]
  fancy a quick drink? tu as/vous
  avez le temps de prendre un
  verre? [too a/voo zavay luh toN
  duh proNdr aN vair]
quickly vite [veet]
quiet (place, hotel) tranquille
  [troNkeel]
  quiet! silence! [seeloNss]
quite (fairly) assez [assay]
  (very) très [tray]
  that's quite right c'est tout à
  fait juste [say too ta fay joost]
  quite a lot pas mal [pa]

R

rabbit le lapin [lapaN]
race (for runners, cars) la course
  [koorss]
racket (tennis, squash etc) la
  raquette [raket]

radiator (of car, in room) le
  radiateur [rad-yaturr]
radio la radio [ra-deeo]
  on the radio à la radio
rail: by rail en train [oN traN]
railway le chemin de fer
  [shuhmaN duh fair]
rain la pluie [plwee]
  in the rain sous la pluie
  [soo]
  it's raining il pleut [eel
  pluh]
raincoat l'imperméable m
  [aNpairmay-abl]
rape le viol [veeol]
rare (steak) saignant [sen-yoN]
rash (on skin) l'éruption f
  [ayroops-yoN]
raspberry la framboise
  [froNbwahz]
rat le rat [ra]
rate (for changing money) le taux
  [toh]
rather: it's rather good c'est
  assez bon [say tassay boN]
  I'd rather ... je préfère ... [juh
  prayfair]
razor le rasoir [razwahr]
razor blades les lames de
  rasoir fpl [lahm duh razwahr]
read lire [leer]
ready prêt [pray]
  are you ready? est-ce que tu
  es/vous êtes prêt? [eskuh too
  ay/voo zet]
  I'm not ready yet je ne suis
  pas encore prêt [juh nuh swee
  pa zoNkor]

•••••• DIALOGUE ••••••

when will it be ready? quand est-ce que ce sera prêt? [kONteskuh suh suhra]

it should be ready in a couple of days ça devrait être prêt dans un ou deux jours [sa duhvray]

real véritable [vayreet-abl]

really vraiment [vraymON]

that's really great c'est vraiment formidable

really? (doubt) vraiment? (polite interest) ah bon?

rearview mirror le rétroviseur [raytroveezurr]

reasonable raisonnable [rezzON-abl]

receipt le reçu [ruhsoo]

recently récemment [ray-samON]

reception (for guests, in hotel) la réception [ray-seps-yON]

at reception à la réception

reception desk le bureau de réception

receptionist le/la réceptionniste [rayseps-yoneest]

recognize reconnaître [ruhkonetr]

recommend: could you recommend ...? pourriez-vous me recommander ...? [pooree-ay-voo muh ruhkomONday]

record (music) le disque [deesk]

red rouge [rooj]

red wine le vin rouge [VAN]

refund le remboursement [rONboorss-mON]

can I have a refund? est-ce que je serai remboursé? [eskuh juh suhray rONboorsay]

region la région [rayjeeON]

registered: by registered mail en recommandé [ON ruhkomONday]

registration number le numéro d'immatriculation [noomayro deematreekoolass-yON]

relative le parent [parON]

religion la religion [ruhleejeeON]

remember: I don't remember je ne me souviens pas [juh nuh muh soov-yAN pa]

I remember je m'en souviens [juh mON]

do you remember? tu te souviens?/vous souvenez-vous? [too tuh .../voo soovnay-voo]

rent (for apartment etc) le loyer [lwy-ay] (verb) louer [loo-ay]

to rent à louer

•••••• DIALOGUE ••••••

I'd like to rent a car j'aimerais louer une voiture [jemray]

for how long? pour combien de temps? [poor kONb-yAN duh tON]

two days deux jours

this is our range voici notre gamme

I'll take the ... je vais prendre la ... [juh vay prONdr]

is that with unlimited mileage? est-ce que ça comprend un

kilométrage illimité? [eskuh sa
KONProN AN keelomaytrahj
eeleemeetay]
it is oui [wee]
can I see your licence please? puis-
je voir votre permis de conduire,
s'il vous plaît? [pweej vwahr votr
pairmee duh KONdweer]
and your passport et votre
passeport [pass-por]
is insurance included? est-ce que
l'assurance est comprise? [eskuh
lassOOrONss ay KONpreez]
**yes, but you pay the first 600
francs** oui, mais vous payez les
six cents francs de départ [voo
pay-ay lay see SON frON duh daypar]
can you leave a deposit of ...?
pouvez-vous me laisser une
caution de ...? [kohss-yON]

rented car la voiture de
location [vwatOOr duh lokass-
yON]
repair (verb) réparer [rayparay]
can you repair it? est-ce que
vous pouvez réparer ça?
[eskuh voo poovay]
repeat répéter [raypaytay]
could you repeat that?
pourriez-vous répéter?
[pooree-ay-voo]
reservation la réservation
[rayzairvass-yON]
I'd like to make a reservation
je voudrais faire une
réservation [juh voodray fair]

•••••• D I A L O G U E ••••••
I have a reservation j'ai réservé
[jay rayzairvay]
yes sir, what name please?
certainement monsieur, à quel
nom s'il vous plaît? [sairten-mON
muh-syuh a kel nON]

reserve réserver [rayzairvay]

•••••• D I A L O G U E ••••••
can I reserve a table for tonight?
j'aimerais réserver une table
pour ce soir [jemray]
yes madam, for how many people?
certainement madame, pour
combien de personnes? [sairten-
mON ... poor KONb-yAN duh pairson]
for two pour deux
and for what time? et pour quelle
heure? [kel urr]
for eight o'clock pour huit heures
**and could I have your name
please?** pourrais-je avoir votre
nom s'il vous plaît? [poorayj
avwahr]
see alphabet

rest: I need a rest j'ai besoin de
repos [jay buh-zwAN duh ruhpo]
the rest of the group le reste
du groupe [rest]
restaurant le restaurant
[restorON]

There's often no difference
between **restaurants** (or
auberges or **relais** as they
sometimes call themselves) and
brasseries in terms of quality
→

ENGLISH ◆ FRENCH | Re

ENGLISH ❖ FRENCH | Re

or price range. The distinction is that **brasseries**, which resemble cafés, serve quicker meals at most hours of the day, while restaurants tend to stick to the traditional meal times. Meals are usually served from 12 to 3 p.m. and from 7.30 to 11.30 p.m. Booking is only required in very busy or upmarket places. Restaurants will normally have a **plat du jour** (dish of the day) and various **menus fixes** (set-price menus) which are good value for money, but you can eat **à la carte** (single dishes chosen from the menu) and this is invariably more expensive. In small towns it may be impossible to get anything other than a sandwich after 10 p.m.; in major cities, town centre **brasseries** will serve until 11 p.m. or midnight and one or two may be open all night.

•••••• DIALOGUE ••••••

what's the dish of the day? quel est le plat du jour? [kel ay luh pla dಠ joor?]

I'll take the 75 franc menu je vais prendre le menu à soixante-quinze francs [juh vay proNdr]

restaurant car le wagon-restaurant [vagON]

rest room les toilettes [twalet] see **toilet**

retired: I'm retired je suis retraité(e) [ruhtretay]

return (ticket) l'aller-retour m [alay-ruhtoor]

Return tickets in France are calculated as twice the price of a single ticket.

reverse charge call le PCV [pay-say-vay]

reverse gear la marche arrière [marsh aree-air]

revolting dégoûtant [daygootON]

rib la côte [koht]

rice le riz [ree]

rich (person) riche [reesh] (food) lourd [loor]

ridiculous ridicule [reedeekಠl]

right (correct) juste [jಠst] (not left) droit [drwa]

you were right vous aviez raison [voo zaveeay rezzON]

that's right c'est juste [say jಠst]

this can't be right ce n'est pas possible [suh nay pa posseebl]

right! d'accord! [dakor]

is this the right road for ...? est-ce bien la route de ...? [ess b-yAN la root]

on the right à droite [drwat]

turn right tournez à droite [toornay]

right-hand drive la conduite à droite [kONdweet a drwat]

ring (on finger) la bague [bag]

I'll ring you je vous appellerai [juh vooz apelray]

ring back rappeler

ripe (fruit) mûr [mOOr]

rip-off: it's a rip-off c'est de
l'arnaque [say duh larnak]

rip-off prices les prix
exorbitants [pree
exorbeetON]

risky risqué [reeskay]

river la rivière [reev-yair]

road la route [root]
is this the road for ...? est-ce
la bonne route pour aller
à ...? [ess la bon root poor alay]
it's just down the road c'est
tout près d'ici [say too pray
dee-see]

road accident l'accident de la
circulation m [axeedon duh la
seerkOOlass-yON]

road map la carte routière [kart
root-yair]

roadsign le panneau de
signalisation [pano duh seen-
yaleezass-yON]

rob: I've been robbed j'ai été
dévalisé [jay aytay dayvaleezay]

rock le rocher [roshay]
(music) la musique rock
[mOOzeek]
on the rocks (with ice) avec des
glaçons [avek day glassON]

roll (bread) le petit pain [puhtee
pAN]

roof le toit [twa]

roof rack la galerie [galree]

room la chambre [shONbr]
in my room dans ma
chambre [dON]

····· DIALOGUE ·····

do you have any rooms? est-ce
que vous avez des chambres?
[eskuh voo zavay day]

for how many people? pour
combien de personnes? [poor
kONb-yAN duh pairson]

for one/for two pour une
personne/deux personnes

yes, we have rooms free oui, nous
avons des chambres libres
[leebr]

for how many nights will it be? ce
serait pour combien de nuits?
[suh suhray – duh nwee]

just for one night pour une nuit
seulement [surlmON]

how much is it? combien est-ce?
[ess]

400 francs with bathroom and 350
francs without bathroom quatre
cents francs avec salle de bain et
trois cent cinquante francs sans
salle de bain [sal duh bAN]

can I see a room with bathroom?
est-ce que je pourrais voir une
chambre avec salle de bain?
[eskuh juh pooray vwahr]

OK, I'll take it d'accord, je la
prends [dakor juh la prON]

room service le service en
chambre [sairveess ON shONbr]

rope la corde [kord]

rosé (wine) le rosé [rozzay]

roughly (approximately) environ
[ONveerON]

round: it's my round c'est ma
tournée [say ma toornay]

roundabout (for traffic) le rond-point [RON-pwAN]

round trip ticket l'aller-retour m [alay-ruhtoor]
see return ticket

route l'itinéraire m [eeteenay-rair]
what's the best route? quel itinéraire nous conseillez-vous? [noo kONsay-ay-voo]

rubber (material) le caoutchouc [ka-oochoo]
(eraser) la gomme [gom]

rubber band l'élastique m [aylasteek]

rubbish (waste) les ordures [ordoor]
(poor quality goods) la camelote [kamlot]

rubbish! (nonsense) n'importe quoi! [nANport kwa]

rucksack le sac à dos [do]

rude grossier [gross-yay]

ruins les ruines fpl [rooeen]

rum le rhum [rum]
rum and coke un rhum coca

run (person) courir [kooreer]
how often do the buses run? à quels intervalles les bus passent-ils? [kel zANtairval lay booss pasteel]
I've run out of money je n'ai plus d'argent [juh nay ploo darjON]

rush hour les heures de pointe [urr duh pwANt]

S

sad triste [treest]

saddle (for bike, horse) la selle [sel]

safe (not in danger) en sécurité [ON saykooreetay]
(not dangerous) sûr [soor]

safety pin l'épingle de sûreté f [aypANgl duh soortay]

sail la voile [vwal]

sailboard la planche à voile [plONsh a vwal]

sailboarding la planche à voile

salad la salade [sa-lad]

salad dressing la vinaigrette

sale: for sale à vendre [vONdr]

salmon le saumon [so-mON]

salt le sel

same: the same le/la même [mem]
the same as he has le/la même que lui
the same again, please la même chose, s'il vous plaît [shohz seel voo play]
it's all the same to me ça m'est égal [sa met aygal]

sand le sable [sabl]

sandals les sandales fpl [sON-dal]

sandwich le sandwich [sOND-weetch]

sanitary napkin la serviette hygiénique [eejee-ayneek]

sanitary towel la serviette hygiénique

sardines les sardines fpl

Saturday samedi [samdee]

sauce la sauce [sohss]

saucepan la casserole

saucer la soucoupe [sookoop]

sauna le sauna [sona]

sausage la saucisse [soseess]

say: how do you say ... in French? comment dit-on ... en français? [komON deet-ON]
what did he say? qu'est-ce qu'il a dit? [keskeel a dee]
he said ... il a dit ...
I said ... j'ai dit ... [jay]
could you say that again? pourriez-vous répéter? [pooree-ay-voo raypaytay]

scarf (for neck) l'écharpe f [aysharp]
(for head) le foulard [foolar]

scenery le paysage [payee-zahj]

schedule (US) l'horaire m [orair]

scheduled flight le vol de ligne [vol duh leeñ]

school l'école f [aykol]

scissors: a pair of scissors une paire de ciseaux [seezo]

scotch le whisky

Scotch tape® le scotch

Scotland l'Écosse f [aykoss]

Scottish écossais [aykossay]
I'm Scottish (man/woman) je suis écossais/écossaise [aykossez]

scrambled eggs les œufs brouillés [uh broo-yay]

scratch l'éraflure f [ayrafloor]

screw la vis [veess]

screwdriver le tournevis [toornuhveess]

scrubbing brush la brosse [bross]

sea la mer [mair]
by the sea au bord de la mer [o bor]

seafood les fruits de mer [frwee duh mair]

seafood restaurant le restaurant de fruits de mer

seafront le bord de la mer [bor duh la mair]
on the seafront au bord de la mer

seagull la mouette [mwet]

search chercher [shairshay]

seashell le coquillage [kokee-yahj]

seasick: I feel seasick j'ai le mal de mer [jay luh mal duh mair]
I get seasick je suis sujet au mal de mer [juh swee sOOjay]

seaside: by the seaside au bord de la mer [o bor duh la mair]

seat le siège [see-ej]
is this anyone's seat? est-ce que cette place est prise? [eskuh set plass ay preez]

seat belt la ceinture de sécurité [sANtOOr duh saykOOreetay]

sea urchin l'oursin m [oorsAN]

seaweed les algues [alg]

secluded isolé [eezolay]

second (adj) second [suhgON]
(of time) la seconde [suhgONd]
just a second! une seconde!

second class (travel) en seconde [ON suhgONd]

second floor le deuxième [duhz-

yem]; (US) le premier
[pruhm-yay]

second-hand d'occasion [dokaz-yON]

see voir [vwahr]
  can I see? est-ce que je peux voir? [eskuh juh puh]
  have you seen ...? est-ce que tu as/vous avez vu ...? [too a/ voo zavay voo]
  I saw him this morning je l'ai vu ce matin [juh lay]
  see you! à bientôt! [b-yANto]
  I see (I understand) je vois [juh vwa]

self-catering apartment l'appartement (de vacances) m [apartmON (duh vakONss)]

self-service le self-service [-sairveess]

sell vendre [vONdr]
  do you sell ...? est-ce que vous vendez ...? [eskuh voo vONday]

Sellotape® le scotch

send envoyer [ONvwy-ay]
  I want to send this to England j'aimerais envoyer ceci en Angleterre [jemray]

senior citizen la personne du troisième âge [pairson doo trwaz-yem ahj]

separate séparé [sayparay]

separated: I'm separated je suis séparé [juh swee sayparay]

separately (pay, travel) séparément [sayparay-mON]

September septembre [septONbr]

septic infecté [ANfektay]

serious (person, situation, problem) sérieux [sayree-uh]
  (illness) **grave** [grahv]

service charge (in restaurant) le service [sairveess]

service station la station-service [stass-yON sairveess]

serviette la serviette [sair-]

set menu le menu (à prix fixe) [muhnoo (a pree feex)]

several plusieurs [plooz-yurr]

sew coudre [koodr]
  could you sew this back on? pouvez-vous recoudre ceci? [poovay-voo ruhkoodr suhsee]

sex le sexe

sexy sexy

shade: in the shade à l'ombre [lONbr]

shake: let's shake hands serrons-nous la main [sairrON-noo la mAN]

shallow (water) peu profond [puh profON]

shame: what a shame! quel dommage! [kel domahj]

shampoo le shampoing [shONpwAN]

shampoo and set le shampoing-mise en plis [ON plee]

share (room, table etc) partager [partajay]

sharp (knife) tranchant [trONshON]
  (taste, pain) **piquant, âpre** [apr]

shattered (very tired) épuisé [aypweezay]

shaver le rasoir [razwahr]
shaving foam la mousse à raser [razay]
shaving point la prise pour rasoirs [preez poor razwahr]
she* elle [el]
sheet (for bed) le drap [dra]
shelf l'étagère f [aytajair]
shellfish les crustacés [kr00stassay]
sherry le sherry
ship le bateau [bato]
  by ship en bateau
shirt la chemise [shuhmeez]
shit! merde! [maird]
shock le choc [shok]
  I got an electric shock from the ... j'ai reçu une décharge en touchant ... [jay ruhs00 00n daysharj ON tosh0N]
shock-absorber l'amortisseur m [amorteessurr]
shocking scandaleux [sk0Ndaluh]
shoe la chaussure [shosh00r]
  a pair of shoes une paire de chaussures
shoelaces les lacets mpl [lassay]
shoe polish le cirage [seerahj]
shoe repairer le cordonnier [kordon-yay]
shop le magasin [magazAN]

Shops generally open between 8.30 and 9.30 a.m. and normally close for lunch around 12.30, re-opening at 2 or 2.30 p.m. They then remain open until →

7 or 8 p.m. **Boulangeries** (baker's shops) usually open earlier than other shops. Some shops and all large department stores and supermarkets are open at lunchtime. Shops in holiday resorts don't always close for lunch and often remain open until very late at night. Nearly all shops are closed on Sunday and for many shops Monday is the additional weekly closing day.

shopping: I'm going shopping je vais faire des courses [juh vay fair day koorss]
shopping centre le centre commercial [s0Ntr komairs-yal]
shop window la vitrine [veetreen]
shore (of sea, lake) le rivage [reevahj]
short (time, journey) court [koor] (person) petit [puhtee]
shortcut le raccourci [rakoorsee]
shorts le short
should: what should I do? que dois-je faire? [kuh dwaj fair]
  he shouldn't be long il devrait revenir bientôt [eel duhvray]
  you should have told me vous auriez dû me le dire [voo zoreeay d00]
shoulder l'épaule f [aypol]
shout crier [kree-ay]
show (in theatre) le spectacle [spekt-akl]

could you show me?
pourrais-tu/pourriez-vous
me montrer? [pooray-too/
pooree-ay-voo muh mONtray]
shower (in bathroom) la douche
[doosh]
with shower avec douche
shower gel le gel douche
shut fermer [fairmay]
when do you shut? à quelle
heure fermez-vous? [kel urr
fairmay-voo]
when do they shut? à quelle
heure est-ce que ça ferme?
[eskuh sa fairm]
they're shut c'est fermé [say
fairmay]
I've shut myself out je me suis
enfermé dehors [juh muh
swee zONfairmay duh-or]
shut up! tais-toi/taisez-vous!
[tay-twa/tezzay-voo]
shutter (on camera) l'obturateur
m [obtOOraturr]
(on window) le volet [volay]
shy timide [teemeed]
sick (US) malade [malad]
I'm going to be sick (vomit) j'ai
envie de vomir [jay ONvee duh
vomeer]
see **ill**
side le côté [kotay]
the other side of town l'autre
côté de la ville
side lights les feux de position
mpl [fuh duh pozeess-yON]
side salad la salade [sa-lad]
side street la petite rue [puhteet
rOO]

sidewalk le trottoir [trotwahr]
see **pavement**
sight: the sights of ... les
endroits à voir à ... [lay
zONdrwa a vwahr]
**sightseeing: we're going
sightseeing** nous allons
visiter la ville [noo zalON
veezeetay]
sightseeing tour l'excursion f
[exkOOrs-yON]
sign (roadsign etc) le panneau de
signalisation [pano duh seen-
yaleezass-yON]
signal: he didn't give a signal
(driver) il n'a pas mis son
clignotant [eel na pa mee sON
kleen-yotON]
(cyclist) il n'a pas fait signe
qu'il allait tourner [fay seeñ
keel alay toornay]
signature la signature [seen-
yatOOr]
signpost le poteau indicateur
[poto ANdeekaturr]
silence le silence [seelONss]
silk la soie [swa]
silly idiot [eed-yo]
silver l'argent m [arjON]
silver foil le papier d'argent
[papyay]
similar semblable [sONbl-abl]
simple simple [sAN-pl]
since: since yesterday depuis
hier [duhp-wee]
since I got here depuis que je
suis arrivé [areevay]
sing chanter [shONtay]
singer le chanteur, la

chanteuse [shONturr, -urz]

single: a single to ... un aller
simple pour ... [alay SAN-pl]

I'm single je suis célibataire
[juh swee sayleebatair]

single bed le lit d'une
personne [lee dOOn pairson]

single room la chambre pour
une personne [shONbr poor OOn
pairson]

sink (in kitchen) l'évier m
[ayv-yay]

sister la sœur [surr]

sister-in-law la belle-sœur
[bel-surr]

sit: can I sit here? est-ce que je
peux m'asseoir ici? [eskuh
juh puh masswahr ee-see]

sit down s'asseoir
sit down assieds-toi/asseyez-
vous [ass-yay-twa/asay-ay-voo]
is anyone sitting here? est-ce
que cette place est prise?
[eskuh set plass ay preez]

size la taille [tī]

ski le ski
(verb) skier [skee-ay]
a pair of skis une paire de
skis

ski boots les chaussures de ski
fpl [shohsOOr]

skiing le ski
we're going skiing nous allons
faire du ski [noo zalON fair]

ski instructor le moniteur (de
ski) [moneeturr]

ski-lift le remonte-pente
[ruhmONt-pONt]

skin la peau [po]

skin-diving la plongée sous-
marine [plONjay soo-mareen]

skinny maigre [megr]

ski-pants le fuseau [fOOzo]

ski-pass le forfait de ski [forfay]

ski pole le bâton de ski [bahtON]

skirt la jupe [jOOp]

ski run la piste de ski

ski slope la pente de ski [pONt]

ski wax le fart [far]

sky le ciel [s-yel]

sleep dormir [dormeer]
did you sleep well? tu as/vous
avez bien dormi? [tOO a/voo
zavay b-yAN dormee]
I need a good sleep j'ai
besoin d'une bonne nuit de
sommeil [jay buh-zwAN dOOn
bon nwee duh somay]

sleeper (rail) le wagon-lit
[vagON-lee]

sleeping bag le sac de
couchage [kooshahj]

sleeping car le wagon-lit [vagON-
lee]

sleeping pill le somnifère
[somneefair]

sleepy: I'm feeling sleepy j'ai
sommeil [jay somay]

sleeve la manche [mONsh]

slide (photographic) la diapositive
[dee-apozeeteev]

slip (under dress) la combinaison
[kONbeenezzON]

slippery glissant [gleessON]

slow lent [lON]
slow down! (driving, speaking)
moins vite! [mwAN veet]

slowly lentement [lONtmON]

could you say it slowly?
pourriez-vous parler plus
lentement? [pooree-ay-voo
parlay ploo]
very slowly très lentement
smell: it smells ça sent mauvais
[mo-vay]
smile sourire [sooreer]
smoke la fumée [foomay]
do you mind if I smoke? est-ce
que ça vous dérange si je
fume? [eskuh sa voo dayronj see
juh foom]
I don't smoke je ne fume pas
do you smoke? tu fumes/vous
fumez? [too foom/voo foomay]
snack: I'd just like a snack
j'aimerais manger un petit
quelque chose [jemray monjay
an puhtee kelkuh shohz]
sneeze l'éternuement m
[aytairnoomon]
snorkel le tuba
snow la neige [nej]
so: it's so good c'est tellement
bien [telmon]
not so fast pas si vite!
so am I moi aussi [mwa o-see]
so do I moi aussi
so-so comme ci, comme ça
[kom see, kom sa]
soaking solution (for contact
lenses) la solution de
trempage [solooss-yon duh
tronpahj]
soap le savon [savon]
soap powder la lessive [lesseev]
sober sobre [sobr]

sock la chaussette [sho-set]
socket (electrical) la prise de
courant [preez duh kooron]
soda (water) le soda
sofa le canapé, le divan
[deevon]
soft doux, f douce [doo, dooss]
soft-boiled egg l'œuf à la
coque m [urf a la kok]
soft drink la boisson non-
alcoolisée [bwasson non-
alkoleezay]
soft lenses les lentilles souples
fpl [lontee soopl]
sole (of shoe, of foot) la semelle
[suhmel]
could you put new soles on
these? pourriez-vous
ressemeler ces chaussures?
[pooree-ay-voo ruh-suhmuhlay
say shohsoor]
some: can I have some water/
peanuts? j'aimerais de l'eau/
des cacahuètes, s'il vous
plaît [jemray duh lo/day]
can I have some? est-ce que
je peux en avoir? [eskuh juh
puh on avwahr]
somebody, someone quelqu'un
[kel-kan]
something quelque chose
[kelkuh shohz]
something to drink quelque
chose à boire
sometimes parfois [parfwa]
somewhere quelque part
[kelkuh par]
son le fils [feess]
song la chanson [shonson]

son-in-law le beau-fils
[bo-feess]
soon bientôt [b-yANto]
I'll be back soon je reviens
bientôt
as soon as possible dès que
possible [day kuh]
sore: it's sore ça fait mal [sa fay
mal]
sore throat le mal de gorge
sorry: (I'm) sorry je suis désolé,
excusez-moi [juh swee
dayzolay, eskoozay-mwa]
sorry? (didn't understand)
pardon? [par-dON]
sort: what sort of ...? quel genre
de ...? [kel jONr duh]
soup le potage [potahj]
sour (taste) acide [aseed]
south le sud [sood]
in the south dans le sud
South Africa l'Afrique du Sud f
[afreek doo sood]
South African (adj) sud-africain
[sood afreekAN]
I'm South African (man/woman)
je suis sud-africain/sud-
africaine [-ken]
southeast le sud-est [sood-est]
South of France le Midi
southwest le sud-ouest [sood-
west]
souvenir le souvenir
Spain l'Espagne f [españ]
Spanish espagnol [espan-yol]
spanner la clé anglaise [klay
ONglez]
spare part la pièce de rechange
[p-yes duh ruhshONj]

spare tyre le pneu de rechange
[p-nuh duh ruhshONj]
spark plug la bougie [boojee]
speak: do you speak English?
parlez-vous l'anglais? [parlay-
voo]
I don't speak ... je ne parle
pas ... [juh nuh parl pa]

•••••• DIALOGUE ••••••

can I speak to Marc? j'aimerais
parler à Marc [jemray parlay]
who's calling? c'est de la part de
qui? [say duh la par duh kee]
it's Patricia c'est Patricia
I'm sorry, he's not in, can I take a
message? désolé, il n'est pas là,
est-ce que je peux prendre un
message [prONdr un messahj]
no thanks, I'll call back later non
merci, je rappellerai plus tard
[mairsee juh rapeluhray ploo tar]
please tell him I called dites-lui
que j'ai appelé, s'il vous plaît
[deet-lwee kuh jay apelay seel voo
play]

spearmint la menthe verte
[mONt vairt]
speciality la spécialité [spayss-
yaleetay]
spectacles les lunettes
[loonet]
speed la vitesse [veetess]
speed limit la limite de vitesse
[leemeet]
speedometer le compteur
[kONturr]
spell: how do you spell it?
comment est-ce que ça

s'écrit? [komON teskuh sa saykree]

see **alphabet**

spend dépenser [daypONsay]

spider l'araignée f [aren-yay]

spin-dryer l'essoreuse f [esrorurz]

splinter l'écharde f [ayshard]

spoke (in wheel) le rayon [ray-ON]

spoon la cuillère [kwee-yair]

sport le sport [spor]

sprain: I've sprained my ... je me suis foulé ... [juh muh swee foolay]

spring (season) le printemps [prANtON]
(of car, seat) le ressort [ruhsor]

square (in town) la place [plass]

stairs l'escalier m [eskal-yay]

stale (taste) pas frais, f pas fraîche [pa fray, pa fresh]
(bread) rassis [rassee]

stall: the engine keeps stalling le moteur cale sans arrêt [moturr kal sON zaray]

stamp le timbre [tANbr]

•••••• DIALOGUE ••••••

a stamp for England, please un timbre pour l'Angleterre, s'il vous plaît

what are you sending? qu'est-ce que vous envoyez? [keskuh voo zONvwy-yay]

it's for this postcard c'est pour cette carte postale

Stamps can either be bought at a post office or at tobacconists' shops (which can be identified by a red diamond-shaped sign with **Tabac** written on it), and sometimes from stalls and shops selling postcards.

standby le vol en stand-by [ON]

star l'étoile f [aytwal]
(in film) la star

start le début [dayboo]
(verb) commencer [kom-ONssay]

when does it start? quand est-ce que ça commence? [kONteskuh sa kom-mONss]

the car won't start la voiture refuse de démarrer [ruhfooz duh daymaray]

starter (of car) le démarreur [daymarurr]
(food) l'entrée f [ONtray]

state (in country) l'état m [ayta]

the States (USA) les États-Unis [ayta-zoonee]

station la gare [gar]

statue la statue

stay: where are you staying? où logez-vous? [oo lojay-voo]

I'm staying at ... je loge au ... [juh loj o]

I'd like to stay another two nights j'aimerais rester deux nuits de plus [jemray restay]

steak le steak

steal voler [volay]

my bag has been stolen on

m'a volé mon sac [ON ma volay]

steep (hill) raide [red]

steering la direction [deereks-yON]

step: on the steps sur les marches [sOOr lay marsh]

stereo stéréo [stayray-o]

sterling la livre sterling [leevr stairleeng]

steward (on plane) le steward

stewardess l'hôtesse de l'air f [otess]

sticking plaster le sparadrap [-dra]

still: I'm still waiting j'attends toujours [toojoor]

is he still there? est-ce qu'il est toujours là? [eskeel ay]

keep still! ne bouge/bougez pas! [nuh booj/boojay pa]

sting: I've been stung j'ai été piqué (par un insecte) [jay aytay peekay (par AN ANsekt)]

stockings les bas mpl [ba]

stomach le ventre, l'estomac m [vONtr, estoma]

stomach ache les maux d'estomac [mo destoma]

stone (rock) la pierre [p-yair]

stop s'arrêter [sa-retay]

to stop the car arrêter la voiture

please, stop here (to taxi driver etc) arrêtez-moi ici, s'il vous plaît [aretay-mwa ee-see]

do you stop near ...? est-ce que vous vous arrêtez près de ...? [eskuh voo voo zaretay]

stop doing that! arrêtez!

stopover la halte [alt]

storm la tempête [tON-pet]

straight: it's straight ahead c'est tout droit [say too drwa]

a straight whisky un whisky sec

straightaway tout de suite [toot sweet]

strange (odd) bizarre, étrange [aytrONj]

stranger l'étranger m, l'étrangère f [aytrONjay, -jair]

I'm a stranger here je ne suis pas d'ici [juh nuh swee pa dee-see]

strap (on watch) le bracelet [braslay]

(on dress) la bretelle [bruhtel]

(on suitcase) la sangle [sONgl]

strawberry la fraise [frez]

stream le ruisseau [rwee-so]

street la rue [rOO]

on the street dans la rue

streetmap le plan de ville [plON duh veel]

string la ficelle [feessel]

strong fort [for]

stuck coincé [kwANsay]

the key's stuck le clé est coincée

student (male/female) l'étudiant m, l'étudiante f [aytOOd-yON, -yONt]

stupid stupide [stOOpeed]

suburb le faubourg [fo-boor]

subway (US) le métro [maytro]

suddenly tout d'un coup [too dAN koo]

suede le daim [dAN]

sugar le sucre [sOOkr]

suit le costume

  it doesn't suit me (colour etc) ça ne me va pas [sa nuh muh va pa]

  it suits you (colour etc) ça vous va bien [b-yAN]

suitcase la valise [valeez]

summer l'été m [aytay]

  in the summer en été

sun le soleil [solay]

  in the sun au soleil [o]

  out of the sun à l'ombre [lONbr]

sunbathe prendre un bain de soleil [prONdr AN bAN duh solay]

sunblock (cream) l'écran total m [aykrON toh-tal]

sunburn le coup de soleil [koo duh solay]

sunburnt: I'm sunburnt j'ai pris un coup de soleil [pree AN]

Sunday dimanche [deemONsh]

sunglasses les lunettes de soleil [lOOnet duh solay]

sun lounger la chaise longue [shez lON-g]

sunny ensoleillé [ONsolay-yay]

  it's sunny il fait soleil [eel fay solay]

sun roof (in car) le toit ouvrant [twa oovrON]

sunset le coucher de soleil [kooshay duh solay]

sunshade le parasol

sunshine le soleil [solay]

sunstroke l'insolation f [ANsolass-yON]

suntan le bronzage [brONzahj]

suntan lotion le lait solaire [lay solair]

suntanned bronzé [brONzay]

suntan oil l'huile solaire f [weel solair]

super super [sOOpair]

  we had a super time c'était super [saytay]

supermarket le supermarché [sOOpairmarshay]

supper le dîner [deenay]

supplement (extra charge) le supplément [sOOplaymON]

sure: are you sure? vous êtes sûr? [voo zet sOOr]

sure! d'accord! [dakor]

surname le nom de famille [nON duh famee]

swearword le juron [jOOrON]

sweater le pullover

sweatshirt le sweatshirt

Sweden la Suède [swed]

Swedish (adj) suédois [swaydwa]

sweet (taste) sucré [sOOkray]

  (dessert) le dessert [dessair]

sweets les bonbons mpl [bONbON]

swelling l'enflure f [ONflOOr]

swim nager [nahjay]

  I'm going for a swim je vais me baigner [juh vay muh benyay]

  let's go for a swim allons nous baigner

swimming costume le maillot de bain [my-o duh bAN]

swimming pool la piscine [peesseen]

swimming trunks le slip de bain
  [sleep duh bAN]
Swiss (adj) suisse [sweess]
  (man) le Suisse
  (woman) la Suissesse
  [sweessess]
switch l'interrupteur m
  [ANtairϾopturr]
switch off (TV, lights) éteindre
  [aytANdr]
  (engine) arrêter [aretay]
switch on (TV, lights) allumer
  [alϾomay]
  (engine) mettre en marche
  [metr ON marsh]
Switzerland la Suisse [sweess]
swollen enflé [ONflay]

T

table la table [tahbl]
  a table for two une table pour
  deux
tablecloth la nappe [nap]
table tennis le ping-pong
table wine le vin ordinaire [vAN
  ordeenair]
tailback (of traffic) le bouchon
  [booshON]
tailor le tailleur [tī-urr]
take (lead) prendre [prONdr]
  (accept) accepter [axeptay]
  can you take me to the airport?
  est-ce que vous pouvez
  m'emmener à l'aéroport?
  [eskuh voo poovay mONmuhnay]
  do you take credit cards?
  acceptez-vous les cartes de
  crédit? [axeptay-voo]

fine, I'll take it d'accord, je le
  prends [juh luh prON]
can I take this? (leaflet etc) je
  peux le prendre? [puh]
how long does it take?
  combien de temps est-ce
  que ça prend? [kONb-yAN duh
  tON eskuh sa prON]
it takes three hours ça prend
  trois heures
is this seat taken? est-ce que
  cette place est occupée?
  [eskuh set plass et okϾopay]
hamburger to take away
  hamburger à emporter
  [ONportay]
can you take a little off here?
  (to hairdresser) pouvez-vous
  couper un peu par ici?
  [koopay AN puh]
talcum powder le talc
talk parler [parlay]
tall grand [grON]
tampons les tampons mpl
  [tONpON]
tan le bronzage [brONzahj]
  to get a tan bronzer [brONzay]
tank (of car) le réservoir
  [rayzairvwahr]
tap le robinet [robeenay]
tape (cassette) la cassette
  (sticky) le scotch®
tape measure le mètre [metr]
tape recorder le magnétophone
  [man-yaytofon]
taste le goût [goo]
  can I taste it? est-ce que je
  peux goûter? [eskuh juh puh
  gootay]

taxi le taxi
 will you get me a taxi?
 pouvez-vous m'appeler un
 taxi? [poovay-voo maplay]
 where can I find a taxi? où y a-
 t-il des taxis? [oo yateel]

•••••• DIALOGUE ••••••

 to the airport/to Hotel ... please à
 l'aéroport/à l'Hôtel ..., s'il vous
 plaît
 how much will it be? combien est-
 ce que ça me coûtera? [kONb-yaN
 eskuh sa muh kootuhra]
 about 75 francs à peu près
 soixante-quinze francs [puh pray]
 that's fine right here thanks vous
 pouvez me déposer ici, merci
 [muh daypozay]

taxi-driver le chauffeur de taxi
taxi rank la station de taxi
 [stass-yON]
tea (drink) le thé [tay]
 tea for one/two please un thé/
 deux thés, s'il vous plaît
 [duh tay]

Ordinary tea usually comes
without milk; to have milk with
it ask for 'un peu de lait frais'
(some fresh milk). Herbal teas
(tisanes or infusions) are very
popular. The more common
ones are verveine (verbena),
tilleul (lime blossom), menthe
(mint) and camomille
(camomile).

---

teabags les sachets de thé mpl

[sashay duh tay]
teach: could you teach me? est-
 ce que vous pouvez
 m'apprendre? [eskuh voo
 poovay maprONdr]
teacher (junior) l'instituteur m,
 l'institutrice f [ANsteetOOturr,
 -treess]
 (secondary) le professeur [-urr]
team l'équipe f [aykeep]
teaspoon la cuillère à café
 [kwee-yair a kafay]
tea towel le torchon à vaisselle
 [torshON a vess-el]
teenager l'adolescent m,
 l'adolescente f [-sON, -sONt]
telegram le télégramme
 [taylay-]
telephone le téléphone [taylay-]
 see phone
television la télévision
 [taylayveez-yON]
tell: could you tell him ...?
 pourriez-vous lui dire ...?
 [pooree-ay-voo lwee deer]
temperature (weather) la
 température [tONpayratOOr]
 (fever) la fièvre [fee-evr]
tennis le tennis [teneess]
tennis ball la balle de tennis
 [bal]
tennis court le court de tennis
 [koor]
tennis racket la raquette de
 tennis [raket]
tent la tente [tONt]
term (at university, school) le
 trimestre [treemestr]
terminus (rail) le terminus

[tairmeenooss]

terrible épouvantable
[aypoovoNt-abl]

terrific fantastique [foNtasteek]

than* que [kuh]
   smaller than plus petit que

thanks, thank you merci
[mairsee]
   thank you very much merci
   beaucoup [bo-koo]
   thanks for the help merci de
   m'avoir aidé
   no thanks non, merci

•••••• DIALOGUE ••••••

   thanks merci
   that's OK, don't mention it il n'y a
   pas de quoi [eel n-ya pa duh kwa]

that: that building ce bâtiment
[suh]
   that woman cette femme [set]
   that one celui-là, f celle-là
   [suhlwee-la, sel-la]
   I hope that ... j'espère que ...
   [kuh]
   that's nice c'est joli [say]
   is that ...? est-ce que c'est ...?
   [eskuh say]
   that's it (that's right) c'est ça
   [say sa]

the* (singular) le, f la [luh]
   (plural) les [lay]

theatre le théâtre [tay-atr]

their* leur [lurr]

theirs* le/la leur [luh/la lurr]

them*: I know them je les
   connais [juh lay konay]
   for them pour eux, f pour
   elles [uh, el]

   with them avec eux/elles
   I gave it to them je le leur ai
   donné [juh luh lurr ay donay]
   who? – them qui? – eux/elles

then (at that time) à cette
   époque [set aypok]
   (after that) alors [alor]

there là
   over there là-bas [la-ba]
   up there là-haut [la-o]
   is there ...? y a-t-il ...? [yateel]
   are there ...? y a-t-il ...?
   there is ... il y a ... [eel ya]
   there are ... il y a ...
   there you are (giving something)
   voilà [vwala]

thermometer le thermomètre
   [tairmometr]

thermos flask le thermos®
   [tairmoss]

these*: these men ces hommes
   [say]
   these women ces femmes
   can I have these? j'aimerais
   ceux-ci/celles-ci, s'il vous
   plaît [suh-see/sel-see]

they* ils, f elles [eel, el]

thick épais [aypay]
   (stupid) bouché [booshay]

thief le voleur, f la voleuse
   [volurr, -urz]

thigh la cuisse [kweess]

thin mince [maNss]

thing la chose [shohz]
   my things mes affaires [may
   zafair]

think penser [poNsay]
   I think so je pense que oui
   [juh poNss kuh wee]

I don't think so je ne crois pas [nuh krwa pa]

I'll think about it je vais y réfléchir [vay zee rayflesheer]

third party insurance l'assurance au tiers f [o t-yair]

thirsty: I'm thirsty j'ai soif [jay swaf]

this: this building ce bâtiment [suh]

   this woman cette femme [set]

   this one celui-ci, f celle-ci [suhlwee-see, sel-see]

   this is my wife je vous présente ma femme [juh voo prayzONt ma fam]

   is this ...? est-ce que c'est ...? [eskuh say]

those: those men ces hommes [say]

   those women ces femmes

   which ones? – those lesquel(le)s? – ceux-là/ celles-là [suh-la/sel-la]

thread le fil [feel]

throat la gorge [gorj]

throat pastilles les pastilles pour la gorge fpl [pastee poor la gorj]

through par

   does it go through ...? (train, bus) est-ce qu'il passe à ...? [eskeel pass]

throw lancer [lONsay]

throw away jeter [juhtay]

thumb le pouce [pooss]

thunderstorm l'orage m [orahj]

Thursday jeudi [juhdee]

ticket (for bus, train, plane) le billet

[bee-yay]

(for cinema, cloakroom) le ticket [teekay]

•••••• DIALOGUE ••••••

a return ticket to Dijon un aller-retour pour Dijon [alay-ruhtoor]

coming back when? avec retour à quelle date? [ruhtoor]

today/next Tuesday aujourd'hui/ mardi prochain

that will be 300 francs trois cents francs, si'il vous plaît

ticket office (bus, rail) le guichet [geeshay]

tide la marée [maray]

tie (necktie) la cravate [kravat]

tight (clothes etc) serré [serray]

   it's too tight ça me serre [sa muh sair]

tights le collant [kollON]

till (cash desk) la caisse [kess]

time* le temps [tON]

   what's the time? quelle heure est-il? [kel urr eteel]

   this time cette fois [set fwa]

   last time la dernière fois

   next time la prochaine fois

   four times quatre fois

timetable l'horaire m [orair]

tin (can) la boîte [bwat]

tinfoil le papier d'aluminium [pap-yay]

tin opener l'ouvre-boîte m [oovr-bwat]

tiny minuscule [meenOOskOOl]

tip (to waiter etc) le pourboire [poorbwahr]

Although service is included (usually 10-20 per cent of the bill), it is customary to leave a tip of about 10 per cent in restaurants when satisfied with the service. A similar tip is usual as well in bars and for taxi drivers.

tired fatigué [fateegay]
  I'm tired je suis fatigué
tissues les kleenex mpl®
to: to Strasbourg/London à
  Strasbourg/Londres
  to Brittany/England en
  Bretagne/Angleterre [ON]
  to the post office à la poste
  to the bar au bar [o]
toast (bread) le pain grillé [pAN
  gree-yay]
today aujourd'hui [ojoordwee]
toe l'orteil m [ortay]
together ensemble [ONSONbl]
  we're together (in shop etc)
  nous sommes ensemble
  can we pay together?
  pouvons-nous payer
  ensemble? [poovON-noo payay]
toilet les toilettes [twalet]
  where is the toilet? où sont
  les toilettes? [oo sON lay]
  I have to go to the toilet
  j'aimerais aller aux toilettes
  [jemray alay o]

Most cities now have a good number of public toilets: they are beige boxes with an →

automatic door that opens when you put two francs in it. The toilet itself gets cleaned automatically after each visitor. If this futuristic toilet doesn't appeal to you, you can use the toilets in restaurants and bars where you stop to eat or drink, or toilets in museums or at railway stations, where an attendant will expect you to leave a coin or two.

toilet paper le papier
  hygiénique [papyay eejee-
  ayneek]
tomato la tomate [tomat]
tomato juice le jus de tomate
  [joo]
tomato ketchup le ketchup
tomorrow demain [duhmAN]
  tomorrow morning demain
  matin
  the day after tomorrow après-
  demain [apray]
toner (cosmetic) la lotion
  tonique [lohss-yON toneek]
tongue la langue [lON-g]
tonic (water) le schweppes®
tonight ce soir [suh swahr]
tonsillitis l'angine f [ONjeen]
too (excessively) trop [tro]
  (also) aussi [o-see]
  too hot trop chaud
  too much trop
  me too moi aussi [mwa]
tooth la dent [dON]
toothache le mal de dents [mal

duh dON]

toothbrush la brosse à dents
[bross]

toothpaste le dentifrice
[dONteefreess]

top: on top of ... sur ... [sOOr]

at the top en haut [ON o]

top floor le dernier étage
[dairn-yay aytahj]

topless seins nus [SAN nOO]

torch la lampe de poche [lONp
duh posh]

total le total [toh-tal]

tour l'excursion f [exkOOrs-yON]
is there a tour of ...? y a-t-il
une visite guidée de ...?
[yateel OOn veezeet geeday duh]

tour guide le guide [geed]

tourist le/la touriste [tooreest]

tourist information office le
centre d'information
touristique [sONtr dANformass-
yON tooreesteek]

tour operator le voyagiste [vwy-
ahjeest]

towards vers [vair]

towel la serviette [sairvee-et]

town la ville [veel]
in town en ville [ON]
just out of town à la sortie de
la ville

town centre le centre-ville
[sONtr-]

town hall la mairie [mairee]

toy le jouet [joo-ay]

track (US) le quai [kay]
see **platform**

tracksuit le survêtement
[sOOrvetmON]

traditional traditionnel
[tradeess-yonel]

traffic la circulation [seerkOOlass-
yON]

traffic jam l'embouteillage m
[ONbootay-ahj]

traffic lights les feux [fuh]

trailer (for carrying tent etc) la
remorque [ruhmork]
(US) la caravane

trailer park le terrain de
camping pour caravanes
[terrAN duh kONpeeng poor]

train le train [trAN]
by train en train [ON]

Don't forget to validate your
ticket by inserting it into the
orange ticket machines in the
station before you board the
train. Also remember that you
need to have a reservation to
travel by **TGV**, and that you are
required to pay a **supplément**
for some trains and if you don't
you will be fined. The French
rail company, SNCF, offers a
whole range of discount fares on
Période Bleue (blue period)
days – in effect most of the year.
A leaflet showing the various
discounts is given out at **gares
SNCF** (train stations). It's worth
asking, before purchasing your
ticket, whether you're entitled to
a **tarif séjour**, which means a
25 per cent reduction on the
normal price if you are buying a
$\rightarrow$

return ticket, are willing to travel on **Période Bleue** days and will be spending Sunday at your destination.

•••••• DIALOGUE ••••••

is this the train for ...? est-ce que ce train va bien à ...? [eskuh suh tRAN va b-yAN a]

sure oui

no, you want that platform there non, il faut que vous alliez sur ce quai là-bas [eel fo kuh voo zalee-ay sŒr suh kay]

trainers (shoes) les tennis fpl [tenneess]

train station la gare [gar]

translate traduire [tradweer]
could you translate that? pourriez-vous me traduire cela? [pooree-ay-voo muh .... suhla]

translation la traduction [tradŒŒks-yON]

translator le traducteur, la traductrice [tradŒŒkturr, -treess]

trashcan la poubelle [poo-bel]

travel voyager [vwyahj-ay]
we're travelling around nous visitons la région [noo veezeetON la rayjeeON]

travel agent's l'agence de voyages f [ajONss duh vwyahj]

traveller's cheque le chèque de voyage [shek duh vwyahj]

tray le plateau [pla-toh]

tree l'arbre m [arbr]

tremendous fantastique [fONtasteek]

trendy à la mode

trim: just a trim please (to hairdresser) pouvez-vous me les égaliser, s'il vous plaît? [poovay-voo muh lay zaygaleezay]

trip le voyage [vwyahj] (excursion) l'excursion f [exkŒŒrs-yON]
I'd like to go on a trip to ... j'aimerais faire une excursion à ... [jemray fair]

trolley le chariot [sharee-o]

trouble les ennuis [ON-nwee]
I'm having trouble with ... j'ai des problèmes de ... [jay day prob-lem]
sorry to trouble you désolé de vous déranger [dayzolay duh voo dayrONjay]

trousers le pantalon [pONtalON]

true vrai [vray]
that's not true ce n'est pas vrai

trunk le coffre [kofr]

trunks (swimming) le maillot de bain [my-o duh bAN]

try essayer [esay-ay]
can I have a try? (at doing something) est-ce que je peux essayer? [eskuh juh puh]
(food) est-ce que je peux goûter? [gootay]

try on essayer [essay-ay]
can I try it on? est-ce que je peux l'essayer?

T-shirt le T-shirt

Tuesday mardi [mardee]

tuna le thon [tON]
Tunisia la Tunisie [tOOneezee]
Tunisian tunisien [tOOneez-yAN]
tunnel le tunnel [tOOnel]
turn: turn left/right tournez à gauche/droite [toornay]
turn off: where do I turn off? où dois-je bifurquer? [oo dwa-juh beefOOrkay]
can you turn the heating off? pouvez-vous arrêter le chauffage? [aretay]
turn on: can you turn the heating on? pouvez-vous mettre le chauffage? [metr]
turning (in road) la bifurcation [beefOOrkass-yON]
TV la télé [taylay]
tweezers la pince à épiler [pANss a aypeelay]
twice deux fois [duh fwa]
twice as much deux fois plus [plOOss]
twin beds les lits jumeaux [lee jOOmo]
twin room la chambre à deux lits [shONbr]
twist: I've twisted my ankle je me suis tordu la cheville [juh muh swee tordOO la shuhvee]
type le type [teep]
a different type of ... une autre sorte de ... [ohtr sort duh]
typical typique [teepeek]
tyre le pneu [p-nuh]

U

ugly (person, building) laid [lay]
UK le Royaume-Uni [rwy-ohm OOnee]
ulcer l'ulcère m [OOlsair]
umbrella le parapluie [paraplwee]
uncle l'oncle m [ONkl]
unconscious sans connaissance [sON konessONss]
under (in position) sous [soo]
(less than) moins de [mwAN duh]
underdone (meat) pas assez cuit [pa zassay kwee]
underground (railway) le métro [maytro]
see bus
underpants le slip [sleep]
understand: I understand je comprends [juh kONprON]
I don't understand je ne comprends pas [pa]
do you understand? comprenez-vous? [kONpruhnay-voo]
unemployed au chômage [o shohmahj]
United States les États-Unis [aytazOOnee]
university l'université f [OOneevairseetay]
unleaded petrol l'essence sans plomb f [essONss sON plON]
unlimited mileage le kilométrage illimité [keelomaytrahj eeleemeetay]
unlock ouvrir [oovreer]

unpack défaire sa valise
[dayfair sa valeez]

until jusqu'à [j00ska]
I'll wait until you're back
j'attendrai jusqu'à ce que tu
reviennes [jatONdray j00ss-kass
kuh]

unusual inhabituel
[eenabeet00el]

up en haut [ON o]
up there là-haut [la-o]
he's not up yet (not out of bed) il
n'est pas encore levé [eel nay
pa zONkor luhvay]
what's up? (what's wrong?) que
se passe-t-il? [kuh suh pasteel]

upmarket chic [sheek]

upset stomach l'indigestion f
[ANdeejest-yON]

upside down à l'envers [a
lONvair]

upstairs en haut [ON o]

urgent urgent [00rjON]

us* nous [noo]
with us avec nous
for us pour nous

USA les USA [00-ess-a]

use utiliser [00teeleezay]
may I use ...? puis-je me
servir de ...? [pweej muh
sairveer duh]

useful utile [00teel]

usual habituel [abeet00el]
the usual (drink etc) comme
d'habitude [kom dabeet00d]

V

vacancy: do you have any
vacancies? (hotel) est-ce que
vous avez des chambres?
[eskuh voo zavay day shONbr]

vacation les vacances fpl

vaccination le vaccin [vaxAN]

vacuum cleaner l'aspirateur m
[aspeeraturr]

valid (ticket etc) valable [val-abl]
how long is it valid for?
jusqu'à quand est-il valable?
[j00ska kON eteel]

valley la vallée [valay]

valuable (adj) précieux [prayss-
yuh]
can I leave my valuables here?
est-ce que je peux laisser
mes objets de valeur ici?
[eskuh juh puh lessay may zobjay
duh valurr ee-see]

value la valeur [valurr]

van la camionnette [kameeonet]

vanilla la vanille [vanee]
a vanilla ice cream une glace
à la vanille [glass]

vary: it varies ça dépend [sa
daypON]

vase le vase [vahz]

veal le veau [vo]

vegetables les légumes mpl
[layg00m]

vegetarian le végétarien, la
végétarienne [vayjaytaree-AN,
-en]

vending machine le
distributeur automatique
[deestreeb00turr otomateek]

very très [tray]
 very little for me un tout petit
 peu pour moi [AN too puhtee
 puh]
 I like it very much ça me plaît
 beaucoup [sa muh play bo-koo]
vest (under shirt) le maillot de
 corps [my-o duh kor]
via par
video (film) la vidéo [veedayo]
 (recorder) le magnétoscope
 [man-yaytoskop]
view la vue [vOO]
villa la villa [veela]
village le village [veelahj]
vinegar le vinaigre [veenegr]
vineyard le vignoble [veen-yobl]
visa le visa
visit visiter [veezeetay]
 I'd like to visit ... j'aimerais
 visiter ... [jemray]
vital: it's vital that ... il faut
 absolument que ... [eel foht
 absolOOmON kuh]
vodka la vodka
voice la voix [vwa]
voltage le voltage [volt-ahj]

The supply is 220V, though anything requiring 240V will work.
Most plugs are two round pins:
a travel plug is useful.

vomit vomir [vomeer]

W

waist la taille [tī]
waistcoat le gilet [jeelay]
wait attendre [atONdr]
 wait for me! attendez-moi!
 [atONday-mwa]
 don't wait for me ne
 m'attendez pas [nuh]
 can I wait until my wife/partner
 gets here? est-ce que je peux
 attendre ma femme/mon
 ami(e)? [eksuh juh puh]
 can you do it while I wait?
 pouvez-vous le faire tout de
 suite? [poovay-voo luh fair toot
 sweet]
 could you wait here for me? (as
 said to taxi driver) est-ce que
 vous pouvez m'attendre ici?
waiter le serveur [sairvurr], le
 garçon [garsON]
 waiter! garçon!
waitress la serveuse [sairvurz]
 waitress! s'il vous plaît! [seel
 voo play]
wake: can you wake me up at
 5.30? pouvez-vous me
 réveiller à cinq heures
 trente? [poovay-voo muh
 rayvayay]
wake-up call le réveil
 téléphonique [ray-vay
 taylayfoneek]
Wales le Pays de Galles [payee
 duh gal]
walk: is it a long walk? est-ce
 loin à pied? [es lwAN a p-yay]
 it's only a short walk c'est à

deux pas d'ici [set a duh pa dee-see]

I'll walk j'y vais à pied [jee vay]

I'm going for a walk je vais faire un tour [juh vay fair AN toor]

Walkman® le walkman®

wall le mur [moor]

wallet le portefeuille [portfuh-ee]

wander: I like just wandering around j'aime bien flâner [jem b-yAN flanay]

want: I want a ... je veux un ... [juh vuh]

I don't want any ... je ne veux pas de ... [juh nuh vuh pa duh]

we want to go home nous voulons rentrer à la maison [noo voolON]

I don't want to non, je ne veux pas

he wants to ... il veut ... [eel vuh]

what do you want? que voulez-vous? [kuh voolay-voo]

ward (in hospital) la salle [sal]

warm chaud [sho]

I'm so warm j'ai tellement chaud

was*: it was ... c'était ... [saytay]

wash laver [lavay]

can you wash these? pouvez-vous laver ceci, s'il vous plaît? [poovay-voo]

washer (for bolt etc) la rondelle [rONdel]

washhand basin le lavabo

washing (clothes) la lessive [lesseev]

washing machine la machine à laver [lavay]

washing powder la lessive [lesseev]

washing-up liquid le produit à vaisselle [prodwee a vess-el]

wasp la guêpe [gep]

watch (wristwatch) la montre [mONtr]

will you watch my things for me? pourriez-vous me garder mes affaires, s'il vous plaît? [pooree-ay-voo muh garday]

watch out! attention! [atONs-yON]

watch strap le bracelet-montre [braslay-mONtr]

water l'eau f [o]

may I have some water? pourriez-vous m'apporter de l'eau, s'il vous plaît? [pooree-ay-voo maportay]

waterproof (adj) imperméable [ANpairmayabl]

waterskiing le ski nautique [skee noteek]

wave (in sea) la vague [vag]

way: it's this way c'est par ici [say par ee-see]

it's that way c'est par là

is it a long way to ...? est-ce que c'est loin d'ici à ...? [eskuh say lwAN dee-see]

no way! pas question! [pa kest-yON]

••••• DIALOGUE •••••

could you tell me the way to ...?
pouvez-vous m'indiquer le
chemin pour aller à ...?
go straight on until you reach the
traffic lights continuez tout droit
jusqu'aux feux [kONteenOO-ay too
drwa jOOsko fuh]
turn left tournez à gauche
[toornay]
take the first on the right prenez la
première à droite [pruhnay]
see also **where**

we* nous [noo]
weak (person) faible [febl]
(drink) pas fort [pa for]
weather le temps [tON]

••••• DIALOGUE •••••

what's the weather forecast?
quelles sont les prévisions de la
météo? [kels sON lay prayveez-yON
duh la maytay-o]
it's going to be fine il va faire
beau [eel va fair bo]
it's going to rain il va pleuvoir
it'll brighten up later ça va
s'éclaircir plus tard [sa va
sayklairseer]

wedding le mariage [maree-ahj]
wedding ring l'alliance f
[aleeONss]
Wednesday mercredi
[mairkruhdee]
week la semaine [suhmen]
a week (from) today
aujourd'hui en huit
[ojoordwee ON weet]

a week (from) tomorrow
demain en huit
weekend le week-end
at the weekend ce week-end
weight le poids [pwa]
weird bizarre
weirdo l'énergumène mf
[aynairgOOmen]
welcome: welcome to ...
bienvenue à ... [b-yAN-vuhnOO]
you're welcome (don't mention
it) je vous en prie [juh voo zON
pree]
well: I don't feel well je ne me
sens pas bien [juh nuh muh
sON pa b-yAN]
she's not well elle ne se sent
pas bien [... sON ...]
you speak English very well
vous parlez très bien
l'anglais
well done! bravo!
this one as well celui-là aussi
[o-see]
well well! (surprise) tiens!
[t-yAN]

••••• DIALOGUE •••••

how are you? comment vas-tu/
allez-vous? [komON va-tOO/alay-voo]
very well, thanks très bien, merci
[tray b-yAN]

well-done (meat) bien cuit
[b-yAN kwee]
Welsh gallois [galwa]
I'm Welsh (man/woman) je suis
gallois/galloise [... galwahz]
were*: we were nous étions
[noo zauteeON]

you were vous étiez [voo zaytee-ay]

they were ils/elles étaient [eel/el zaytay]

west l'ouest m [west]

in the west à l'ouest

West Indian (adj) antillais [ONteeyay]

wet mouillé [mooyay]

what? quoi? [kwa]

what's that? qu'est-ce que c'est? [keskuh say]

what should I do? que dois-je faire? [kuh dwahj fair]

what a view! quelle vue magnifique! [kel]

what bus do I take? je prends quel bus?

wheel la roue [roo]

wheelchair le fauteuil roulant [fotuh-ee roolON]

when? quand? [kON]

when we get back à notre retour [a notr ruhtoor]

when's the train/ferry? à quelle heure part le train/ferry? [kel urr par]

where? où? [oo]

I don't know where it is je ne sais pas où il est

•••••• DIALOGUE ••••••

where is the cathedral? où est la cathédrale? [oo ay]

it's over there c'est par là [say]

could you show me where it is on the map? pouvez-vous me montrer où ça se trouve sur la carte?

it's just here c'est ici

which: which train? quel train? [kel]

•••••• DIALOGUE ••••••

which one? lequel (laquelle)? [luhkel, lakel]

that one celui-là (celle-là) [suhlwee-la, sel-la]

this one? celui-ci (celle-ci)? [suhlwee-see]

no, that one non, celui-là (celle-là)

while: while I'm here pendant que je suis ici [pondON kuh]

whisky le whisky

white blanc, f blanche [blON, blONsh]

white wine le vin blanc [VAN blON]

who? qui? [kee]

who is it? qui est-ce? [ess]

the man who ... l'homme qui ...

whole: the whole week toute la semaine [toot]

the whole lot le tout [luh too]

whose: whose is this? à qui est ceci? [a kee ay suhsee]

why? pourquoi? [poorkwa]

why not? pourquoi pas? [pa]

wide large [larj]

wife: my wife ma femme [fam]

will*: will you do it for me? pouvez-vous faire ça pour moi? [poovay-voo]

wind le vent [vON]

window la fenêtre [fuhnetr]

near the window près de la fenêtre

in the window (of shop) en vitrine [ON veetreen]

window seat le siège près de la fenêtre [pray duh la fuhnetr]

windscreen le pare-brise [par-breez]

windscreen wiper l'essuie-glace m [eswee-glass]

windsurfing la planche à voile [plONsh a vwal]

windy: it's so windy il y a beaucoup de vent [eelya bo-koo duh vON]

wine le vin [vAN]

can we have some more wine? encore un peu de vin, s'il vous plaît [ONkor AN puh]

wine list la carte des vins [kart day vAN]

wine merchant le marchand de vins [marshON duh vAN]

wine-tasting la dégustation [daygoostass-yON]

winter l'hiver m [eevair]

in the winter en hiver [ON]

winter holiday les vacances d'hiver [vakONss deevair]

wire le fil de fer [feel duh fair]

(electric) le fil (électrique) [aylektreek]

wish: best wishes meilleurs vœux [mayurr vuh]

with avec [avek]

I'm staying with ... j'habite chez ... [jabeet shay]

without sans [sON]

witness le témoin [taymwAN]

will you be a witness for me? voulez-vous me servir de témoin? [voolay-voo muh sairveer duh]

woman la femme [fam]

---

women

Women are bound to experience sexual harassment in France, where many men make a habit of looking you up and down, and more often than not, passing comment. A 'bonjour' or 'bonsoir' on the street is almost always a pick-up line. If you so much as return the greeting, you've left yourself open to a persistent monologue and a difficult brush-off job.

---

wonderful merveilleux [mairvayuh]

won't*: the car won't start la voiture ne veut pas démarrer [nuh vuh pa]

wood (material) le bois [bwa]

woods (forest) la forêt [foray]

wool la laine [len]

word le mot [mo]

work le travail [trav-ī]

I work in ... je travaille dans ... [juh trav-ī]

it's not working ça ne marche pas [sa nuh marsh pa]

world le monde [mONd]

worried inquiet, f inquiète [ANkee-ay, -et]

worse: it's worse c'est pire [say peer]

worst le pire [luh peer]

worth: is it worth a visit? est-ce que ça vaut le détour? [eskuh sa vo luh daytoor]

would: would you give this to ...? pourriez-vous donner ceci à ...? [pooree-ay-voo donay suhsee]

wrap: could you wrap it up? pourriez-vous me l'emballer? [pooree-ay-voo muh lONbalay]

wrapping paper le papier d'emballage [pap-yay dONbalahj]

wrist le poignet [pwAN-yay]

write écrire [aykreer]

  could you write it down? pouvez-vous me l'écrire? [poovay-voo muh laykreer]

  how do you write it? comment est-ce que ça s'écrit? [komON teskuh sa saykree]

writing paper le papier à lettres [pap-yay a letr]

wrong: it's the wrong key ce n'est pas la bonne clef [suh nuh pa la bon klay]

  this is the wrong train ce n'est pas le bon train

  the bill's wrong il y a une erreur dans la facture [eelya OOn air-rurr dON la faktOOr]

  sorry, wrong number excusez-moi, j'ai fait un mauvais numéro [exkOOzay-mwa jay fay AN movay

nOOmayro]

  sorry, wrong room excusez-moi, je me suis trompé de chambre [juh muh swee trONpay]

  there's something wrong with ... ... ne marche pas bien [nuh marsh pa b-yAN]

  what's wrong? qu'y a-t-il? [k-yateel]

X

X-ray les rayons X mpl [rayON eex]

Y

yacht le voilier [vwal-yay]

yard* le jardin [jardAN]

year l'année f [anay]

yellow jaune [jo-n]

yes oui [wee]

  you're not going already, are you? – yes tu ne t'en vas pas déjà, hein? – si [tOO nuh tON va pa day-ja AN – see]

yesterday hier [yair]

  yesterday morning hier matin

  the day before yesterday avant-hier [avONt-yair]

yet encore [ONkor]

  have you heard from him yet? est-ce que vous avez déjà eu de ses nouvelles? [eskuh voo zavay day-ja OO duh say noovel]

•••••• DIALOGUE ••••••

is it here yet? est-ce que c'est
arrivé? [eskuh say]

no, not yet non, pas encore
[pa zONkor]

you'll have to wait a little longer yet
il vous faudra attendre encore
un peu

yoghurt le yaourt [ya-oor]

you* (polite or plural) vous [voo]
(singular, familiar) tu [tOO]

this is for you c'est pour toi/
vous [twa]

with you avec toi/vous

In French, when you address
strangers or people with whom
you have a semi-formal
relationship (e.g. shopkeepers,
hotel staff), and when you are
speaking to more than one
person, you should use the **vous**
form of 'you', which takes the
second person plural of the verb.
The familiar **tu** form, which
takes the second person
singular of the verb, is used to
address family, friends, children
and informal acquaintances.

young jeune [jurn]

your* votre, pl vos [votr, vo]
(singular, familiar) ton, f ta, pl
tes [tON, ta, tay]

yours* le/la vôtre [luh/la vohtr],
pl les vôtres
(singular, familiar) le tien, f la
tienne [t-yAN, t-yen], pl les

tiens/tiennes

youth hostel l'auberge de
jeunesse f [obairj duh jur-ness]

Z

zero zéro [zayro]

zip la fermeture éclair
[fairmtOOr ayklair]

could you put a new zip on?
pourriez-vous mettre une
nouvelle fermeture éclair?
[pooree-ay-voo metr OOn noovel]

zoo le zoo [zo]

French-English

A

a: il/elle a he/she/it has

à [a] to; at; in; by

à la gare at the station

abcès m [absay] abscess

abeille f [abay] bee

abonnements mpl [abonnuh-mON] season tickets

abord: d'abord [dabor] first

absolument [absolooMON] absolutely

accélérateur m [axaylayraturr] accelerator

accélérer [axaylayray] to accelerate

accepter [axeptay] to accept

accès autorisé pour livraisons deliveries only

accès aux quais to the platforms

accès aux trains to the trains

accès interdit no entry

accès réservé au personnel staff entrance only

accès réservé aux riverains no entry except for access

accès réservé aux voyageurs munis de billets ticket holders only

accompagner [akONpan-yay] to accompany

accord: d'accord [dakor] OK

je suis d'accord I agree

accotement non stabilisé soft verge

accueil m [akuh-ee] reception

accusé de réception m [akOOzay duh rayseps-yON]

acknowledgement of receipt

achat m [a-sha] purchase

faire des achats to go shopping

acheter [ashtay] to buy

acide [a-seed] sour

acteur m [akturr] actor

actrice f [aktreess] actress

adaptateur m [adaptaturr] adaptor

addition f [adeess-yON] bill

adolescent m [adolessON] teenager

s'adresser à ... [sadressay] ask ...

adressez-vous à la réception ask at reception

aérogare f [a-airogar] air terminal

aéroglisseur m [a-airogleessurr] hovercraft

aéroport m [a-airopor] airport

affaires fpl [affair] business

affichage m [affeeshahj] display

affiche f [affeesh] poster

afficher [affeeshay] to display

affranchir [affrONsheer] to stamp

affranchissement m [affrONsheess-mON] postage

affreux [affruh] awful

afin que [afAN kuh] so that

âge m [ahj] age

agence f [ajONss] agency

agence de voyages f [duh vwyahj] travel agent's

agenda m [ajANda] diary

agent conservateur [ajON kONsairvaturr] preservative

agent de police m [duh poleess] policeman

agiter avant l'emploi shake before use

agrandissement m [agroNdeess-moN] enlargement

agréable [agray-abl] pleasant

agriculteur m [agreekꝏlturr] farmer

ai: j'ai [jay] I have

aide f [ed] help

aider [ayday] to help

aiguille f [aygwee] needle

aile f [el] wing

ailleurs [ī-yur] elsewhere

aimable [aymabl] kind

aimer [aymay] to like; to love
ne pas aimer to dislike

aimerais: j'aimerais [jemray] I would like

ainsi [ANsee] so; like this
ainsi que (just) as

air m [air] air
avoir l'air [avwahr] to look

air conditionné [kondeess-yonay] air conditioning

aire de croisement f [air duh krwaz-moN] passing place

aire de repos [ruhpo] rest area

aire de service [sairveess] service area

aire de stationnement [stass-yonuh-moN] parking area

ajouter [ajootay] to add

alimentation f [aleemoNtass-yon] food; grocer

alimentation générale [jaynayral] grocer

allaiter [alaytay] to breastfeed

Allemagne f [almañ] Germany

allemand [almoN] German

aller [alay] to go
comment allez-vous? [komoN alay voo] how are you?
s'en aller [soN] to go away
allez-vous-en! [alay-voo zoN] go away!

aller chercher [shairshay] to go and get, to fetch

aller-retour m [alay ruhtoor] return/round trip ticket

aller simple m [sANpl] single ticket

aller voir [vwahr] to go and see, to go and visit

allumage m [alꝏmahj] ignition

allumer [alꝏmay] to light; to switch on

allumette f [alꝏmet] match

allumez vos phares switch on your lights

allumez vos veilleuses switch on your sidelights/parking lights

alors [alor] then; well

alpinisme m [alpeeneess-muh] mountaineering

ambassade f [ONbasad] embassy

améliorer [amayleeoray] to improve

amende f [amoNd] fine

amener [amuhnay] to bring

amer [amair] bitter

américain [amayreekAN] American

Amérique f [amayreek] America

ameublement m [amurbluhmoN] furniture

ami m, amie f [amee] friend

amortisseur m [amorteessurr]

shock-absorber

amour m [amoor] love
faire l'amour [fair] to make
love

ampoule f [ONpool] light bulb;
blister

s'amuser [samoozay] to have
fun

an m [ON] year

analgésique m [an-aljayzeek]
painkiller

ancien [ONss-yAN] ancient; old

ancien franc [frAN] old French
franc (= 1 centime)

ancre f [ONkr] anchor

anémique [anaymeek] anaemic

anesthésie générale f [anestayzee
jaynayral] general anaesthetic

anesthésie locale [lo-kal] local
anaesthetic

angine f [ONjeen] tonsillitis

angine de poitrine [pwatreen]
angina

anglais [ONglay] English

Anglais m Englishman
les Anglais the English

Anglaise f [ONglez]
Englishwoman

Angleterre f [ONgluhtair] England

année f [anay] year

anniversaire m [aneevairsair]
birthday

anniversaire de mariage [maree-
ahj] wedding anniversary

annuaire m [anoo-air] phone
book*

annulé [anoolay] cancelled

annuler [anoolay] to cancel

antigel m [ONtee-jel] antifreeze

antihistaminique m
[ONteeheestameeneek]
antihistamine

**anti-insecte: la crème anti-
insecte** [krem ONtee-ANsekt]
insect repellent

antiquaire m [ONteekair] antique
shop

août [oo] August

apparaître [aparetr] to appear

appareil m [aparay] device;
camera
qui est à l'appareil? who's
speaking?
Madame ... à l'appareil
Madame ... speaking
cet appareil ne rend pas la
monnaie this machine does
not give change
cet appareil rend la monnaie
this machine gives change

appareil acoustique m hearing
aid

appareil-photo m camera

appartement m [apartmON] flat,
apartment

appartenir [apartuhneer] to
belong

appeler [aplay] to call
comment vous appelez-vous?
[komON voo zaplay-voo] what's
your name?
je m'appelle ... [juh mapel] my
name is ...

appendicite f [apANdeesseet]
appendicitis

apporter [aportay] to bring
on peut apporter son repas
you may eat your own

food here

apprendre [aproNdr] to learn

s'approcher (de) [saproshay] to go/come near

appuyer [apwee-yay] to lean, to push

appuyer ici press here

appuyez pour ouvrir press to open

après [apray] after

après-demain [-duhmAN] the day after tomorrow

après-midi m afternoon

arabe [a-rab] Arabic

araignée f [aren-yay] spider

arbre m [arbr] tree

arc-en-ciel m [arkONss-yel] rainbow

argent m [arjON] money; silver

argent massif solid silver

armoire f [armwahr] cupboard

arnaque f [arnak] rip-off, swindle

arôme m [arohm] flavour

arôme naturel/artificiel natural/artificial flavouring

arrêt m [aray] stop

arrêt d'autobus bus stop

arrêt de bus bus stop

arrêté: par arrêté préfectoral by order

arrêter [aretay] to stop; to arrest

s'arrêter to stop

arrêtez! stop!

arrêtez votre moteur switch off your engine

arrêt facultatif request stop

arrêt interdit no stopping

arrière m [aree-air] back

la roue arrière the back wheel

le siège arrière the back seat

arrivée(s) f(pl) [areevay] arrival(s)

arriver [areevay] to arrive; to happen

arrondissement m [aroNdeess-mON] administrative district of Paris

arthrite f [artreet] arthritis

articles mpl [arteekl]: les articles soldés ne sont ni repris ni échangés no refund or exchange of reduced price goods

articles de camping camping accessories

articles de sport sports goods

articles de voyage travel accessories

articles ménagers [mayna-jay] household goods

artisanat m [arteezana] crafts

arts ménagers mpl [ar mayna-jay] household goods

as: tu as [a] you have

as-tu ...? do you have ...?

ascenseur m [asONsurr] lift, elevator

aspirateur m [aspeeraturr] hoover®

s'asseoir [sasswahr] to sit down

asseyez-vous [asay-ay-voo] sit down

assez (de) [assay] enough; quite

j'en ai assez [jON ay assay] I have enough; I'm fed up

assieds-toi [ass-yay-twa] sit
down

assiette f [ass-yet] plate

assurance f [assOOrONss]
insurance

assure la correspondance avec ...
connects with ...

asthme m [ass-muh] asthma

astucieux [astOOss-yuh] clever

athée m/f [atay] atheist

athlétisme m [atlayteess-muh]
athletics

Atlantique m [atlONteek] Atlantic

attachez vos ceintures fasten
your seat belt

attaque f [atak] attack; stroke

atteindre [atANdr] to reach

attendez ici wait here

attendez-moi! wait for me!

attendez votre ticket wait for
your ticket

attendre [atONdr] to wait

attendre la sonorité wait for the
dialling tone

attention! [atONss-yON] look out!;
caution!

attention à la marche mind the
step

attention, chien méchant
beware of the dog

attention, enfants caution,
children

attention, fermeture automatique
des portes caution, doors
close automatically

attention, peinture fraîche wet
paint

atterrir [ataireer] to land

attraper [atrapay] to catch

au [o] to the; at the; in the; by
the; with

auberge f [obairj] inn

auberge de jeunesse [jur-ness]
youth hostel

aucun [okAN] none, not any

au-dessous de [o-duhsoo duh]
below

au-dessus de [o-duhsOO duh]
above

audiophone m [odeeo-fon]
hearing aid

aujourd'hui [ojoordwee] today

aujourd'hui en huit a week
today

auprès de [opray duh] near

auquel [okel] to which; at
which

aurai: j'aurai [joray] I will have

aura: il/elle aura [ora] he/she/it
will have

aurais: j'aurais/tu aurais [oray] I/
you would have

auras: tu auras [ora] you will
have

au revoir goodbye

aurez: vous aurez [oray] you will
have

auriez: vous auriez [oree-ay] you
would have

aurions: nous aurions [oree-ON]
we would have

aurons: nous aurons [orON] we
will have

auront: ils/elles auront [orON]
they will have

aussi [o-see] also

aussi grand que as big as

moi aussi me too

aussi ... que possible as ... as possible

aussitôt [o-seeto] at once
aussitôt que as soon as

Australie f [ostralee] Australia

australien [ostralee-AN] Australian

autant (de) [otON duh] as much; as many

autobus m [otob∞ss] bus

autocar m coach, bus

automne m [otON] autumn

automobiliste m/f [otomobeeleest] car driver; motorist

autoradio m [otorad-yo] car radio

autoroute f [otoroot] motorway, highway

autoroute à péage toll motorway/highway

auto-stop m [otostop] hitch-hiking
faire de l'autostop to hitchhike

autre [ohtr] other
un/une autre another

autre chose [shohz] something else

autres destinations other destinations

autres directions other destinations

Autriche f [otreesh] Austria

autrichien [otreeshee-AN] Austrian

aux [o] to the; at the; in the; by the; with

auxquel(le)s [okel] to which; at which; in which; by which

avaler [avalay] to swallow

avance: d'avance [davONss] in advance
en avance early

avancer [avONsay] to move forward, to advance

avant m [avON] front

avant before
avant JC BC

avant-hier [avON-tee-air] the day before yesterday

avec [avek] with

averse f [avairss] shower

aveugle [avurgl] blind

avez: vous avez [voo zavay] you have
avez-vous ...? do you have ...?

avion m [av-yON] plane
par avion by airmail

avis m [avee] notice

avocat m [avoka] lawyer

avoir* [avwahr] to have

avons: nous avons [noo zavON] we have

avril [avreel] April

ayant [ay-yON] having

B

bac m ferry

bagages mpl [bagahj] luggage
faire ses bagages to pack

bagages à main [MAN] hand luggage

bagarre f [ba-gar] fight

bagnole f [ban-yol] car (familiar word)

bague f [bag] ring

baignade dangereuse danger,

do not swim here

baignade interdite no swimming

se baigner [suh ben-yay] to go swimming

baignoire f [beñ-wahr] bathtub

bain m [bAN] bath

bains douches municipaux public baths

baiser m [bezzay] kiss

bal m dance

bal du 14 juillet open air dance on the French national holiday

balade f [bal-ad] walk, stroll

se balader [suh baladay] to go for a stroll

baladeur m [baladurr] personal stereo

balcon m [balkON] balcony

balle f [bal] ball

balles [bal] francs (familiar word)

ballon m [balON] ball; balloon

bande d'arrêt d'urgence hard shoulder

bande magnétique f [man-yayteek] tape

bande médiane [mayd-yan] central reservation

banlieue f [bON-l-yuh] suburbs

en banlieue in the suburbs

banque f [bONk] bank

barbe f [barb] beard

barque f [bark] small boat

barrière f [baree-air] fence

barrière de dégel road closed to heavy vehicles during thaw

bas mpl [ba] stockings

bas low

en bas [ON] downstairs

baskets fpl [bass-ket] trainers

bateau m [bato] boat

bateau à rames [ram] rowing boat

bateau à vapeur [vapurr] steamer

bateau à voile [vwahl] sailing boat

bateau-mouche [-moosh] pleasure boat on the Seine

bâtiment m [bateemON] building

batterie f [batree] battery

se battre [suh batr] to fight

baume après-shampoing m [bohm apray-shONpwAN] conditioner

bd boulevard

BD (bande dessinée) f [bay-day (bONd desseenay)] comic strip

beaucoup [bo-koo] a lot; much

beaucoup de ... a lot of ...

beau, f **belle** [bo, bel] beautiful; fine

il fait beau the weather is good

beau-fils m [-feess] son-in-law

beau-père m [-pair] father-in-law

bébé m [bay-bay] baby

belge [belj] Belgian

Belgique f [beljeek] Belgium

belle [bel] beautiful

belle-fille f [-fee] daughter-in-law

belle-mère f [-mair] mother-in-law

béquilles fpl [baykee] crutches

besoin: j'ai besoin de ... [jay buhzwAN duh] I need ...

bibliothèque f [beebleeo-tek] library

bibliothèque municipale public library

bicyclette f [beesseeklet] bicycle

bien [b-yAN] well, fine

bien du/de la/des many, a lot of

bien portant [portON] in good health

bien que [kuh] although

bien sûr [sOOr] of course

bientôt [b-yanto] soon

à bientôt see you later

bienvenue! [b-yAN-vuhnOO] welcome!

bienvenue à ... welcome to ...

bienvenue sur notre réseau welcome to our network

bijouterie f [beejootuhree] jeweller's

bijoux mpl [beejoo] jewellery

billet m [bee-yay] ticket

billet de banque [bONK] banknote, bill

billets tickets; (bank)notes

billet Section Urbaine ticket valid for suburban train and métro and all RER

billets internationaux international tickets

billets périmés used tickets

blaireau m [blairo] shaving brush

blanc, f blanche [blON, blONsh] white

blanchisserie f [blONsheesree] laundry

blessé [blessay] injured; hurt

blessure f [blessOOr] wound

bleu [bluh] blue

bleu m bruise

boire [bwahr] to drink

bois m [bwa] wood

boîte f [bwat] box; can; nightclub

boîte à/aux lettres [letr] letterbox

boîte de nuit [nwee] nightclub

boîte de vitesses [veetess] gearbox

bol m bowl

bombe f [bONb] bomb

bon [bON] good

bon! right!, OK!

bon anniversaire! happy birthday!

bon appétit! enjoy your meal!

bon après-midi! have a good afternoon!

bonbon m [bON-bON] sweet

bondé [bONday] crowded

bonde f [bONd] plug

bonjour [bONjoor] hello; good morning

bon marché [bON marshay] cheap

bonne année! [bon anay] happy New Year!

bonne chance! [shONss] good luck!

bonne journée! [joornay] have a good day!

bonne nuit [nwee] good night

bonne route! [root] safe
journey!

bonnet de bain m [bonay duh
bAN] bathing cap

bonsoir [bONswahr] good
evening

bon voyage! have a good trip!

bord m [bor] edge
au bord de la mer [o] at the
seaside

borne f [born] kilometre
(familiar word)

botte f [bot] boot

bottin m [botAN] telephone
directory

bouche f [boosh] mouth

bouché [booshay] blocked

boucherie f [booshree] butcher's

boucherie-charcuterie
[-sharkOOtree] butcher's (also
selling pâté and sausages)

boucherie chevaline horsemeat
butcher

bouchon m [booshON] cork;
stopper; traffic jam

bouclé [booklay] curly

boucles d'oreille fpl [bookl doray]
earrings

bouée f [boo-ay] buoy

bouffe f [boof] grub, food

bouger [boojay] to move

bougie f [boojee] candle; spark
plug

bouillotte f [boo-ee-yot] hot-
water bottle

boulangerie f [boolONjree]
baker's

boulangerie-pâtisserie baker
and confectioner

boules fpl [bool] (French-style)
bowling

boules Quiès® [kee-ess]
earplugs

boulevard périphérique m ring
road

bourré [booray] pissed

boussole f [boossol] compass

bouteille f [bootay] bottle

boutique f small shop

boutique de mode clothes
boutique

boutique hors-taxe [or tax] duty
free shop

bouton m [bootON] button; spot

boxe f [box] boxing

BP (boîte postale) PO Box

bras m [bra] arm

brasserie f pub/bar/café
serving food

brave [brahv] good; brave

bref brief

Bretagne f [bruhtañ] Brittany

bricolage m [breekolahj] do-it-
yourself, DIY (supplies)

bricoler [breekolay] to do DIY

briller [bree-yay] to shine

briquet m [breekay] lighter

brise f [breez] breeze

britannique British

brocante secondhand goods

broche f [brosh] brooch

bronchite f [brONsheet]
bronchitis

bronzage m [brONzahj] suntan

bronzer [bronzay] to tan
se bronzer to sunbathe

brosse f [bross] brush

brosse à cheveux [shuhvuh]

hairbrush

brosse à dents [dON] toothbrush

brosser [brossay] to brush

brouillard m [broo-ee-yar] fog

brouillard fréquent risk of fog

bruit m [brwee] noise

brûler [brOOlay] to burn

brûlure f [brOOlOOr] burn

brume f [brOOm] mist

brun [brAN] brown

brushing m blow-dry

bruyant [brwee-yON] noisy

bu [bOO] drunk

buffet à volonté unlimited buffet

bureau m office

bureau d'accueil [dakuh-ee] reception centre

bureau de poste [posst] post office

bureau des objets trouvés [objay troovay] lost property office

bureautique f office automation

butagaz m camping gas

buvette f [bOOvet] refreshment room; refreshment stall

buvez: vous buvez [bOOvay] you drink

buvons: nous buvons [bOOvON] we drink

C

ça* [sa] it; that

ça alors! well really!; I don't believe it!

ça va? how's things?

ça va it's OK, I'm OK; that's fine

ça va mieux I'm feeling better; things are better

cabas m [kaba] shopping bag

cabine f [kabeen] cabin

cabine téléphonique phone box

cabines d'essayage fitting rooms

cabinet dentaire m dentist's surgery

cabinet médical doctor's surgery

cacher [kashay] to hide

cacher m [kashair] kosher

cachet m [kashay] tablet

caddie m (supermarket) trolley

cadeau m [kado] present

cadeaux-souvenirs gift shop

cafard m [kafar] cockroach

j'ai le cafard I feel a bit down

café m [kafay] coffee, black coffee; café, bar

café complet [kONplay] continental breakfast

cahier m [ky-yay] notebook

caisse f [kess] till, cashier's desk, cash desk

caisse d'épargne [dayparñ] savings bank

caissier m cashier

calculette f [kalOOlet] calculator

calendrier m [kalONdree-ay] calendar

calmant m [kalmON] tranquillizer

caméra f [kamayra] cine-camera; (TV) camera

camion m [kam-yON] lorry

camionnette f [kam-yonet] van

campagne f [kONpañ]
countryside
à la campagne in the country

camping m [kONpeeng] camping;
campsite

camping-car m mobile home

camping-caravaning site for
camping and caravans

camping interdit no camping

canadien [kanadee-AN] Canadian

canif m [kaneef] penknife

canne à pêche f [kan a pesh]
fishing rod

canoë m [kano-ay] canoe;
canoeing

canton m [kONtON]
administrative district of
Switzerland

caoutchouc m [ka-oochoo]
rubber

capitaine m [kapeeten] captain

capot m [kapo] bonnet

car m coach, bus

car for, because

caravane f caravan

carburateur m carburettor

cardiaque: être cardiaque to
have a heart condition

carie f [karee] caries

carnet m [karnay] book (of
tickets)

carnet d'adresses [dadress]
address book

carnet de tickets [teekay] book
of tickets

carnet de timbres [tANbr] book
of stamps

carrefour m [karfoor] crossroads

carrefour dangereux dangerous
crossroads

carrosserie f garage that does
bodywork repairs

carte f [kart] card; map; pass

carte d'anniversaire birthday
card

carte de crédit [kraydee] credit
card

carte d'embarquement
[ONbarkmON] boarding pass

carte de réduction [raydOOx-yON]
card entitling the holder to
price reductions

carte de visite [veezeet]
(business) card

carte d'identité [eedONteetay] ID
card

carte grise [greez] car
registration book

carte orange [orONj] season
ticket for transport in Paris
and its suburbs

carte postale [poss-tal] postcard

carte refusée card rejected

carte routière [root-yair] road
map

carte vermeille [vair-may] senior
citizen's railcard

carte verte [vairt] green card

carton m [kartON] box;
cardboard

cascade f [kaskad] waterfall

casquette f [kasket] cap

cassé [kassay] broken

casser [kassay] to break

casserole f saucepan

cauchemar m [kohsh-mar]

nightmare

cause f [kohz] cause
à cause de because of

CCP (compte de chèques
postaux) giro account

ce* [suh] this; that; it
ce serait [suhray] it would be

CE (Communauté européenne) f
[say-uh] EC, European
Community

ceci [suhsee] this

cédez le passage give way,
yield

ceinture f [sANtOOr] belt

ceinture de sécurité
[saykOOreetay] seat belt

cela [suhla] that

célèbre [saylebr] famous

célibataire m [sayleebatair]
bachelor

célibataire single

celle-ci [sel-see] this one

celle-là [-la] that one

celles-ci [sel-see] these

celles-là those

celui-ci [suhlwee-see] this one

celui-là that one

cendrier m [sONdree-ay] ashtray

cent [sON] hundred

centime m [sONteem] centime
(1/100 franc)

centre m [sONtr] centre

centre commercial shopping
centre

centre culturel arts centre

centre sportif sports centre

centre-ville city centre

cependant [suhpONdoN]
however

ce que [suh kuh] what

ce qui [kee] what

certain [sairtAN] sure, certain;
some

ces* [say] these

c'est [say] it is; that's
c'est ça that's it

c'est-à-dire [setadeer] that is to
say

cet [set] this; that

c'était [saytay] it was

cette* [set] this; that

cette cabine peut être appelée
au numéro: ... incoming calls
can be made to this
phonebox using the
following number: ...

ceux-ci* [suh-see] these

ceux-là* those

CFF (Chemins de fer fédéraux)
Swiss railways

chacun [shakAN] each one;
everyone

chaîne f [shen] chain; channel;
stereo

chaise f [shez] chair

chaise longue deck chair

chaleur f [shalurr] heat

chambre f [shONbr] room

chambre à air inner tube

chambre à coucher [kooshay]
bedroom

chambre à deux lits [duh lee]
twin room

chambre pour deux personnes
[pairson] double room

chambre pour une personne
[OOn] single room

chambres à louer rooms to let

champ m [shoN] field

chance f [shoNss] luck; chance

change m [shoNj] change; exchange; currency exchange

change de devises currency exchange

changement à ... change at ...

changer [shonjay] to change

se changer to change

changer de train to change trains

changer de vitesse to change gear

changeur de monnaie m change machine

chanson f [shoNSON] song

chanter [shoNtay] to sing

chantier m roadworks; building site

chantilly f [shontee-yee] whipped cream

chapeau m [shapo] hat

chapeau de soleil [solay] sun hat

chapellerie f hat shop

chaque [shak] each, every

charcuterie f [sharkootree] butcher selling meat that has been treated such as sausages, salami, pâtés etc and prepared salads

chariot m [sharee-o] trolley

chariot obligatoire you must take a trolley

charter m charter flight

chasse gardée hunting preserve

chat m [sha] cat

châtain [shatAN] chestnut, brown

château m [shato] castle

château fort fortified castle

chaud [sho] warm, hot

chauffage m [shofahj] heating

chauffage central [soN-tral] central heating

chauffard! [shofar] learn to drive!

chauffe-eau m [shohf-o] water heater

chaussée déformée uneven road surface

chaussée glissante slippery road surface

chaussée rétrécie road narrows

chaussée verglacée icy road

chaussettes fpl [sho-set] socks

chaussures fpl [sho-soor] shoes

chaussures de ski ski boots

chaussures de tennis gym shoes

chauve [shohv] bald

CH (Confédération Helvétique) Switzerland

chemin m [shuhmAN] path

chemin de fer [duh fair] railway

chemise f [shuhmeez] shirt

chemise de nuit [duh nwee] nightdress

chemiserie menswear

chemisier m [shuhmeez-yay] blouse

chèque m [shek] cheque, (US) check

les chèques ne sont acceptés qu'à partir de 100 F cheques accepted for amounts over

100F only

les chèques ne sont pas acceptés we do not accept cheques

chèque de voyage [duh vwyahj] traveller's cheque

chéquier m [shaykee-ay] cheque book

cher [shair] expensive; dear

chercher [shairshay] to look for

cheveux mpl [shuhvuh] hair

cheville f [shuhvee] ankle

chez [shay] at; among

chez Nadine at Nadine's

faites comme chez vous make yourself at home

chez Marcel/Mimi Marcel's/ Mimi's

chien m [shee-AN] dog

les chiens doivent être tenus en laisse dogs must be kept on a leash

choc m [shok] shock

chocolat à croquer m [shokola a krokay] plain chocolate

chocolat au lait [o lay] milk chocolate

chocolatier m chocolate shop

choisir [shwazeer] to choose

choix m [shwa] choice

chômage: au chômage [o shohmahj] unemployed

chose f [shohz] thing

Chronopost express mail

chute de neige f [shoot duh nej] snowfall

chute de pierres falling rocks

ciel m [see-el] sky; heaven

cigare m [seegar] cigar

cimetière m [seemt-yair] cemetery

cinémathèque f film theatre, movie theater

cinglé m [SANglay] nutter, nutcase

cinq [SANk] five

cinquante [SANkONt] fifty

cinquième [SANk-yem] fifth

cintre m [SANtr] coathanger

cirage m [seerahj] shoe polish

circuit touristique tourist route

circulation f [seerkoolass-yON] traffic

circulation alternée single line traffic

circuler [seerkoolay] to run

circule le … runs on …

ne circule pas le samedi/ dimanche does not run on Saturdays/Sundays

circulez! move along!

circulez sur une file single line traffic

cire pour voiture f [seer poor vwatoor] car wax

cirque m [seerk] circus

ciseaux mpl [seezo] scissors

cité universitaire f university halls of residence

clair clear

bleu clair light blue

classe f [klass] class

clé f [klay] key

clé anglaise [ONglez] wrench

clignotant m [kleen-yotON] indicator

climat m [kleema] climate

climatisation f [kleemateezassyON] air-conditioning

climatisé air-conditioned

clinique f clinic

cloche f bell

clôture électrifiée electric fence

clou m [kloo] nail

cochon m [koshON] pig

code de la route m [kod duh la root] highway code

code postal [poss-tal] postcode

coffre m [kofr] boot

coiffer [kwafay] to comb

se coiffer to do one's hair

coiffeur m, **coiffeuse** f [kwafurr, -urz] hairdresser

coiffeur pour dames [poor dam] ladies' hairdresser

coiffeur pour hommes [om] men's hairdresser, barber's

coiffure f [kwafOOr] hairstyle; hairdresser's

coin m [kwAN] corner

coincé [kwANsay] stuck

col m collar; (mountain) pass

col fermé pass closed

col ouvert pass open

col roulé [roolay] polo neck (jumper)

colis m [kolee] parcel, package

colis France parcels for France only

collant m [kolON] tights

colle f [kol] glue

collectionner [kolex-yonay] to collect

collier m [kol-yay] necklace

colline f [koleen] hill

combien? [kONb-yAN] how many?, how much?

commander [komONday] to order

comme [kom] like; as; how

commencer [komONsay] to begin

comment? [komON] how?; pardon?; sorry?

comment allez-vous? [talay-voo] how are you?

comment ça va? [sa] how are things?

comment vas-tu? [va-tOO] how are you?

commerçant m [komairsON] shopkeeper

commissariat m [komeessaree-a] police station

commissariat de police police station

commotion cérébrale f [komoss-yON sayray-bral] concussion

communication f [komOOneekass-yON] call

communication internationale international call

communication interurbaine long-distance call

communication locale local call

communication urbaine local call

compagnie aérienne f [kompan-yee a-ayree-en] airline

comparer [kONparay] to compare

compartiment fumeurs smoking compartment

compartiment non-fumeurs non-smoking compartment

complet m [kONplay] suit

complet full, no vacancies

complètement [kONpletmON]

totally

compliqué [kONpleekay] complicated

composer le numéro dial the number

composez le ... dial ...

composez sur le clavier numérique le montant choisi pour la vignette enter selected value of postage label on numerical keyboard (francs, comma, centimes)

composez votre code confidentiel à l'abri des regards indiscrets type your PIN without letting anybody see it

composition contents

composition du train order of cars

compostage: le compostage des billets est obligatoire tickets are valid only if punched

compostez votre billet validate/ punch your ticket in the machine

comprendre [kONproNdr] to understand; to include

comprimé m [kONpreemay] tablet

comprimé effervescent effervescent tablet

comptable m [kONtabl] accountant

comptant: payer comptant [kONtON] pay cash

compteur m [kONturr] speedometer

con m [kON] stupid idiot; stupid bastard

concessionnaire m agent

concierge m/f caretaker

conditions d'enneigement snow conditions

conditions pour skier skiing conditions

conducteur m [kONdookturr] driver

conductrice f [kONdooktreess] driver

conduire [kONdweer] to drive

confirmer [kONfeermay] to confirm

confiserie f confectioner, sweet shop

congé annuel m annual holiday

congélateur m [kONjaylaturr] freezer

connaître [konetr] to know

conseiller [kONsay-yay] to advise

conserver: se conserve au moins ... après la date-limite de vente keeps for at least ... after the sell-by date

conserver au frais (et au sec) keep in a cool (dry) place

conservez votre ticket sur vous keep your ticket with you

conservez votre titre de transport jusqu'à la sortie keep your ticket till you leave the station

consigne f [kONseeñ] left luggage

consigne automatique left luggage lockers

consommation f [kONsomass-yON] drink

consommation au comptoir

drink at the bar

consommation en salle drink in the lounge

consommer avant le ... eat by ..., best before ...

constipé [kONsteepay] constipated

consulat m [kONsɔɔla] consulate

contacter [kONtaktay] to contact

contagieux [kONtah-jyuh] contagious

contenir [kONtuhneer] to contain

ne contient pas de ... contains no ...

content [kONtON] pleased

contenu contents

continuer [kONteenɔɔ-ay] to continue, to go on

contraceptif m contraceptive

contractuel m traffic warden

contraire m [kONtrair] opposite

contre [kONtr] against

contre les ... for ...

contre-indications contra-indications

contrôle des bagages m baggage security check

contrôle des passeports passport control

contrôles radar radar speed checks

convoi exceptionnel long vehicle

copain m [kopAN] pal, mate; boyfriend

copine f [kopeen] friend; girlfriend

coqueluche f [kok-lɔɔsh]

whooping cough

coquillage m [kokee-ahj] shell

Corail m intercity train

cor au pied m [o p-yay] corn

corde f rope

cordonnerie f cobbler's

cordonnier m cobbler, shoe repairs

corps m [kor] body

correspondance f [koresspONdONss] connection

correspondance Porte d'Orléans all stops on the line to Porte d'Orléans

Corse f [korss] Corsica

costume m suit

côté m [kotay] side

à côté de next to

mettre de côté to put aside

côte f [koht] coast; rib

Côte d'Azur French Riviera

côté non stabilisé soft verge

coton m [kotON] cotton

coton hydrophile [eedrofeel] cotton wool

cou m [koo] neck

couche f [koosh] nappy

coucher: aller se coucher [alay suh kooshay] to go to bed

au coucher seulement only when you go to bed

couchette f couchette; reclining seat; bunk bed

coude m [kood] elbow

coudre [koodr] to sew

couette f [kwet] continental quilt; bunch (in hair)

couler [koolay] to sink; to run

couleur f [koolurr] colour

couloir bus et taxis bus and taxi lane

coup m [koo] blow, knock; stroke

tout d'un coup suddenly

coup de fil phonecall

coup de soleil [solay] sunburn

coupe f [koop] haircut

coupe de cheveux [duh shuhvuh] haircut

couper [koopay] to cut

coupure f [koopOOr] cut

coupure de courant [duh koorON] power cut

courageux [koorahj-uh] brave

courant d'air m [koorON dair] draught

courant dangereux dangerous current

courir [kooreer] to run

courrier m [kooree-ay] mail; letters and postcards

courrier recommandé registered mail

courroie du ventilateur f [koorwa dOO vONteelaturr] fan belt

cours du change m [koor dOO shONj] exchange rate

course f [koorss] race

faire des courses to go shopping

course automobile racing track

court [koor] short

court de tennis m tennis court

cousin m, cousine f [koozAN, -een] cousin

couteau m [kooto] knife

coûter [kootay] to cost

coutume f [kootOOm] custom

couture f dressmaking; couture

couvent m [koovON] convent

couvercle m [koovairkl] lid

couvert [koovair] covered; overcast

couverts mpl [koovair] cutlery

couverts à poisson fish cutlery

couverture f [koovairtOOr] blanket

couverture chauffante [shohfONt] electric blanket

couvre-lit m [koovr-lee] bedspread

cracher [krashay] to spit

crachin m [krashAN] drizzle

craindre [krANdr] to fear

crampe f [krONp] cramp

crâne m [krahn] skull

cravate f tie

crayon m pencil

crédit ... unités ... units remaining, credit ...

crème de beauté f [botay] cold cream

crème démaquillante [daymakee-yONt] cleansing cream

crème hydratante [eedratONt] moisturizer

crémerie f dairy

crêperie f [krepuhree] pancake restaurant

crevaison f [kruhvezzON] puncture

crevé [kruhvay] knackered; punctured

cric m jack

crier [kree-ay] to shout

crise f [kreez] fit, attack; crisis

crise cardiaque heart attack

crise de foie [duh fwa] upset
stomach
crise d'épilepsie epileptic fit
croire [krwahr] to believe
croisement m [krwazmON]
junction, intersection
croisière f [krwaz-yair] cruise
crosse de golf f golf club
CRS (Compagnie républicaine de
sécurité) f [say-air-ess] riot
police; m riot policeman
cuiller f, cuillère f [kwee-yair]
spoon
cuillère à café teaspoon
cuillère à dessert dessert spoon
cuillère à soupe soup spoon
cuillerée f spoonful
cuir m [kweer] leather
cuisine f kitchen; cooking
cuisiner [kweezeenay] to cook
cuisinier m [kweezeen-yay] cook
cuisinière f [kweezeen-yair]
cooker; cook
cuisse f [kweess] thigh; leg (of
chicken)
cycles cycle shop
cyclisme m [seekleess-muh]
cycling
cycliste m/f [seekleést] cyclist
cyclotourisme m cycle touring
cystite f [seess-teet] cystitis

D

daim m [dAN] suede
dame f [dam] lady
dames ladies' (toilets);
draughts, checkers
dancing m [dONseeng] dance

hall, night club
danger m [dONjay] danger
danger de mort danger of
death
dangereux [dONjuhruh]
dangerous
dans [dON] in; into
danse f [dONss] dance; dancing
danser [dONsay] to dance
date f [dat] date
date de naissance [nessONss]
date of birth
date limite de vente sell-by date
de [duh] of; from
debout [duhboo] standing
début m beginning
débutant m beginner
décembre [daysONbr] December
décider [dayseeday] to decide
déclarer [dayklaray] to declare,
to state
décoller [daykolay] to take off
déconseillé aux personnes
sensibles unsuitable for
people of a nervous
disposition
décontracté [daykONtraktay]
casual; laid-back
découpez suivant le pointillé cut
along the dotted line
découvrir [daykoovreer] to
discover
décrire [daykreer] to describe
décrochez lift the receiver
déçu [daysOO] disappointed
dedans [duhdON] inside
défaire sa valise [dayfair] to
unpack
défectueux [dayfektOO-uh] faulty

défendu [dayfONdω] forbidden

défense de ... [dayfONss] ...
forbidden, no ..., do not ...

défense d'afficher stick no
bills

défense de déposer des ordures
no litter, no dumping

défense de fumer no smoking

défense de laisser des bagages
dans le couloir bags must not
be left in the corridor

défense de marcher sur la
pelouse keep off the grass

défense d'entrer no entrance

défense de parler au conducteur
do not talk to the driver

défense de ... sous peine
d'amende ... will be fined

défense de stationner no
parking

défense de traverser les voies it
is forbidden to cross the
railway/railroad lines

dégagé clear

dégoûtant [daygootON]
disgusting

degré m [duhgray] degree

dégueulasse [daygurlass]
disgusting

dégustation (de vin) f
[daygωstass-yON] wine tasting

dégustation gratuite free wine-
tasting

dehors [duh-or] outside
dehors! get out!

déjà [dayja] already

déjeuner m [dayjuhnay] lunch;
breakfast

delco m distributor

délicieux [dayleess-yuh]
delicious

deltaplane m [-plan] hang-
gliding

demain [duhmAN] tomorrow
à demain see you tomorrow

demander [duhmONday] to ask

demandez à la caisse ask at the
cash desk

démangeaison f [daymONjezzON]
itch

démaquillant m [daymakee-yON]
skin cleanser

se démaquiller [daymakee-yay] to
remove one's make-up

démarrer [daymaray] to start up

demi [duhmee] half

demi-litre m half a litre

demi-heure f [-urr] half an hour

demi-journée f [-joornay] half a
day

demi-pension f [-pONss-yON] half
board, American plan

demi-tour m U-turn

dent f [dON] tooth

dentier m [dONt-yay] dentures,
false teeth

dentifrice m [dONteefreess]
toothpaste

dentiste m/f [dONteest] dentist

dépanneuse f [daypanurz]
breakdown lorry

département m [daypartmON]
administrative district of
France

départementale f [daypartmONtal]
B road

départ(s) departure(s)

dépasser [daypassay] to pass

se **dépêcher** [suh daypeshay] to
hurry
dépêchez-vous! hurry up!
dépendre: ça dépend [sa daypON]
it depends
dépenser [daypONsay] to spend
dépliant m [dayplee-ON] leaflet
dépression (nerveuse) f
[daypress-yON nairvurz] nervous
breakdown
déprimé [daypreemay]
depressed
depuis (que) [duhpwee (kuh)]
since
dérangement: en dérangement
out of order
déranger [dayrONjay] to disturb
ça vous dérange si ...? [sa voo
dayrONj] do you mind if ...?
déraper [dayrapay] to skid
dermatologue m/f [dairmatolog]
dermatologist
dernier [dairn-yay] last
l'année dernière last year
derrière [dairyair] behind
derrière m bottom
des* [day] of the; from the;
some
des biscuits some biscuits
dès [day] from
dès que as soon as
désagréable [dayzagray-abl]
unpleasant
désastre m [dayzastr] disaster
descendre [duhsONdr] to go
down; to get off
se **déshabiller** [suh dayzabee-yay]
to undress
désinfectant m [dayzANfektON]

disinfectant; antiseptic
désirer [dayzeeray] to want, to
wish for
désolé: je suis désolé [dayzolay]
I'm sorry
desquels [daykel] of which;
from which
dessert m [desair] dessert
dessert ... stops at ...
dessin m [duhsAN] drawing
dessiner [duhseenay] to draw
dessous [duhsoo] underneath;
under it
dessus [duhsoo] above; on top;
on it
destinataire m/f addressee;
consignee
détaxe à l'exportation f tax
refund on export goods
détendre: se détendre [suh
daytONdr] to relax
détester [daytestay] to hate
deux [duh] two
deuxième étage m [duhz-yem
aytahj] second floor, (US)
third floor
devant [duhvON] in front of; in
front
**développement de pellicules/
photos** film processing
développer [dayvlopay] to
develop
devenir [duhvuhneer] to become
déviation f diversion
devises étrangères fpl [duhveez
aytrONjair] foreign currency
devoir m [duhvwahr] duty
devoir to have to
devrai: je devrai [duhvray] I will

have to

devrais: je/tu devrais [duhvray] I/
you should

devras: tu devras [duhvra] you
will have to

devrez: vous devrez [duhvray]
you will have to

devriez: vous devriez [duhvree-
ay] you should

diabétique diabetic

diamant m [dee-amON] diamond

diapositive f [dee-apozeeteev]
slide

diarrhée f [dee-aray] diarrhoea

dictionnaire m [deex-yonair]
dictionary

diététique health food

Dieu m [d-yuh] God

différent [deefayrON] different

difficile [deefeesseel] difficult

Diligo® pre-stamped parcel,
for France only

diluer [deeloo-ay] to dissolve

diluer dans un peu d'eau
dissolve in water

dimanche [deemONsh] Sunday

dimanches et jours fériés
Sundays and public holidays

dîner m [deenay] dinner

dîner to have dinner

dîner-spectacle dinner during
the show (in cabaret)

dingue [dAN-g] crazy

dire [deer] to say; to tell

directeur m [deerekturr]
manager; director;
headteacher

direction f [deerex-yON] steering;
direction

dis: je/tu dis [dee] I/you say

disent: il/elles disent [deez] they
say

disons: nous disons [deezON] we
say

disparaître [deesparetr] to
disappear

disquaire m [deeskair] record
shop

disque m [deesk] record

disque compact compact disc

disque obligatoire parking disk
compulsory

dissolvant m [deessolvON] nail-
polish remover

Distingo® envelope with pre-
printed address box

**distributeur automatique de
billets** m ticket machine

**distributeur (automatique) de
billets (de banque)** autobank,
cash point

distributeur de boissons drinks
vending machine

dit [dee] says; said

dites: vous dites [deet] you
say

divorcé [deevorsay] divorced

divorcer [deevorsay] to get a
divorce

dix [deess] ten

dix-huit [deez-weet] eighteen

dixième [deez-yem] tenth

dix-neuf [deez-nuhf] nineteen

dix-sept [deesset] seventeen

d'occasion [dokaz-yON]
secondhand

docteur m [dokturr] doctor

doigt m [dwa] finger

dois: je/tu dois [dwa] I/you
  must
doit: il/elle doit [dwa] he/she/it
  must
doivent: ils/elles doivent [dwav]
  they must
dolmen m megalithic tomb
domicile m home address
dommage: c'est dommage
  [domahj] it's a pity
donc [doNk] then, therefore
donner [donay] to give
dont [doN] of which; whose
dormir [dormeer] to sleep
dos m [doh] back
dose pour adultes/enfants dose
  for adults/children
douane f [dwan] Customs
doubler [dooblay] to overtake
douce [dooss] soft; sweet
douche f [doosh] shower
douleur f [doolurr] pain
douloureux [doolooruh] painful
douter [dootay] to doubt
doux, f douce [doo, dooss] soft;
  sweet
douzaine f [doozen] dozen
douze [dooz] twelve
drap m [dra] sheet
drapeau m [drapo] flag
draps de lit mpl [dra duh lee] bed
  linen
drogue f [drog] drug
droguerie f [drogree] drugstore,
  sells aspirins, toiletries,
  household goods etc
droit [drwa] straight
droit m right
droite f [drwat] right

à droite (de) on the right (of)
drôle funny
du* [doo] of the; from the;
  some
du vin some wine
dû: j'ai dû [doo] I had to; I must
  have
duquel [dookel] of which; from
  which
dur [door] hard
dur d'oreille [doray] hard of
  hearing
durer [dooray] to last; to keep
durée de conservation … keeps
  for …

E

eau f [o] water
eau de javel [duh javel] bleach
eau non potable not drinking
  water
eau potable drinking water
échanger [ayshoNjay] to
  exchange
échange/remboursement
  exchange/refund
échantillon gratuit – ne peut être
  vendu free sample – not for
  sale
échecs mpl [ayshek] chess
écharpe f [aysharp] scarf
échelle f [ayshel] ladder
école f [aykol] school
école de langues [duh loN-g]
  language school
économique [aykonomeek]
  economy; economy-rate
Écopli® m [aykoplee] economy-

rate letter for France

écossais [aykossay] Scottish

Écosse f [aykoss] Scotland

écouter [aykootay] to listen (to)

écrire [aykreer] to write

écrou m [aykroo] nut

édifice public m [aydeefeess pOObleek] public building

édredon m [aydruhdON] duvet

égal [aygal] equal
    ça m'est égal I don't mind

égaliser [aygaleezay] to equalize; to trim

église f [aygleez] church

élastique m [aylasteek] rubber band

électricité f [aylektreesseetay] electricity

électroménager m household appliances

électrophone m [aylektrofon] record player

élever [ayluhvay] to raise

elle* [el] she; her; it

elle-même [el-mem] herself; speaking

elles* [el] they; them

emballer [ONbalay] to wrap

embarquement (immédiat) boarding (now)

embouteillage m [ONbootay-ahj] traffic jam

embranchement m [ONbrONshmON] fork

embranchement d'autoroutes motorway junction

embrasser [ONbrassay] to kiss

embrayage m [ONbray-ahj] clutch

émission f [aymeess-yON]

programme

emmener [ONmuhnay] to give a lift to; to take away

Empire [Onpeer] Napoleon's reign (1804-14)

emplacement m [ONplassmON] site

emplacement réservé no parking

employer [ONplwy-yay] to use; to employ

emporter [ONportay] to take

emprunter [ONprANtay] to borrow

empruntez le passage souterrain use the underpass

en [ON] in; to; by
    en 1945 in 1945
    en France in France
    en bas [ba] downstairs
    en haut [o] upstairs
    en cas d'incendie in the event of fire
    en cas d'urgence in an emergency
    en cas d'affluence ne pas utiliser les strapontins do not use fold-down seats when the train is crowded
    en face de opposite

enceinte [ONsANt] pregnant

enchanté [ONshONtay] pleased to meet you

encolure f [ONkolOOr] collar size

encore [ONkor] again; still
    encore plus beau even more beautiful
    encore une bière another beer

endommager [ONdoma-jay] to damage

endormi [ONdormee] asleep

enfant m/f [ONfON] child

enfin [ONfAN] at last

enflé [ONflay] swollen

enjoliveur m [ONjoleevurr] hub cap

enlever [ONluhvay] to take away; to remove

ennuyer [ON-nwee-yay] to bother; to bore
s'ennuyer to be bored

ennuyeux [ON-nwee-yuh] annoying; boring

énorme [aynorm] enormous

énormément [aynormaymON] enormously

enregistrement des bagages m check in

enrhumé: je suis enrhumé [ONroomay] I've got a cold

enseignant m [ONsen-yON] teacher

enseigner [ONsen-yay] to teach

ensemble [ONsONbl] together

ensemblier-décorateur m interior decorator

ensoleillé [ONsolay-yay] sunny

ensuite [ONsweet] afterwards

entendre [ONtONdr] to hear

enterrement m [ONtairmON] funeral

entier [ONteeyay] whole

entièrement [ONtee-yairmON] entirely

entorse f [ONtorss] sprain

entracte m interval

entraînement m [ONtrenmON] training

entre [ONtr] between; among

entrée f [ONtray] entrance, way in; entrée

entrée à l'avant entry at the front

entrée des artistes stage door

entrée de service tradesman's entrance

entrée gratuite admission free

entrée interdite no admittance, no entry

entrée libre admission free

entrejambe m inside leg measurement; crutch

entrer [ONtray] to go in; to come in; to enter
vous entrez dans un espace non fumeur you are entering a no smoking area

entrez! [ONtray] come in!

entrez sans frapper enter without knocking

entrez sans sonner enter without ringing the bell

envers [ONvair] to, towards

envie: j'ai envie de [ONvee] I feel like

environ [ONveerON] about

envoi d'un objet recommandé avec/sans avis de réception mailing of a registered item with/without receipt note

envoi recommandé m recorded delivery

envoyer [ONvwy-ay] to send

épais [aypay] thick

épaule f [aypol] shoulder

épeler [ayplay] to spell

épicerie f [aypeesree] grocer's

épicerie fine delicatessen

épingle f [aypANgl] pin

épingle de nourrice [duh nooreess] safety pin

épouse f [aypooz] wife

épouser [aypoozay] to marry

épouvantable [aypoovONtabl] terrible

épuisé [aypweezay] exhausted

équipage m [aykeepahj] crew

équipe f [aykeep] team

équipements sportifs sporting facilities

équitation f [aykeetass-yON] horse riding

erreur f [air-rurr] mistake

éruption f [ayrOOps-yON] rash

es: tu es [ay] you are

escale f [eskal] stop-over

escalier m [eskal-yay] stairs

escalier roulant [roolON] escalator

Espagne f [españ] Spain

espagnol [espan-yol] Spanish

espèce de con! [espess duh kON] you stupid bastard!

espérer [espayray] to hope

espoir m [espwahr] hope

esquimau m [eskeemo] ice cream on a stick, ice lolly

essayer [essay-ay] to try; to try on

essence f [essONss] petrol, gas

essieu m [ess-yuh] axle

essuie-glace m [ess-wee-glass] windscreen wiper

est: il/elle est [ay] he/she/it is

est m east

à l'est de east of

est-ce que ...? [eskuh] to form questions

est-ce que vous pensez ...? do you think ...?

est-ce qu'il y a ...? [eskeel ya] is there ...?; are there ...?

estomac m [estoma] stomach

et [ay] and

et ... et both ... and

étage m [aytahj] floor

1er étage first floor, (US) second floor

étage inférieur lower floor

étage supérieur upper floor

étang m [aytON] pond

étant [aytON] being

état m [ayta] state

États-Unis mpl [ayta zOOnee] United States

été m [aytay] summer

été been

éteignez vos phares switch off your lights

éteignez vos veilleuses switch off your sidelights/parking lights

éteindre [aytANdr] to switch off

éteint [aytAN] switched off; out

s'étendre [saytONdr] to lie down; to extend

éternuer [aytairnOO-ay] to sneeze

êtes: vous êtes [et] you are

étiquette f label

étoile f [aytwal] star

étonnant [aytonON] astonishing

étranger m [aytrONjay] foreigner

à l'étranger abroad

étranger foreign

étranger service prioritaire overseas priority mail

être* [etr] to be

étroit [aytrwa] narrow; tight

études fpl [aytood] studies

étudiant m, étudiante f [aytood-yON, -yONt] student

étudier [aytood-yay] to study

eu [oo] had

européen [urropay-AN] European

eux* [uh] them

s'évanouir [sayvanweer] to faint

évidemment [ayveedamON] obviously

évident [ayveedON] obvious

évier m [ayv-yay] sink

exagérer [exajayray] to exaggerate

examiner [exameenay] to examine

excédent de bagages m excess baggage

excès de vitesse m speeding

s'excuser [sexkoozay] to apologize

excusez-moi [exkoozay mwa] sorry; excuse me

exemple m [exONpl] example
par exemple for example

exiger [exeejay] to demand

exigez votre reçu ask for a receipt

expliquer [expleekay] to explain

exposition f exhibition; exposure

exprès [expray] deliberately
par exprès [express] special delivery

express m ordinary fast train

extincteur m [extANkturr] fire extinguisher

F

fabriqué en/au ... made in ...

fâché [fashay] angry

facile [fasseel] easy

façon f [fassON] way
de façon que so that

facteur m postman

facultatif optional; request

faible [febl] weak

faim: j'ai faim [fAN] I'm hungry

faire* [fair] to do; to make
ça ne fait rien [san fay ree-AN] it doesn't matter

faisons: nous faisons [fuhzON] we do; we make

fait: il/elle fait [fay] he/she/it does; he/she/it makes

fait did; made

faites: vous faites [fet] you do; you make

faites attention! be careful!

faites l'appoint have the right change ready

faites vérifier votre niveau d'huile have your oil checked

fait main hand-made

falaise f [falez] cliff

falloir [falwahr] to be necessary
il va falloir ... it will be necessary to ...

famille f [fameel] family

fard à paupières m [far a pohp-yair] eye-shadow

fatigué [fateegay] tired

fauché [fohshay] broke

fausse [fohss] wrong

faut: il faut que je/vous ... [eel fo kuh] I/you must ...

faute f [foht] mistake; fault

fauteuil roulant m [fotuh-ee roolON] wheelchair

faux, f fausse [fo, fohss] wrong

faux numéro wrong number

favori favourite

FB (franc belge) Belgian franc

félicitations! [fayleesseetass-yON] congratulations!

femelle [fuhmel] female

femme f [fam] woman; wife

femme d'affaires [dafair] businesswoman

femme de chambre [duh shONbr] chambermaid

fenêtre f [fuhnetr] window

fer m [fair] iron

   fer à repasser [ruhpassay] iron

ferai: je ferai [fuhray] I will do; I will make

fera: il/elle fera [fuhra] he/she/it will do; he/she/it will make

feras: tu feras [fuhra] you will do; you will make

ferez: vous ferez [fuhray] you will do; you will make

fermé [fairmay] closed

   fermé jusqu'au ... closed until ...

   fermé le ... closed on ...

ferme f [fairm] farm

fermer [fairmay] to close

fermer à clé [klay] to lock

fermer la grille [gree] close the outside door

fermeture annuelle f annual holiday, annual closure

fermeture automatique des portes doors close automatically

fermeture éclair f [fairmuhtOOr ayklair] zip

fermeture hebdomadaire le lundi closed on Mondays

fermez le volet svp please close the flap

ferons: nous ferons [fuhrON] we will do; we will make

feront: ils/elles feront [fuhrON] they will do; they will make

fête f [fet] party; feast day

fête des vendanges [vONdONj] grape harvest festival

fête de village [veelajh] village fair

fête nationale 14 July (national holiday)

feu m [feu] fire

   vous avez du feu? [voo zavay dOO] have you got a light?

feuille f [fuh-ee] leaf

feux arrière mpl [fuh aree-yair] rear lights

feux d'artifice fireworks

feux de camp interdits no campfires

feux de position sidelights

feux de signalisation traffic lights

février [fayvree-ay] February

FF (franc français) French franc

fiancé engaged

se fiancer [suh fee-ONsay] to get engaged

fibres naturelles natural fibres

ficelle f [feessel] string

fier [fee-air] proud

fièvre f [fee-evr] fever
avoir de la fièvre to have a
temperature

fil m [feel] thread

fil de fer [duh fair] wire

file f [feel] lane

fille f [fee] girl; daughter

film en VO m film in the
original language

fils m [feess] son

filtre m [feeltr] filter

fin f [fAN] end

fin fine

fin d'autoroute end of
motorway

fin de ... end of ...

fin de série oddment

finir [feeneer] to finish

fleur f [flurr] flower

fleuriste m [flurreest] florist's

foire f [fwahr] fair

foire à la brocante [brokONt]
street market for antiques
and bric-à-brac

fois f [fwa] time
une fois once

folle [fol] mad

fonctionnaire m/f [fONks-yonair]
civil servant

fond m [fON] bottom
au fond de at the bottom of

fond de teint [duh tAN]
foundation cream

fontaine f [fONten] fountain

font: ils/elles font [fON] they do;
they make

footing m jogging

forêt f [foray] forest

forme: en forme [form] fit

formellement interdit strictly
prohibited

formez le ... dial ...

formidable [formeedabl] great

formulaire m [formOOlair] form

fort [for] strong; loud; loudly

fou, f folle [foo, fol] mad

foulard m [foolar] scarf

foule f [fool] crowd

foulure f [foolOOr] sprain

four m [foor] oven

fourchette f [foorshet] fork

fournitures de bureau office
supplies

fourreur m furrier

fous: je m'en fous [juh mON foo] I
don't give a damn
fous le camp! [kON] get lost!

foutre [footr] to put; to do
allez vous faire foutre! [alay voo
fair] go to hell!

fraîche [fresh] fresh

frais mpl [fray] charges

frais, f fraîche [fray, fresh] fresh

franc m [frON] franc

français [frONsay] French

Français m Frenchman

Française f [frONsez] French
woman

franc belge [belj] Belgian franc

franc français [frONsay] French
franc

franc suisse [sweess] Swiss
franc

frapper [frapay] to hit

frappez avant d'entrer knock

before entering

frein m [frAN] brake

frein à main [mAN] handbrake

freiner [frenay] to brake

frein moteur: utilisez votre frein moteur engage lower gear

frère m [frair] brother

fr (franc) franc

frigo m fridge

frisé [freezay] curly

frissonner [freessonay] to shiver

froid [frwa] cold

fromager m [fromajay], **fromages** [fromahj] cheese shop

front m [frON] forehead

frontière f [frONt-yair] border

FrS (franc suisse) Swiss franc

fuite f [fweet] leak

fumée f [foomay] smoke

fumer [foomay] to smoke

fumeurs [foomurr] smokers

fusible m [foozeebl] fuse

fusil m [foozee] gun

G

gagner [gan-yay] to win; to earn

galerie f roof rack; circle

galerie d'art [dar] art gallery

gallois [galwa] Welsh

gallo-romain civilization following Roman conquest of Gaul

ganterie f glove shop

gants mpl [gON] gloves

garçon m [garson] boy; waiter

garder [garday] to keep

gare f [gar] train station

gare routière [root-yair] bus station

se garer [suh garay] to park

gare SNCF [ess-en-say-ef] French train station

gas-oil m diesel, fuel

gauche f [gohsh] left

à gauche (de) on the left (of)

gaucher [gohshay] left-handed

Gaulois Gauls (original inhabitants of France)

gazoil m fuel

gel m [jel] gel; frost

gelé [juhlay] frozen

gelée f [juhlay] frost

geler [juhlay] to be freezing

gélule f [jayl∞l] capsule

gênant [jenON] embarrassing

gendarme m policeman

gendarmerie f police station

gendre m [jONdr] son-in-law

gêner [jenay] to embarrass; to hinder

généralement [jaynayralmON] generally

généraliste m/f [jaynayraleest] GP

génial! [jayn-yal] great!, fantastic!

genou m [juhnoo] knee

gens mpl [jON] people

gentil [jONtee] kind; nice

gérant m [jayrON] manager

gilet m [jeelay] cardigan

gilet de corps [duh kor] vest

gîte et petit déjeuner [jeet ay puhtee dayjuhnay] bed and breakfast

gîte m rural holiday accommodation in the

countryside
glacier m [glassee-ay] ice cream
  shop; glacier
glissant [gleessON] slippery
Golfe de Gascogne m Bay of
  Biscay
gomme f [gom] rubber
gorge f [gorj] throat
goût m [goo] taste
goûter [gootay] to taste
goûter m tea (meal)
gouttes fpl [goot] drops
grâce à [grass] thanks to
grand [grON] large; tall; great
Grande-Bretagne f [grON-
  bruhtañ] Great Britain
grandes lignes main lines
grande surface f [sOOrfass]
  superstore
grandes vacances fpl [grOND
  vakONss] summer holidays
grand magasin m [magazAN]
  department store
grand-mère f [grON-mair]
  grandmother
grand-père m [-pair]
  grandfather
gras m [gra] fat
gras, f grasse [gra, grass] greasy
gratuit [gratwee] free
grave [grahv] serious; deep
gravillons loose chippings
grec, f grecque [grek] Greek
grêle f [grel] hail
grippe f [greep] flu
gris [gree] grey
gros [gro] big; fat
grossier [gross-yay] rude
grotte f [grot] cave

groupe sanguin m [groop sONgAN]
  blood group
guêpe f [gep] wasp
guère [gair] hardly
guérir [gay-reer] to heal, to
  cure; to recover
guerre f [gair] war
gueule de bois f [gurl duh bwa]
  hangover
guichet m [geeshay] ticket
  office; box office; counter
guichet automatique cash
  dispenser
guichet fermé position closed
guide touristique m/f [geed
  tooreesteek] tourist guide
gymnase m [jeemnaz]
  gymnasium
gynécologue m/f [jeenaykolog]
  gynaecologist

H

habillé [abeeyay] formal;
  dressed
habiller [abeeyay] to dress
  s'habiller to get dressed
habiter [abeetay] to live
habitude f [abeetOOd] habit
  d'habitude usually
habituel [abeetOOel] usual
s'habituer à [sabeetOO-ay] to get
  used to
haïr [a-eer] to hate
hall d'arrivée m arrival hall,
  arrivals
hall (de) départ departures,
  departure hall
hall de gare station concourse

halte stop
hameau m [amo] hamlet
hanche f [ONsh] hip
handicapé [ONdeekapay]
  disabled
hasard: par hasard [azar] by
  chance
haut [o] high
  en haut upstairs
hauteur limitée à ... maximum
  height ...
herbe f [airb] grass
heure f [urr] hour; time
  quelle heure est-il? [kel urr
  ayteel] what time is it?
  à l'heure on time
  3 heures de l'après-midi 3
  p.m.
  5 heures du matin 5 a.m.
  11 heures du soir 11 p.m.
heure limite d'enregistrement
  check-in deadline
heures d'affluence rush hour
heures des levées collection
  times
heures de visite visiting hours
heures d'ouverture opening
  times
heureusement [urrurzmON]
  fortunately
heureux [ur-ruh] happy
hexagone: l'hexagone m France
  (colloquial name)
hier [yair] yesterday
hippisme m [eepeess-muh]
  horse-riding
histoire f [eestwahr] history;
  story
hiver m [eevair] winter

HLM (habitation à loyer modéré)
  f [ash-el-em] council flat,
  public housing unit
hollandais [olONday] Dutch
homme m [om] man
homme d'affaires [dafair]
  businessman
hommes [om] gents (toilet)
honnête [onet] honest
honteux [ONtuh] ashamed
hôpital m [opeetal] hospital
hoquet m [okay] hiccups
horaire m [orair] timetable,
  schedule
horaire d'ouverture opening
  times
horloge f [orloj] clock
horlogerie f watchmaker
horlogerie-bijouterie
  watchmaker and jeweller
horodateur m parking meter,
  pay and display
hors-bord m [or-bor] motorboat
hors de [or duh] out of
hors saison off season
hors service out of order
hors taxes [tax] duty-free
hôtel m [otel] hotel
hôtel de ville [duh veel] town
  hall, city hall
hôtesse de l'air f [otess] air
  hostess
huile f [weel] oil
huile solaire suntan oil
huit [weet] eight
huitième [weet-yem] eighth
humeur f [OOmurr] mood
humide [OOmeed] damp
humidité f [OOmeedeetay]

dampness

hypermarché m [eepairmarshay] supermarket; hypermarket

I

I tourist information

ici [ee-see] here

idée f [eeday] idea

il* [eel] he; it

île f [eel] island

il est interdit de … … is prohibited

il est interdit de déposer des ordures no litter, no tipping

il est interdit de donner à manger aux animaux do not feed the animals

il est interdit de marcher sur les pelouses keep off the grass

il n'y a pas … [eel nya pa] there isn't …; there aren't …

il n'y a pas de quoi! [duh kwa] don't mention it!

ils* [eel] they

il y a … [eelya] there is …; there are …

   il y a trois jours three days ago

   est-ce qu'il y a …? [eskeel ya] is there …?; are there …?

imbécile! [ANbayseel] idiot!

immédiatement [eemaydee-atmoN] immediately

immeuble m [eemurbl] block (of flats); building

impasse cul-de-sac, dead end

imperméable m [ANpairmay-abl] raincoat

imprimé printed matter

incroyable [ANkrwyabl] incredible

indicatif m [ANdeekateef] dialling code, area code; country code

indiquer [ANdeekay] to indicate

s'infecter [sANfektay] to become infected

infirmerie f [ANfeermuhree] infirmary

infirmière f [ANfeerm-yair] nurse

informations fpl [ANformass-yoN] news; information

informatique f [ANformateek] information technology; computing

informer [ANformay] to inform

infraction f [ANfrax-yoN] offence

insérer le jeton insert token

insérez votre carte insert your card

insolation f [ANsolass-yoN] sunstroke

insomnie f [ANsomnee] insomnia

institut de beauté m [ANsteetoo duh botay] beauty salon

instrument de musique m [ANstroomoN duh moozeek] musical instrument

insupportable [ANsooportabl] obnoxious

interdiction de … [ANtairdeex-yoN] no …

interdiction de fumer no smoking

interdiction de marcher sur la voie do not walk on the track interdiction de parler au conducteur do not speak to the driver

interdiction de stationner no parking

interdit [ANtairdee] forbidden, prohibited

interdit à tous véhicules no access to any vehicle

interdit aux forains et aux nomades no gypsies

interdit aux mineurs no admittance to minors

interdit aux moins de ... ans children under ... not admitted

interdit aux voyageurs no access for passengers; staff only

intéressant [ANtayressON] interesting

s'intéresser à [sANtayressay] to be interested in

intérieur: à l'intérieur [ANtayree-urr] inside

interrupteur m [ANtairOOpturr] switch

intoxication alimentaire f [ANtoxeekass-yON aleemONtair] food poisoning

introduire [ANtrodweer] to introduce; to insert

introduire carte ou composer numéro libre insert card or dial freephone number

introduire les pièces ici insert coins here

introduisez une pièce de 2 francs et tournez la poignée insert a 2 franc coin and turn the handle

introduisez votre pièce ici insert coin here

invité m [ANveetay] guest

inviter [ANveetay] to invite

irai: j'irai [eeray] I will go

ira: il/elle ira [eera] he/she/it will go

iras: tu iras [eera] you will go

irez: vous irez [eeray] you will go

irlandais [eerlONday] Irish

Irlande du Nord f [eerlOND dOO nor] Northern Ireland

irons: nous irons [eerON] we will go

iront: ils/elles iront [eerON] they will go

issue de secours emergency exit, fire escape

italien [eetalyAN] Italian

itinéraire m [eeteenayrair] route

itinéraire bis alternative route

itinéraire conseillé recommended route

itinéraire de délestage alternative route

itinéraire obligatoire compulsory route (for heavy vehicles etc)

ivre [eevr] drunk

ivresse f [eevress] drunkenness

J

jaloux [jaloo] jealous

jamais [jamay] never; ever

jambe f [jONb] leg

janvier [joNvee-ay] January

jardin m [jardAN] garden

jardin public public gardens,
park

jardin zoologique zoo

jauge f [johj] gauge

jaune [jo-n] yellow

je* [juh] I

jean m jeans

j'écoute [jaykoot] speaking

jetable [juhtahbl] disposable

jeter [juhtay] to throw (away)

jeton m [juhtON] token

jeu m [juh] game

jeu de société board game

jeudi [juhdee] Thursday

jeun: le matin à jeun first thing
in the morning on an empty
stomach

jeune [jurn] young

jeune femme f [fam] young
woman

jeune fille f [fee] girl

jeune homme m [om] young
man

jeux mpl [juh] games

jeux électroniques computer
games

jeux interdits aux moins de 16
ans use of gaming machines
forbidden for those under
16

joindre [jwANdr] to join

joli [jolee] pretty

jouer [joo-ay] to play

jouet m [joo-ay] toy

jour m [joor] day

jour férié [fayree-ay] public
holiday

journal m [joornal] newspaper

journaux newspapers,
stationer

journée f [joornay] day

journée continue open all day

journées à tarif réduit cheap
travel days

jours de semaine uniquement
weekdays only

jours impairs odd dates of the
month (parking allowed)

jours ouvrables weekdays

jours pairs/impairs parking
allowed only on even/odd
days of the month

joyeuses Pâques! [jwy-urz pak]
happy Easter!

juif, f juive [jweef, jweev] Jewish

juillet [jwee-yay] July

juin [jwAN] June

juive [jweev] Jewish

jumeaux mpl [jOOmo] twins

jumelé [jOOmuhlay] twinned

jumelles fpl [jOOmel] binoculars;
twins

jupe f [jOOp] skirt

jupon m [jOOpON] petticoat

jusqu'à (ce que) [jOOska(ss kuh)]
until

jusque [jOOsk] up to, as far as;
till

juste [jOOst] fair; right

K

kermesse f [kairmess] fair

kiosque à journaux m
newspaper stand

klaxon m horn

klaxonner [klaxonay] to hoot
K-way m [ka-way] cagoule

L

l'* the; him; her; it
la* the; her; it
là [la] there
là-bas [laba] over there
lac m lake
lacets mpl [lassay] shoe laces
laid [lay] ugly
laine f [len] wool
laisser [lessay] to let; to leave
lait m [lay] milk
laiterie dairy (Switzerland)
lait solaire [solair] suntan lotion
lame de rasoir f [lahm duh razwahr] razor blade
lampe de poche f [lONp duh posh] torch
lancer [lONsay] to throw
landau m [lONdo] pram
langue f [lON-g] tongue; language
laque f [lak] hair spray
laquelle [lakel] which one
large [larj] wide
lavabo m washbasin
lavage à la main hand wash
lavage du pare-brise screen wash
lave-auto m [lav-oto] car wash
laver [lavay] to wash
  se laver to wash, to have a wash
laverie automatique f [lavree otomateek] launderette, laundromat

laver séparément wash separately
lave-vaisselle m [lav-vess-el] dish washer
lavoir m [lavwahr] wash house
lavomatic m launderette, laundromat
layette f babywear
le* [luh] the; him; it
leçon f [luhsON] lesson
lecteur de cassettes m [lekturr] cassette player
lendemain m [lONduhmAN] the next day
lent [lON] slow
lentement [lONtuhmON] slowly
lentilles de contact fpl [lONtee duh] contact lenses
lentilles dures [dOOr] hard lenses
lentilles semi-rigides [-reejeed] gas-permeable lenses
lentilles souples [soopl] soft lenses
lequel [luhkel] which one
les* [lay] the; them
lesquel(le)s [laykel] which ones
lessive f [lesseev] washing powder; washing
  faire la lessive do the washing
lettre f [letr] letter
leur* [lurr] their; (to) them
  le/la leur theirs
leurs* [lurr] their
  les leurs theirs
lever [luhvay] to lift, to raise
  se lever to get up
levier de vitesses m [luhv-yay duh veetess] gear lever

lèvre f [levr] lip

lézard m [layzar] lizard

libellez votre chèque à l'ordre de ... please make out your cheque to ...

librairie f [leebrairee] bookshop, bookstore

libre [leebr] free, vacant

libre-service self-service

libre-service affranchissement self-service stamping facility

libre-service bancaire autobank, cashpoint

lieu m [l-yuh] place

ligne f [leeñ] line
la ligne est encombrée the line is busy

lignes de banlieue suburban lines

lime à ongles f [leem a ONgl] nailfile

limitation de vitesse f [leemeetass-yON duh veetess] speed limit

limite de validité des billets expiry of validity of tickets

lin m [lAN] linen

linge de maison m [lANj duh mezzON] household linen

lingerie f underwear

linge sale m [lANj sal] laundry

lire [leer] to read

liste f [leest] list

lit m [lee] bed

lit de camp [kON] campbed

lit d'enfant [dONfON] cot

literie f [leetuhree] bedding

lit pour deux personnes [duh pairson] double bed

lit pour une personne [OOn] single bed

lits superposés mpl [lee sOOpairpozay] bunk beds

living m living room

livraison f [leevrezzON] delivery

livraison à domicile home deliveries

livraisons interdites de ... à ... no deliveries between ... and ...

livre f [leevr] pound

livre m book

livres et journaux books and newspapers

livre sterling f pound sterling

localité f [lokaleetay] place

location f [lokass-yON] rental; theatre tickets

location à la semaine charge per week

location de ... ... for hire

location de bateaux [bato] boat hire

location de vélos [vaylo] bicycles for hire/rent

location de voitures [vwatOOr] car hire/rental

loft m warehouse conversion

logement m [lojmON] accommodation

loger [lojay] to stay

loges des artistes artists' dressing rooms

logiciel m [lojeess-yel] software

loi f [lwa] law

loin [lwAN] far away
plus loin further

loisirs mpl [lwazeer] free time; leisure

Londres [loNdr] London

long, f longue [loN, loN-g] long

longtemps [loNtoN] a long time

longue [loN-g] long

longueur f [loNgurr] length

lorsque [lorskuh] when

louer [loo-ay] to rent
  à louer to let, for rent, for
  hire

lourd [loor] heavy; rich; muggy

loyer m [lwy-ay] rent

lui* [lwee] him; to him; to her

lui-même [-mem] himself;
  speaking

lumière f [loom-yair] light

lundi [laNdee] Monday

lune f [loon] moon

lunettes fpl [loonet] glasses

lunettes de soleil [duh solay]
  sunglasses

lycée m [leessay] secondary
  school

M

M, M° (métro) underground

M (Monsieur) Mr

m'* (to) me; myself

ma* my

machine à écrire f [aykreer]
  typewriter

machine à laver [lavay] washing
  machine

mâchoire f [mashwahr] jaw

Mademoiselle [mad-mwazel]
  Miss

magasin m [magazaN] shop,
  store

magasin d'alimentation grocery
  store

magasin de chaussures shoe
  shop

magasin de disques record
  shop

magasin de vins et spiritueux
  off-licence, liquor store

magasin diététique health food
  store

magnétoscope m [man-yaytoskop]
  video recorder

mai [may] May

maigre [megr] skinny

maigrir [megreer] to lose weight

maillot de bain m [my-o duh baN]
  swimming costume

main f [maN] hand

maintenant [maNtnoN] now

mairie f [mairee] town hall

mais [may] but

maison f [mezzoN] house
  à la maison at home
  la maison n'accepte pas les
  chèques we do not accept
  cheques
  la maison ne fait pas crédit we
  do not give credit

maison de la culture arts centre

maison des jeunes youth club

maison d'hôtes [doht]
  guesthouse

mal badly
  se faire mal à la main to hurt
  one's hand
  avoir mal au cœur to feel sick
  ça fait mal it hurts

malade [malad] ill

maladie f [maladee] disease

maladie vénérienne

[vaynayree-en] VD

mal de gorge m [gorj] sore throat

mal de mer [duh mair] seasickness

mal de tête [tet] headache

mal d'oreilles [doray] earache

mal du pays [payee] homesickness

mâle [mahl] male

malentendu m [malONtONdoo] misunderstanding

malgré [malgray] in spite of

malheureusement [malurr-urzmON] unfortunately

maman f [mamON] mum

Manche f [mONsh] English Channel

manche f sleeve

mandat postal m [mONda poss-tal] postal order

manette du signal d'alarme pull for alarm

manger [mONjay] to eat

manquer [mONkay] to miss
... **me manque** [muh mONk] I miss ...

manteau m [mONto] coat

manuel de conversation m [mONooel duh konvairsass-yON] phrase book

maquillage m [makee-ahj] make-up

se maquiller [makee-ay] to put one's make-up on

marchand m [marshON] shopkeeper; merchant; dealer

marchand de légumes greengrocer

marchand de vins wine merchant

marchandise: les marchandises dangereuses sont interdites dangerous items are prohibited

marche f [marsh] walking; step; march; running, working

marché m [marshay] market

marche arrière [aree-air] reverse gear

marcher [marshay] to walk; to work, to function
ça marche? OK?

mardi [mardee] Tuesday

marée f [maray] tide

mari m [maree] husband

mariage m [maree-ahj] wedding

marié [maree-ay] married

se marier (avec) [suh maree-ay] to get married, to marry

maroquinerie f leather goods

marque déposée registered trademark

marrant [marON] funny

marre: j'en ai marre (de) [jON ay mar] I'm fed up (with)

marron [marON] brown

mars [marss] March

marteau m [marto] hammer

massepain m [massuhpan] marzipan

matelas m [matuhla] mattress

matin m [matAN] morning
le matin in the morning

mauvais [mo-vay] bad

maux de dents mpl [mo duh dON] toothache

maux d'estomac stomach ache

me* [muh] me; to me; myself

mec m bloke, guy

mécanicien m [maykaneess-yAN] mechanic

mèches fpl [mesh] highlights

médecin m [maydsAN] doctor

médicament m [maydeekamON] medicine

Méditerranée f [maydeetairanay] Mediterranean

méduse f [maydOOz] jellyfish

meilleur [mayurr] better
le meilleur the best
meilleur que better than

meilleurs vœux! [vuh] best wishes!

mélanger [maylONjay] to mix

même [mem] even; same
le/la même the same

ménage: faire le ménage [maynahj] to do the housework

mener [muhnay] to lead

menhir m [mayneer] standing stone

mentir [mONteer] to lie

menton m [mONtON] chin

menu à ... F set menu costing ... francs

mer f [mair] sea

mercerie f haberdasher's, (US) notions store

merci [mairsee] thank you; no thank you

merci beaucoup [bo-koo] thank you very much

merci de votre visite thanks for your visit

merci, pareillement [paraymON] thank you, the same to you

mercredi [mairkruhdee] Wednesday

merde! [maird] shit!

mère f [mair] mother

merveilleux [mairvay-uh] wonderful

mes* [may] my

messe f [mess] mass

messieurs [mess-yuh] gentlemen; gents, men's restroom

mesure f [muhzOOr] measure
à mesure que as
sur mesure to measure

météo f [maytay-o] weather forecast

métier m [maytee-ay] job

mètre m [metr] meter

métro m [maytro] underground, subway

mettre [metr] to put
se mettre à to begin to

meublé m [murblay] furnished accommodation

meubles mpl [murbl] furniture

Midi m South of France

midi m midday

mien*: le mien [luh m-yAN] mine

mienne*: la mienne [m-yen] mine

mien(ne)s*: les mien(ne)s [m-yen, m-yen] mine

mieux [m-yuh] better
le mieux (the) best

mignon, mignonne [meen-yON, meen-yon] sweet, cute

milieu m [meel-yuh] middle

mille m [meel] thousand

million f [meel-YON] million

mince [mANss] thin

minuit m [meen-wee] midnight

mirroir m [meer-wahr] mirror

mis [mee] put

mise en fourrière immédiate
illegally parked cars will be
removed

mise en marche automatique,
placez vos mains sous le volet
starts automatically, place
your hands under the flap

Mlle (Mademoiselle) Miss

Mme (Madame) Mrs

mobylette f [mobeelet] moped

mode f [mod] fashion
à la mode fashionable

mode d'emploi directions for
use

modèle m [mo-del] model;
design; style

modes ladies' fashions

moi [mwa] me

moi-même [mwa-mem] myself

moindre [mwANdr] smaller
le moindre the smallest

moins: à moins que [mwAN kuh]
unless
au moins at least [o]
moins (de) less
le moins (the) least

mois m [mwa] month

moitié f [mwatee-ay] half
à moitié prix [pree] half price

molle [mol] soft

mollet m [molay] calf

mon* [mON] my

monde m [mONd] world

tout le monde [too luh]
everyone

moniteur m, monitrice f
[moneeturr, -treess] instructor

monnaie f [monay] change

monsieur m [muhss-yuh]
gentleman, man

Monsieur sir

montagne f [mONtañ] mountain

montant m [mONtON] amount

montant exact exact change

monter [mONtay] to go up; to
get in

montre f [mONtr] watch

montrer [mONtray] to show

monument aux morts war
memorial

moquette f [moket] carpet

morceau m [morso] piece

mordre to bite

morsure f [morsoor] bite

mort f [mor] death

mort dead

mosquée f [moskay] mosque

mot m [mo] word

moteur m [moturr] engine

moto f motorbike

mou, f molle [moo, mol] soft

mouche f [moosh] fly

mouchoir m [moosh-wahr]
handkerchief

mouillé [mooyay] wet

mourir [mooreer] to die

mousse à raser f [razay] shaving
foam

moustique m [moosteek]
mosquito

mouton m [mootON] sheep

moyen âge m Middle Ages

mur m [mOOr] wall

mûr [mOOr] ripe

musée m [mOOzay] museum; art gallery

musée d'art [dar] art gallery

muséum m [mOOzay-om] natural history museum

musique f [mOOzeek] music

musulman [mOOzOOlmON] Muslim

myope [mee-op] shortsighted

N

nager [nahjay] to swim

naître [netr] to be born

nana f bird, girl

nappe f [nap] tablecloth

natation f [natass-yON] swimming

nationalité f [nass-yonaleetay] nationality

nature f [natOOr] nature

yaourt nature natural yoghurt

naturel [natOOrel] natural

naturellement [natOOrelmON] naturally, of course

navette f [navet] shuttle service

navette de l'aéroport airport bus

ND (Notre Dame) Our Lady

né born

néanmoins [nay-ONmwAN] nevertheless

ne ... aucun [nuh ... okAN] no, not any, none

nécessaire [naysessair] necessary

négatif m [naygateef] negative

ne ... guère [gair] hardly

neige f [nej] snow

neiger [nejay] to snow

ne ... jamais [jamay] never

ne ... ni neither ... nor

ne ... nulle part [nOOl par] nowhere, not ... anywhere

ne ... pas* [pa] not

ne pas ... do not ...

ne pas affranchir freepost, do not affix stamp

ne pas avaler do not swallow

ne pas congeler do not freeze

ne pas dépasser ... comprimés par jour do not take more than ... tablets a day

ne pas dépasser la dose prescrite do not exceed the prescribed dose

ne pas déranger do not disturb

ne pas essorer do not spin dry

ne pas laisser à la portée des enfants keep out of the reach of children

ne pas repasser do not iron

ne pas se pencher au dehors do not lean out of the window

ne pas se pencher par la fenêtre do not lean out of the window

ne pas ... sous peine d'amende ... will be fined

ne pas tordre do not wring

ne pas toucher à ... do not touch ...

ne ... personne [pairson] nobody, not anybody

ne ... plus [plOO] no more, no longer

ne ... que [kuh] only

ne quittez pas [nuh keetay pa] hold the line, hold on

ne ... rien [ree-AN] nothing, not anything

ne rien jeter dans les WC do not flush objects down the toilet

ne rien jeter par la fenêtre do not throw anything out of the window

ne tirer la poignée qu'en cas de danger pull handle only in case of emergency

nerveux [nairvuh] nervous

n'est-ce pas? [ness-pa] didn't he/she/it?; isn't it?; isn't that so?

nettoyage à sec dry cleaner, dry clean only

nettoyer [net-wy-ay] to clean

neuf, f neuve [nuhf, nuhv] new

neuf nine

neveu m [nuhvuh] nephew

neuvième [nuhv-yem] ninth

névralgies headaches

névrosé [nayvrozay] neurotic

nez m [nay] nose

ni neither

ni ... ni ... neither ... nor ...

nids-de-poule potholes

nièce f [nee-ess] niece

nocturne late night opening

Noël [no-el] Christmas

noir [nwahr] black

noir et blanc black and white

nom m [nON] name

nom de famille [duh famee] surname, family name

nom de jeune fille [jurn fee] maiden name

nommer: se nommer [suh nomay] to be called

non [nON] no; not

non-fumeurs [-foomurr] no smoking

non merci [mairsee] no thank you

nord m [nor] north

au nord de north of

nos* [no] our

note f [not] bill; note

notez le numéro de votre emplacement make a note of the number of your parking space

notre* [notr] our

nôtre*: le/la nôtre [luh/la nohtr] ours

nôtres*: les nôtres ours

n'oubliez pas de composter votre billet do not forget to punch/validate your ticket

n'oubliez pas le guide don't forget to tip the guide

n'oubliez pas votre reçu don't forget your receipt

nourriture f [nooreetoor] food

nous* [noo] we; (to) us

nous acceptons les cartes de crédit credit cards welcome

nous n'acceptons pas les chèques cheques not accepted

nouveau, f nouvelle [noovo, -vel] new

de nouveau again

nouveau franc new French franc (100 old francs)

Nouvel An m [ON] New Year

nouvelle [noovel] new
nouvelles fpl [noovel] news
novembre [no-vONbr] November
nu [n∞] naked
nuage m [n∞-ahj] cloud
nuageux [n∞-ahjuh] cloudy
nuit f [nwee] night
nul [n∞l] no; lousy
nulle part [n∞l par] nowhere
numéro m [n∞mayro] number
numéro de téléphone phone
  number
numéro direct direct dialling
numérotez dial
numéro vert freephone
nu-pieds mpl [n∞-p-yay] flip-
  flops

O

objectif m [objekteef] lens;
  objective
objets trouvés mpl [objay
  troovay] lost property office,
  lost and found
objets volumineux large
  parcels/packages
oblitérez votre billet punch your
  ticket
obtenir [obtuhneer] to get
obturateur m [obt∞raturr]
  shutter
occasion f [okaz-yON]
  opportunity; occasion;
  bargain
  d'occasion second-hand
occupé [ok∞pay] engaged;
  occupied; busy
s'occuper de [sok∞pay] to take

care of
octobre [oktobr] October
oculiste m/f eye specialist
odeur f [odurr] smell
œil m [uh-ee] eye
office à … service at …
office du tourisme tourist office
offre spéciale special offer
offrir [ofreer] to offer; to give
oiseau m [wazo] bird
ombre f [ONbr] shade
  à l'ombre in the shade
ombre à paupières [pohp-yair]
  eye shadow
on* [ON] one; someone; you;
  they; people; we
oncle m [Onkl] uncle
ondulé [ONd∞lay] wavy
ongle m [ONgl] nail
ont: ils/elles ont [ON] they have
onze [ONz] eleven
opératrice f [opayratreess]
  operator
opérer [opayray] to operate
ophtalmologue m/f
  ophthalmologist
opticien m [opteess-yAN] optician
optimiste optimistic
optique optician's
or m gold
or massif solid gold
orage m [orahj] thunderstorm
orageux [orahjuh] stormy
orchestre m [orkestr] orchestra;
  stalls
ordinaire [ordeenair] ordinary;
  equivalent of two-star petrol
ordinateur m [ordeenaturr]
  computer

ordonnance f [ordonONss]
prescription
ordures fpl [ordOOr] litter;
refuse; filth
oreille f [oray] ear
oreiller m [oray-yay] pillow
oreillons mpl [orayON] mumps
organiser [organeezay] to
organize
orteil m [ortay] toe
os m [oss] bone
oser [ozay] to dare
oto-rhino-laryngologiste m/f ear,
nose and throat specialist
ou [oo] or
ou bien [b-yAN] or else
où [oo] where
oublier [ooblee-ay] to forget
ouest m [west] west
à l'ouest de west of
oui [wee] yes
outil m [ootee] tool
ouvert [oovair] open
ouvert de ... à ... open from ...
to ...
ouverture f [oovairtOOr] opening
ouverture des guichets hours of
opening
ouvre-boîte m [oovr-bwat] tin-
opener
ouvre-bouteille m [-bootay]
bottle-opener
ouvreuse f [oovrurz] usherette
ouvrier m [oovree-ay] (factory)
worker
ouvrir [oovreer] to open
ouvrir ici open here

P

pages jaunes fpl [pahj jo-n]
yellow pages
paire f [pair] pair
palais m [palay] palace
pâle [pahl] pale
panier m [pan-yay] basket
panier (à provisions) shopping
basket
panique f panic
panne f [pan] breakdown
en panne [ON] out of order;
broken down
tomber en panne [tONbay] to
break down
panneau de signalisation m
roadsign
pansement m [pONssmON]
bandage
pansement adhésif [adayzeef]
Elastoplast®
panser [pONsay] to dress
pantalon m [pONtalON] trousers
pantoufles fpl [pONtoofl] slippers
papa m dad
papeterie f stationer's,
stationery
papier m [pap-yay] paper
papier à lettres writing paper
papier collant [kolON]
sellotape®
papier d'aluminium
[dalOOmeenee-um] silver foil
papier d'emballage [dONbalahj]
wrapping paper
papier hygiénique [eejee-ayneek]
toilet paper
papiers papers; litter

papiers, s'il vous plaît your identity papers, please

papillon m [papee-yoN] butterfly

Pâques [pak] Easter

paquet m [pakay] package, packet

par by; through

parachute ascensionnel m [assoNsee-onel] parascending

parachutisme m parachuting

parages: dans les parages [doN lay parahj] in the vicinity

paraître [paretre] to seem; to come out, to be published

parapluie m [paraplwee] umbrella

parc m park

parce que [parss-kuh] because

parcmètre m parking meter

parcotrain m parking for train users

pardessus m [par-duhsoo] overcoat

par-dessus over

par-dessous [-duhsoo] under

pardon [par-doN] excuse me, pardon me; thank you; sorry; pardon

pare-brise m [par-breez] windscreen

pare-chocs m [-shok] bumper

parents mpl [paroN] parents; relatives

paresseux [paressuh] lazy

parfait [parfay] perfect

parfois [parfwa] sometimes

parfum m [parfAN] perfume

parfumerie f perfume and cosmetics shop

parking m [parkeeng] car park, (US) parking lot

parking à étages [aytahj] multi-storey car park

parking courte durée short-term car park

parking longue durée long-term car park

parking non gardé unsupervised parking

parking payant paying car park

parking privé private car park

parking public public car park

parking réservé aux clients de l'hôtel parking for hotel guests only

parking souterrain underground car park

parking surveillé car park with attendant

parler [parlay] to speak

parler ici talk here

parmi among

pars: je/tu pars [par] I/you leave, I/you go away

part f [par] piece; share

à part except

de la part de from; on behalf of

de la part de qui? [duh kee] who shall I say is calling?

partager [partahjay] to share

parterre m stalls

partir [parteer] to leave

partout [partoo] everywhere

pas* [pa] not

pas de ... no ...

pas de remboursement we cannot give cash refunds

pas encore not yet

passage à niveau m [passahj a neevo] level crossing, (US) railroad crossing

passage à niveau gardé/non gardé manned/unmanned level crossing

passage clouté pedestrian crossing

passage interdit no entry

passage piétons pedestrian crossing

passage protégé priority road

passager m [passahjay] passenger

passage souterrain underpass

passeport m [pass-por] passport

passer [passay] to pass

qu'est-ce qui se passe? [keskee suh pass] what's happening?

passer par to go through

passerelle f gangway

passe-temps m [pass-tON] pastime

passionnant [pass-yonON] exciting

passionné de [pass-yonay] very keen on

pastilles pour la gorge fpl [pastee poor la gorj] throat pastilles

patientez svp please wait

patinage m [pateenahj] skating

patiner [pateenay] to skate

patinoire f [pateenwahr] ice rink

patins à glace mpl [patAN a glass] ice skates

patron m [pa-trON] manager

pauvre [pohvr] poor

payer [pay-ay] to pay

payer comptant to pay cash

payez à la caisse pay at the cash desk

payez à la sortie pay on your way out

payez à l'ordre de ... payable to ...

payez ici pay here

pays m [payee] country

paysage m [payee-zahj] scenery

Pays de Galles m [payee duh gal] Wales

PCV m [pay-say-vay] collect call, reverse charge call

péage m [payahj] toll

peau f [po] skin

pêche f [pesh] fishing; peach

pêche interdite no fishing

pêcher [peshay] to fish

pêche sous-marine underwater fishing

peigne m [peñ] comb

se peigner [suh pen-yay] to comb one's hair

peindre [pANdr] paint

peine: à peine [pen] hardly

ce n'est pas la peine it's not worth it; it's not necessary

peinture f [pANtoor] painting

peinture fraîche wet paint

pelle f [pel] spade

pellicule f film

pelouse f [puhlooz] lawn

pénalité pour abus penalty for misuse

pendant [pONdON] during

pendant que while

penser [pONsay] to think

pension f [pONs-yON] guesthouse

pension complète [kONplet] full board, European plan

pension de famille guesthouse

pente f [pONt] slope

perdre [pairdr] to lose
se perdre to get lost

père m [pair] father

périphérique m [payreefayreek] ring road

permanente f [pairmanONt] perm

permettre [pairmetr] to allow

permis [pairmee] allowed

permis de conduire m [duh kONdweer] driving licence, driver's license

perruque f [pairOOk] wig

personne f [pairson] person

personne nobody
personne ne sait ... nobody knows ...

personnes handicapées disabled

peser [puhzay] to weigh

pétanque f [paytONk] French bowling game

petit [puhtee] small

petit ami m [tamee] boyfriend

petit déjeuner m [dayjuhnay] breakfast

petite amie f [tamee] girlfriend

petite cuillère f teaspoon

petite-fille f [puhteet-fee] granddaughter

petit-fils m [puhtee-feess] grandson

petit nom m [nON] pet name

petits-enfants mpl [puhtee-zONfON] grandchildren

peu: peu de ... [puh] few ...

un peu (de) a bit (of)

peur f [purr] fear
de peur que for fear that
j'ai peur (de) I'm afraid (of)

peut-être [puht-etr] maybe

peut: il/elle peut [puh] he/she/it can
il peut y avoir ... there may be ...

peuvent: ils/elles peuvent [puhv] they can

peux: je/tu peux [puh] I/you can

phallocrate m [falokrat] male chauvinist pig

phare m [far] headlight; lighthouse

phare antibrouillard [ONtee-brooyar] fog lamp

pharmacie f chemist's, pharmacy

pharmacie de garde duty chemist/pharmacy, latenight chemist

pharmacie de service duty chemist

photographe m photographer; camera shop

photographie f [foto-grafee] photograph

photographier [foto-grafyay] to photograph

photomètre m [foto-metr] light meter

pièce f [p-yess] coin; room

pièce de théâtre [duh tay-atr] play

pièces de rechange [ruhshONj] spare parts

pièces détachées [daytashay]

parts

pièces rejetées reject coins

pied m [p-yay] foot
à pied on foot

pierre f stone

piéton m [p-yaytON] pedestrian
piétons passez en deux temps
pedestrians cross in two
stages

pile f [peel] battery; pile

pilote m [peelot] pilot

pilule f [peel00l] pill

pince f [pANss] pliers; clip

pince à épiler [aypeelay]
tweezers

pince à linge [lANj] clothes peg

pince à ongles [ONgl] nail
clippers

pinceau m [pANso] paint brush

piquant [peekON] hot, spicy

piquer [peekay] to sting

piqûre f [peek00r] injection; bite

piqûre d'insecte [dANsekt] insect
bite

pire [peer] worse
le pire worst

piscine f [peesseen] swimming
pool

pissoir m public urinal

piste balisée f [baleezay] marked
ski path

piste cyclable [seeklabl] cycle
path

piste de ski ski track, piste

piste pour débutants [dayb00tON]
nursery slope

place f [plass] seat; square

place principale [prANseepal]
main square

placer [plassay] to place

place réservée aux ... this seat is
intended for ...

place(s) assise(s) seat(s)

places debout standing
passengers

places libres spaces free (in car
park)

plafond m [plafON] ceiling

plage f [plahj] beach

plaindre: se plaindre [suh plANdr]
to complain

plaire [plair] to please

plaisanterie f [plezzONtree] joke

plaît: s'il vous plaît [seel voo play]
please

plan m [plON] map

planche de surf f [plONsh]
surfboard

planche à voile [vwal] sailboard

plancher m [plONshay] floor

plan de métro underground
map

plan de ville map of the town

plan du quartier map of the
district

plan du réseau network map

planning familial m [pla-neeng]
family planning

plante f [plONt] plant

plaque minéralogique f
[meenayralojeek] number plate

plat m [pla] dish

plat flat

plateau m tray

plateaux-repas light meals
served on trains

plâtre m plaster; plaster cast

plats à emporter take-away

meals

plein [plAN] full
faire le plein to fill up

pleurer [plurray] to cry

pleut: il pleut [pluh] it's raining

pleuvoir [pluhvwahr] to rain

plombage m [plONbahj] filling

plombier m plumber

plongée f [plONjay] diving

plongée interdite no diving

plongée sous-marine skin-diving

plonger [plONjay] to dive

pluie f [plwee] rain

plupart: la plupart de [plOOpar duh] most of

plus [plOO] more
plus jamais never again
plus de ... more; no more ...
plus ... que ...-er than
le plus [plOOss] (the) most

plusieurs [plOOz-yurr] several

plutôt [plOOto] rather

pluvieux [plOOv-yuh] rainy

PMU betting on horses

pneu m [p-nuh] tyre

pneu crevé [kruhvay] flat tyre

pneu de rechange [duh ruhshONj] spare tyre

poche f [posh] pocket

poche en plastique plastic bag

poêle f [pwal] frying pan

poids m [pwa] weight

poids lourds [pwa loor] heavy vehicles

poids maximum maximum weight

poids net net weight

poignée f [pwan-yay] handle

poignet m [pwan-yay] wrist

point de rencontre m [pwAN duh rONkONtr] meeting point

point de vue [vOO] viewpoint

point noir accident blackspot; blackhead

point panoramique viewpoint

point phone pay-phone

pointure f [pwANtOOr] shoe size

poissonnerie f fishmonger

poitrine f [pwatreen] chest; breast

poli [polee] polite

police f police

police de l'aéroport airport police

police de la route traffic police

police du port harbour police

police secours emergency police

politique f politics

politique political

pollué [polOO-ay] polluted

pommade f [pomahd] ointment

pompiers mpl [pONp-yay] fire brigade

poney m pony

pont m [pON] bridge; deck

pont à péage [payahj] toll bridge

port de pêche m [por duh pesh] fishing port

porte f [port] door; gate

porte-bébé m [-baybay] carry-cot

portefeuille m [portfuh-ee] wallet

porte-jarretelles fpl suspenders

porte-monnaie m [port-monay] purse

porter [portay] to carry
  bien se porter to be well
portes automatiques automatic
  gates
portier m [port-yay] porter
portière f [port-yair] door
portillon automatique m
  automatic gate
posologie directions for use,
  dosage
posséder [possayday] to own; to
  possess
poste f [posst] post office
poste de police m police
  station
poster [postay] to post
poste restante poste restante;
  (US) general delivery
pot m [po] jug
pot d'échappement
  [dayshapmON] exhaust
poterie f [potree] pottery
poubelle f [poobel] dustbin
poudre f [poodr] powder
pouls m pulse
poumons mpl [poomON] lungs
poupée f [poopay] doll
pour [poor] for
pourboire m [poorbwahr] tip
pourboire interdit please do not
  tip
pour cent [sON] per cent
pour entrer ..., to enter ...
pour ouvrir appuyer push to
  open
pour que [kuh] in order that, so
  that
pourquoi [poorkwa] why
pourrai: je pourrai [pooray] I will

be able
pourra: il/elle pourra [poora] he/
  she/it will be able
pourras: tu pourras [poora] you
  will be able
pourrez: vous pourrez [pooray]
  you will be able
pourri [pooree] rotten
pourrons: nous pourrons
  [poorON] we will be able
pourront: ils/elles pourront
  [poorON] they will be able
pourtant [poortON] however
pour tous renseignements,
  s'adresser à ... for enquiries,
  please see ...
pourvu que [poorvoo kuh]
  provided that
pousser [poossay] to push
poussette f pushchair
poussez [poossay] push
pouvoir m [poovwahr] power
pouvoir to be able to
pratique practical
précautions d'emploi
  instructions for use
préfecture f [prayfektoor]
  regional administrative
  headquarters
préfecture de police police
  headquarters
préféré [prayfayray] favourite
préférence f [prayfayrONss]
  preference
préférer [prayfayray] to prefer
premier m [pruhm-yay] first
  floor; (US) second floor
premier first
première f first class; première

premier étage first floor

premiers secours mpl [pruhm-yay suhkoor] first aid

premiers soins [swAN] first aid

prendre [proNdr] to take; to catch

à prendre à jeun to be taken on an empty stomach

à prendre après les repas to be taken after meals

à prendre au coucher to be taken at bedtime

à prendre avant le coucher to be taken before going to bed

à prendre avant les repas to be taken before meals

à prendre ... fois par jour to be taken ... times a day

prendre ... comprimés à la fois take ... pills/tablets at a time

prendre ... comprimés ... fois par jour take ... pills/tablets ... times a day

prenez: vous prenez [pruhnay] you take

prenez un caddy take a trolley/cart

prenez un chariot take a trolley/cart

prenez un jeton à la caisse buy a token at the cash desk

prenez un panier take a basket

prenez un ticket take a ticket

prénom m [praynoN] Christian name, first name

prenons: nous prenons [pruhnoN] we take

préparer [prayparay] to prepare, to get ready

préparez votre monnaie have your change ready

presbyte [prezbeet] long-sighted

prescrire [preskreer] to prescribe

près de [pray duh] near

présenter [prayzoNtay] to introduce; to present

préservatif m [prayzairvateef] condom

presque [presk] almost

pressing m dry-cleaner's

pression f [press-yoN] blood pressure; draught beer

pression de l'air air pressure

pression des pneus tyre pressure

prêt [pray] ready

prêt-à-porter ready-to-wear clothes

prêter [pretay] to lend

prêtre m [pretr] priest

prier [pree-ay] to ask; to pray

je vous en prie [juh voo zoN pree] don't mention it, you're welcome

prière f [pree-air] prayer

prière de ... please ...

prière de frapper avant d'entrer please knock before entering

prière de ne pas déranger please do not disturb

prière de ne pas faire de bruit après 22 heures please do not make any noise after 10 p.m.

prière de ne pas fumer please

do not smoke

prière de ne pas toucher please do not touch

prière de refermer la porte please close the door

prière de s'essuyer les pieds avant d'entrer please wipe your feet

prière de tenir les chiens en laisse please keep dogs on a lead

primeurs fruit shop, greengrocer's

principal [prANseepal] main

printemps m [prANtoN] spring

prioritaire [pree-oreetair] priority; priority-rate; having right of way

priorité f [pree-oreetay] right of way; priority

priorité à droite right of way for traffic coming from the right

pris [pree] taken

prise f [preez] plug; socket

prise en charge minimum charge

prise multiple [mOOlteepl] adaptor

privé [preevay] private

prix m [pree] price; fee; prize

prix cassés reduced prices

prix coûtant at cost price

prix des places ticket prices

prix par jour price per day

prix par personne price per person

prix par semaine price per week

prix réduit reduced price

prix sacrifiés prices slashed

probablement [prob-abluhmON] probably

prochain [proshAN] next

à la prochaine [proshen] see you soon

prochaine levée next collection

prochaine séance à ... heures next performance at ...

produits de beauté cosmetics

produits d'entretien household cleaning materials

produits naturels health food

produit toxique poison

professeur m [professurr] teacher; lecturer; professor

profond [profON] deep

profondeur f [profONdurr] depth

promenade f walk

promenades à cheval horse riding

promener: aller se promener [alay suh promnay] to go for a walk

promettre [prometr] to promise

promotion: en promotion on special offer

prononcer [prononsay] to pronounce

propre [propr] clean; own

propriétaire m/f [propee-aytair] owner

propriété privée private property

propriété privée défense d'entrer private property, keep out; no trespassing

prospectus m brochure

protège-couches mpl [protej-koosh] nappy-liners

protéger [protejay] to protect

provenance: en provenance de (arriving) from

prudence f [prOOdONss] caution

prudent [prOOdON] careful

P & T (Postes et Télécommunications) post office (with telephone)

PTT (Postes, Télégraphes, Téléphones) [pay-tay-tay] post office (with telephone)

pu: il a pu [pOO] he was able to

public m [pOObleek] audience; public

puce f [pOOss] flea

puis [pwee] then

puisque [pweess-kuh] since

pull(over) m sweater

pure laine vierge pure new wool

puzzle m [pOOsl] jigsaw

PV (procès verbal) m [pay-vay] parking ticket

Q

quai m [kay] platform; track; quay

quand [kON] when

quand même [-mem] anyway; all the same

quant à [kONta] as for

quarante [karONt] forty

quart m [kar] quarter

quartier m [kart-yay] district

quatorze [katorz] fourteen

quatre [katr] four

quatre-vingt-dix [katr-vAN-deess] ninety

quatre-vingts [katr-vAN] eighty

quatrième [katree-em] fourth

que [kuh] that; what; than; who(m); which

que …? what …?

que désirez-vous? what would you like?

quel [kel] which

quelque chose [kelkuh shohz] something

quelque part [par] somewhere

quelque(s) [kelkuh] some

quelques-uns [kelkuh-zAN] some, a few

quelqu'un [kelkAN] somebody

qu'est-ce que …? [keskuh] what …?

qu'est-ce que vous avez dit? what did you say?

qu'est-ce qu'il y a? [keskeel ya] what's the matter?

qu'est-ce qui …? [keskee] what …?

queue f [kuh] tail; queue

faire la queue to queue

qui [kee] who

quincaillerie f [kAN-ky-ree] ironmonger, hardware store

quinzaine f [kANzen] fortnight; about fifteen

quinze [kANz] fifteen

quitter [kitay] to leave

ne quittez pas [nuh kitay pa] hold the line

quoi? [kwa] what?

quoique [kwa-kuh] although

R

rabais m [rabay] discount, reduction

raccourci m [rakoorsee] shortcut

raccrochez: ne raccrochez pas [nuh rakroshay pa] hold the line

raccrochez svp replace the receiver

radiateur m [rad-yaturr] heater; radiator

radio(graphie) f X-ray

radiographier to X-ray

raide [red] steep; straight

raison f [rezzON] reason
  avoir raison [avwahr] to be right

raisonnable [rezzonabl] sensible; reasonable

ralentir [ralONteer] to slow down

ralentisseurs speed bumps; rumble strip

ralentissez slow down

rallonge f [ralONj] extension lead

rame f [ram] train (on underground)

randonnée f [rONdonay] rambling

ranger [rONjay] to tidy; to put away

rapide [rapeed] fast

rapide m inter-city train

rappel m reminder, reminder sign

rappeler [rapuhlay] to call back
  se rappeler to remember, to recall

raquette de tennis f tennis racket

rarement [raruhmON] seldom

se raser [suh razay] to shave

rasoir m [razwahr] razor

rasoir électrique electric shaver

rater [ratay] to miss

RATP (Régie autonome des transports parisiens) Paris public transport company

ravi de faire votre connaissance [ravee duh fair votr konessONss] how do you do, nice to meet you

ravissant [raveessON] lovely

rayon m [rayON] spoke; department

rayon jouets toy department

rayons X mpl [rayON eex] X-ray

récépissé m [raysaypeessay] receipt note

recette f [ruhset] recipe

recevoir [ruhsuhvwahr] to receive; to have guests

recharge f [ruhsharj] refill

réchaud à gaz m [raysh] camping gas stove

réclamations fpl [rayklamass-yON] complaints; faults service

recommander [ruhkomONday] to recommend
  envoyer une lettre en recommandé to send a letter by recorded delivery

reconnaissant [ruhkonessON] grateful

reconnaître [ruhkonetr] to recognize

reçu m [ruhsoo] receipt

réductions familles nombreuses special rates for large families

regarder [ruhgarday] to look (at); to watch

régime m [rayjeem] diet
être au régime to be on a diet

règlement m [reglmON] regulation

règles fpl [regl] period

rein m [rAN] kidney

reine f [ren] queen

reins mpl [rAN] back

relâche [ruhlahsh] closed

relais routier m [ruhlay root-yay] transport café (often quality restaurant)

relevez lift up

remarquer [ruhmarkay] to notice

remboursement m [rONboorsmON] refund

rembourser [rONboorsay] to refund

remercier [ruhmairs-yay] to thank

remettez mes amitiés à ... [ruhmetay may zameet-yay] give my regards to ...

remise f [ruhmeez] reduction

remonte-pente m [ruhmONt-pONt] ski lift; ski tow

remorque f [ruhmork] trailer

remorquer [ruhmorkay] to tow

remplir [rONpleer] to fill in, to fill

rencontrer [rONkONtray] to meet

rendez-vous m appointment
prendre rendez-vous to make an appointment

rendre [rONdr] to give back; to make
se rendre à to go to

renouveler [ruhnoovuhlay] to renew

renseignement m [rONsen-yuhmON] information

renseignements information desk; directory enquiries

renseignements internationaux international directory enquiries

renseigner [rONsen-yay] to inform
se renseigner to find out; to enquire

rentrer [rONtray] to return
rentrer à la maison to go home

renverser [rONvairsay] to knock over

réparations fpl [rayparass-yON] repairs

réparer [rayparay] to repair

repas m [ruhpa] meal

repasser [ruhpassay] to iron; to come back

répéter [raypaytay] to repeat

répondre [raypONdr] to answer

réponse f [raypONss] answer

repos m [ruhpo] rest

reposer: se reposer [suh ruhpozay] to take a rest

représentant m [ruhprayzONtON] agent

représentation f [ruhprayzONtass-yON] representation; performance

reprise f [ruhpreez] revival; renewal; resumption

RER (Réseau express régional) m
[air-uh-air] fast, limited-stop
metro line in Paris

résa f [rayza] reservation ticket
on TGV

réservation obligatoire booking
essential

réservé [rayzairvay] reserved

réservé au personnel staff only

réservé aux clients patrons only

réservé aux clients de l'hôtel
hotel patrons only

réservé aux membres de
l'équipage reserved for the
crew, crew only

réserve de chasse hunting
preserve

réserver [rayzairvay] to book, to
reserve

réservoir m [rayzairvwahr] tank

respectez le silence de ces lieux
please respect the sanctity
of this place

respectez les pelouses please
do not walk on the grass

respirer [respeeray] to breathe

responsable [respONsabl]
responsible

resquilleur m [reskeeyurr] fare
dodger

ressembler à [ruhsONblay] to
look like

ressort m [ruhsor] spring

restaurant de poisson fish
restaurant

restauration à votre place meal
served at your seat (1st class
only)

reste m [rest] rest

rester [restay] to stay

resto m restaurant

restoroute m roadside café

retard m [ruhtar] delay
en retard late

retardé [ruhtarday] delayed;
retarded

retirer [ruhteeeray] to withdraw

retirez votre argent take your
money

retirez votre carte remove your
card

retirez votre reçu (d'opération)
take your receipt

retour m [ruhtoor] return
de retour dans une heure back
in an hour

retour de suite back soon

retourner [ruhtoornay] to return

retrait de colis et lettres
recommandées collection of
parcels and recorded
delivery letters

retrait des bagages m [ruhtray
day bagahj] baggage claim

retrait d'espèces cash
withdrawal

retraité(e) m/f [ruhtretay] old-age
pensioner

retraits withdrawals

rétroviseur m [raytroveezurr]
rearview mirror

réunion f [ray-OOn-yON] meeting

réussir [rayOOseer] to succeed

rêve m [rev] dream

réveil m [rayvay] alarm clock;
waking up

réveillé [rayvay-yay] awake

réveiller [rayvay-yay] to wake

FRENCH ◆ ENGLISH | Re

se réveiller to wake up

revenir [ruhvuhneer] to come back

revêtement temporaire temporary road surface

revue f magazine

rez-de-chaussée m [rayd-shoh-say] ground floor

RF (République française) French Republic

rhume m [room] cold

rhume des foins [day fwAN] hay fever

riche [reesh] rich

rideau m [reedo] curtain

rien [ree-AN] nothing
de rien you're welcome

rien à déclarer nothing to declare

rire [reer] to laugh

risque d'avalanche danger of avalanche

rivage m [reevahj] shore

rive f [reev] bank

riverains autorisés no entry except for access, residents only

rivière f river

RN (route nationale) f [air-en] national highway

robe f [rob] dress

robe de chambre [duh shONbr] dressing gown

robinet m [robeenay] tap

rocher m [roshay] rock

roi m [rwa] king

Roi-Soleil [solay] Louis XIV (The Sun King)

roman m [romON] novel

roman Romanesque

rond [rON] round

rond-point m [-pwAN] roundabout; (US) traffic circle

ronfler [rONflay] to snore

rose f [roz] rose

rose pink

rôtisserie f [roteesree] steak-house

roue f [roo] wheel

roue de secours [duh suhkoor] spare wheel

rouge [rooj] red

rouge à lèvres m [rooj a levr] lipstick

rougeole f [roojol] measles

roulez au pas drive at walking pace

roulez sur une file single lane traffic

rousse [rooss] red-haired

route f [root] road; route

route barrée road closed; road blocked

route départementale secondary road

route du vin route taking in vineyards, wine route

route nationale [nass-yonal] national highway, main road

route verglacée black ice

routier m [root-yay] lorry; lorry-driver; roadside café

roux, f rousse [roo, rooss] red-haired

Royaume-Uni m [rwy-ohm oonee] United Kingdom

RU (Royaume Uni) UK

rubéole f [rOObayol] German
  measles
rue f [rOO] street
rue commerçante [komairsONt]
  shopping street
rue piétonne [p-yayton]
  pedestrian precinct
rue piétonnière [p-yayton-yair]
  pedestrian precinct
ruisseau m [rweesso] stream

S

sa* his; her; its
sable m [sabl] sand
  sables mouvants quicksand
sac m bag
sac à dos [doh] rucksack
sac à main [mAN] handbag
sac de couchage [duh kooshahj]
  sleeping bag
sac en plastique [ON plasteek]
  plastic bag
saignement m [sen-yuhmON]
  bleeding
saigner [sen-yay] to bleed
sais: je/tu sais [say] I/you know
  je ne sais pas I don't know
saison f [sezzON] season
  en haute saison in the high
  season
sait: il/elle sait [say] he/she/it
  knows
salaud [salo] bastard
sale [sal] dirty
salé [salay] salty; savoury
salle à manger f [sal a mONjay]
  dining room
salle climatisée [kleemateezay]
  dining room with air
  conditioning
salle d'attente [datONt] waiting
  room
salle de bain [duh bAN]
  bathroom
salle de cinéma [duh seenayma]
  cinema
salon m [salON] lounge
salon de coiffure [duh kwafOOr]
  hairdressing salon
salon d'essayage [dessayahj]
  fitting room
salon de thé [duh tay] tearoom
salon privé [preevay] private
  lounge
salut! [salOO] hi!; cheerio!
samedi [samdee] Saturday
SAMU (Service d'Aide Medicale
  d'Urgence) m [samOO]
  emergency medical service
sang m [sON] blood
sanisette f [saneezet] automated
  public toilet on the street
sanitaires mpl [saneetair] toilets
  and showers
sans [sON] without
sans agent de conservation
  contains no preservatives
sans alcool non-alcoholic
sans doute [doot] undoubtedly
sans issue no through road,
  dead end
sans plomb lead-free
santé! [sontay] cheers!; bless
  you!
santé f health
  en bonne santé healthy, in
  good health

bon pour la santé healthy

SARL (société à responsabilité limitée) Ltd, Inc

SA (société anonyme) [ess-ah] Ltd, Inc

satellite m [-eet] section of airport terminal; satellite

sauf [sohf] except; safe

sauf indication contraire du médecin unless otherwise stated by your doctor

sauf le ... except on ...

sauf riverains access only

saurai: je saurai [soray] I will know

saura: il/elle saura [sora] he/she/it will know

sauras: tu sauras [sora] you will know

saurez: vous saurez [soray] you will know

saurons: nous saurons [soronN] we will know

sauront: ils sauront [soronN] they will know

sauter [sotay] to jump

sauvage [sovahj] wild

savoir [savwahr] to know

savon m [savonN] soap

scandaleux [skoNdaluh] shocking

se* [suh] him; to him; himself; her; to her; herself; each other

séance f [say-oNss] showing

seau m [so] bucket

sec, f sèche [sek, sesh] dry

sèche-cheveux m [sesh-shuhvuh] hair dryer

sécher [sayshay] to dry

second m [suhgoN] second floor

seconde f [suhgoNd] second; second class

secours: au secours! [o suhkoor] help!

secours de montagne m [duh moNtañ] mountain rescue

Secours routier français [root-yay] French motoring organization

secrétaire m/f [suhkraytair] secretary

sécurité: en sécurité [oN saykooreetay] safe

séduisant [saydweezoN] attractive

sein m [saN] breast
au sein de in

seize [sez] sixteen

seizième: le seizième [sez-yem] the 16th arrondissement, up-market area of Paris

séjour m [sayjoor] stay

self m self-service restaurant

selle f [sel] saddle

selon [suhloN] according to

sels de bain mpl [sel duh baN] bath salts

semaine f [suhmen] week
par semaine per week

semblable [soNblabl] similar

sembler [soNblay] to seem

semelle f [suhmel] sole

semi-remorque m [suhmee-ruhmork] articulated lorry

sens m [soNss] direction

sens giratoire [jeeratwahr] roundabout; (US) traffic

circle

sensible [sONseebl] sensitive

sens interdit one-way street; no
entry

sens unique one-way street

sentier m [sONt-yay] path

sentier balisé marked footpath

sentiment m [sONteemON] feeling

sentir [sONteer] to feel; to smell

séparé [sayparay] separate

séparément [sayparaymON]
separately

sept [set] seven

septembre [septONbr]
September

septième [set-yem] seventh

serai: je serai [suhray] I will be

sera: il/elle sera [suhra] he/she/
it will be

serais: je/tu serais [suhray] I/you
would be

seras: tu seras [suhra] you will
be

serez: vous serez [suhray] you
will be

sérieux [sayree-uh] serious

seriez: vous seriez [suhree-ay]
you would be

serions: nous serions [suhree-ON]
we would be

serons: nous serons [suhrON] we
will be

seront: ils/elles seront [suhrON]
they will be

serpent m [sairpON] snake

serrez à droite keep to the right

serrure f [sair-rOOr] lock

serveur m [sairvurr] waiter

serveuse f [sairvurz] waitress

servez-vous please take one

service m [sairveess] service;
service charge; ward;
department

service! not at all! (Switzerland)

service après vente after-sales
service

service de retouches alteration/
tailoring service

service des urgences casualty
department

service d'urgence emergency
ward, emergencies

service non-stop 24-hour
service

serviette f [sairvee-et] briefcase;
serviette, napkin

serviette (de table) serviette,
napkin

serviette de toilette [twalet]
towel

serviette hygiénique [eejee-
ayneek] sanitary towel

servir [sairveer] to serve

se servir to help oneself

se servir de to use

ses* [say] his; her; its

seul [surl] alone; single; only

seulement [surlmON] only

sexe m [sex] sex

shamp(o)oing m [shONpwAN]
shampoo

shamp(o)oing - mise en plis
[meez ON plee] shampoo and
set

si if; so; yes

SIDA m [seeda] AIDS

siècle m [see-ekl] century

siège m [see-ej] seat

sien*: le sien [luh s-yAN] his; hers; its

sienne*: la sienne [s-yen] his; hers; its

sien(ne)s*: les sien(ne)s [s-yAN, s-yen] his; hers; its

signal d'alarme m alarm; emergency lever

signer [seen-yay] to sign

signifier [seen-yeefee-ay] to mean

silence m [seelONss] silence

silencieux [seelONssee-uh] silent

s'il te plaît [seel tuh play] please; excuse me

s'il vous plaît [seel voo play] please; excuse me

simple [SANpl] simple; mere

sinon [seenON] otherwise

sirop pour la toux m [too] cough mixture

site historique m [seet eestoreek] place of historical interest

six [seess] six

sixième [seez-yem] sixth

ski m ski; skiing
faire du ski to go skiing

ski de descente [duh dessONt] downhill skiing

ski de fond [fON] cross-country skiing

skier [skee-ay] to ski

ski nautique waterski

slip m [sleep] underpants

slip de bain [duh bAN] swimming trunks

snack m snack bar

SNCB (Société Nationale des Chemins de Fer Belges) f [ess-en-say-bay] Belgian railways/

railroad

SNCF (Société Nationale des Chemins de Fer Français) f [ess-en-say-ef] French railways/railroad

société f [sos-yay-tay] company; society

sœur f [surr] sister

soi [swa] oneself

soie f [swa] silk

soif: j'ai soif [jay swaf] I'm thirsty

soigner [swan-yay] to treat, to nurse, to tend

soir m [swahr] evening
le soir in the evening
ce soir tonight

soirée f [swahray] evening; evening performance

soirée privée private party

sois [swa] be

soit ... soit ... [swa] either ... or ...

soixante [swassONt] sixty

soixante-dix [-deess] seventy

sol m ground

soldé [solday] reduced

solde: en solde [ON sold] reduced

solder [solday] to sell at a reduced price

soldes fpl [sold] sale

soldes d'été [daytay] summer sale

soleil m [solay] sun
au soleil in the sun

sombre [sONbr] dark

sommeil: j'ai sommeil [jay somay] I'm sleepy

sommes: nous sommes [som] we are

sommet m [somay] summit

somnifère m [somneefair] sleeping pill

son* [SON] his; her; its

son m sound

sonnette f bell

sonnette d'alarme alarm bell

sonnette de nuit night bell

sont: ils/elles sont [SON] they are

sorte f [sort] sort
de sorte que so that

sortie f [sortee] exit, way out

sortie de camions vehicle exit

sortie de secours emergency exit

sortie piétons exit for pedestrians

sortir [sorteer] to go out; to take out

SOS Femmes [ess-o-ess fam] Women's Aid Centre

SOS Médecin [mayd-SAN] 24-hour emergency medical service found in large towns

souci m [soossee] worry
se faire du souci (pour) to worry (about)

soucoupe f [sookoop] saucer

soudain [soodAN] suddenly

souffrant [soofrON] unwell

souffrir [soofreer] to be in pain; to suffer

souffrir de to suffer from

souhait: à vos souhaits [soo-ay] bless you

souhaiter [soo-ettay] to wish

(for)

souliers mpl [sool-yay] shoes

sourcil m [soorseel] eyebrow

sourd [soor] deaf

sourire [sooreer] to smile

souris f [sooree] mouse

sous [soo] under

sous réserve de toute modification subject to modifications

sous-sol m basement

sous-titré [-teetray] subtitled

sous-titres mpl [-teetr] subtitles

sous-vêtements mpl [-vetmON] underwear

soutien-gorge m [soot-yAN-gorj] bra

souvenir: se souvenir de [suh soovuhneer duh] to remember

souvent [soovON] often

soyez [swy-yay] be

soyez le bienvenu [luh b-yAN-vuhn∞] welcome

sparadrap m [sparadra] sticking plaster

spécialement [spays-yalmoN] especially

spectacle m [spektakl] show

spéléologie f pot-holing

sports d'hiver mpl [spor deevair] winter sports

stade m [stad] stadium

stage m [stahj] training course

standardiste m/f [stONdardeest] operator

starter m choke

station de métro f [stass-yON duh maytro] underground station

station de taxis taxi rank

stationnement à durée limitée restricted parking

stationnement alterné parking on alternate sides of the street on 1st-15th and 16th-31st of the month

stationnement en épis interdit no angle parking

stationnement gênant no parking please

stationnement interdit no parking

stationnement limité à 30 minutes parking restricted to 30 minutes

stationnement payant pay to park here

stationnement réglementé limited parking

stationnement toléré 2 minutes parking for 2 minutes only

stationner [stass-yonay] to park

station-service f [stass-yon-sairveess] petrol/gas station

station thermale [tairmahl] spa

stérilet m [stayreelay] IUD, coil

strapontin m [strapontAN] fold-down seat

studio m flatlet

stylo m [steelo] pen

stylo à bille [bee] biro®

stylo-feutre [furtr] felt-tip pen

su [soo] known

substance dangereuse dangerous substance

sucette f [soosset] lollipop

sucré [sookray] sweet

sud m [sood] south
au sud de south of

suffire [soofeer] to be sufficient
ça suffit [sa soofee] that's enough

suis: je suis [swee] I am

Suisse f [sweess] Switzerland

suisse Swiss

Suisse romande [romOnd] French-speaking Switzerland

suivant [sweevON] next

suivre [sweevr] to follow
faire suivre to forward

sujet: au sujet de [o soojay duh] about

super m [soopair] 4 star petrol; (US) premium (gas)
super! great!

supermarché m [soopairmarshay] supermarket

supplément m [sooplaymON] extra fare, extra charge, supplement

supporter [sooportay] to tolerate, to stand; to support

supposer [soopozay] to suppose

sur [soor] on

sûr [soor] sure

surgelé [soorjelay] frozen

surgelés mpl frozen foods

surnom m [soornON] nickname

surprenant [soorpruhnON] surprising

surtout [soortoo] above all; especially

surveillant m [soorvayON] supervisor; guard

surveillant de plage [duh plahj] lifeguard

survêtement de sport m

[soorvetmON duh spor] tracksuit

SVP (s'il vous plaît) please

sympa [sANpa] nice

sympathique [sANpateek] nice

syndicat d'initiative m [sANdeeka deeneess-yateev] tourist information centre

T

t'* (to) you; yourself

ta* your

tabac m [taba] tobacco; tobacconist and newsagent (also sells stamps)

tabac-journaux m newsagent, tobacco store and news vendor (also sells stamps); newspaper kiosk

tableau m [tablo] painting

tableau de bord [duh bor] dashboard

tache f [tash] stain

taille f [tī] size; waist

tailleur m [tī-urr] tailor; lady's suit

taisez-vous [tezzay-voo] shut up

tais-toi [tay-twa] shut up

talc m talcum powder

talon m [talON] heel

talon-minute heel bar

tandis que [tONdee kuh] whereas; while

tant (de) [tON] so much; so many

tant mieux [m-yuh] so much the better

tant pis [pee] too bad

tant que as long as

tante f [tONt] aunt

tapis m [tapee] rug

tapis roulant [roolON] moving walkway; baggage carousel

tard [tar] late

tarif m [tareef] price

tarif des consommations price list

tarif normal first class mail

tarif réduit reduced fare; second class mail

tarifs postaux postage rates

tarifs postaux intérieurs inland postage rates

tarifs postaux pour l'étranger overseas postage rates

tasse f [tass] cup

taureau m [toro] bull

taux m [toh] rate

taux à l'achat buying rate

taux à la vente selling rate

taux de change [duh shONj] exchange rate

taxis - tête de station taxi rank, queue here

TCF (Touring club de France) m [tay-say-ef] French automobile association

te* [tuh] (to) you; yourself

TEE (Trans-Europe-Express) m [tay-uh-uh] first class trans-European express

teint m [tAN] complexion

teint dyed

teinte f [tANt] colour, shade

teinturerie f [tANtoor-uhree] dry cleaner's

teinturier m [tANtooree-ay] dry-cleaner's

télé f [taylay] TV

télécarte f [taylay-kart] phonecard

télécartes en vente ici phonecards sold here

télécopie f fax

téléférique m [taylayfayreek] cable car

téléphone à carte m cardphone

téléphone interurbain long-distance telephone

téléphoner (à) [taylayfonay] to phone

télésiège m [taylaysee-ej] chairlift, ski lift

téléski m ski tow

Télétel® free computerized service available in post offices instead of the phonebook

téléviseur m [taylayveezurr] television set

tellement [telmON] so

tellement (de) so much; so many

tel(s) such

témoin m [taymwAN] witness

tempête f [tONpet] storm

tempête de neige [duh nej] snowstorm

temple m [tONpl] Protestant church

temps m [tON] time; weather de temps en temps from time to time

tenez votre droite keep to the right

tenir [tuhneer] to hold; to keep

tennis fpl [tenneess] trainers

tente f [tONt] tent

terminer [tairmeenay] to finish

terrain m [terrAN] pitch, field, ground

terrain de camping [duh kONpeeng] campsite

terrain pour caravanes [poor karavan] caravan site

terre f [tair] earth

tes* [tay] your

tête f [tet] head

tête de station taxi rank, queue here

TGV (Train à grande vitesse) m [tay-jay-vay] high-speed train

théière f [tay-air] teapot

tiède [t-yed] lukewarm

tien*: le tien [luh t-yAN] yours

tienne*: la tienne [t-yen] yours à la tienne! your health!

tiennent: ils/elles tiennent [t-yen] they hold

tien(ne)s*: les tien(ne)s [t-yAN, t-yen] yours

tiens: je/tu tiens [t-yAN] I/you hold

tient: il/elle tient [t-yAN] he/she/it holds

timbre m [tANbr] stamp

timbres de collection collectors' stamps

tir m [teer] shooting

tire-bouchon m [teer-booshON] corkscrew

tirer [teeray] to pull; to shoot

tirez [teeray] pull

tissu m [teessoo] material

tissus fabrics

titre de transport ticket

toi* [twa] you

toile de tente f [twal duh tONt] tent

toilette: faire sa toilette [twalet] to have a wash

toilettes fpl [twalet] toilets; (US) restroom
les toilettes sont dans la cour the toilet is in the back yard

toit m [twa] roof

tomber [tONbay] to fall

tomber en panne [ON pan] to break down

tomber en panne d'essence to run out of petrol

tomber malade to fall ill

ton* [tON] your

tonalité f [tohnaleetay] ringing tone

tonnage limité weight limit

tonnerre m [tonair] thunder

torchon à vaisselle m [torshON a vess-el] tea towel

tort: avoir tort [avwahr tor] to be wrong

tôt [toh] early

toucher [tooshay] to touch

toujours [toojoor] always; still

tour m tour; turn

tour f tower

tour de hanches m [duh ONsh] hip measurement

tour de poitrine [pwatreen] bust/chest measurement

tour de taille [tī] waist measurement

tour en voiture [vwatoor] drive

tourner [toornay] to turn

tournevis m [toornuhvee] screwdriver

tous [too] all; every
tous les deux both of them
tous les jours every day
tous les jours sauf ... every day except ...
tous les matins every morning

tousser [toossay] to cough

tout [too] everything; all; every
du tout at all
en tout altogether
à tout à l'heure! [a toota lurr] see you later!

tout à fait [too ta fay] entirely; altogether

tout compris [kONpree] all inclusive

tout de suite [toot sweet] immediately

tout droit [drwa] straight ahead

toute [toot] all; every
toute la journée all day

toutefois [tootfwa] however

toute personne prise en flagrant délit de vol sera poursuivie all shoplifters will be prosecuted

toutes [toot] all; every

toutes directions all directions

toutes opérations all transactions

toutes taxes comprises inclusive of taxes

tout le monde [too luh mONd] everyone

toux f [too] cough

traduction f [tradOOx-yON] translation

FRENCH ◆ ENGLISH |Tr

traduire [tradweer] to translate

train m [trAN] train

un train peut en cacher un autre there may be another train hidden behind this one

être en train de faire quelque chose to be doing something

train à supplément train for which you must pay a supplement

train auto-couchettes motorail

train direct direct train

train en partance pour ... train leaving for ...

train omnibus slow train

train rapide express train

trains au départ departures

train supplémentaire extra train

traitement m [tretmON] (course of) treatment

traitement de texte word processing; word processor

traiteur m [treturr] delicatessen

tranche f [trONsh] slice

tranquille [trONkeel] quiet

transactions avec l'étranger overseas business

transpirer [trONspeeray] to sweat

travail m [travī] work

travailler [travī-ay] to work

travaux mpl [travō] roadworks; building work

traversée f [travairsay] crossing

traverser [travairsay] to cross, to go through

treize [trez] thirteen

trembler [trONblay] to tremble

trente [trONt] thirty

très [tray] very

très bien, merci [b-yAN] very well, thank you

tribunal m [treebOOnal] court

tricot m [treeko] knitting; jumper

tricoter [treekotay] to knit

tricots knitwear

triste [treest] sad

trois [trwa] three

troisième [trwaz-yem] third

tromper [trONpay] to deceive

se tromper to be wrong

se tromper de numéro to dial the wrong number

trop [tro] too; too much

trop de too much; too many

trottoir m [trotwahr] pavement

trou m [troo] hole

trouver [troovay] to find

truc m [trOOk] thing

TTC (toutes taxes comprises) inclusive of tax

tu* [tOO] you

tuer [tOO-ay] to kill

tunnel de lavage m [tOOnel duh lavahj] car-wash tunnel

tutoyer [tOOtwy-ay] to use the familiar 'tu' form

tuyau m [twee-yo] pipe

TVA (taxe sur la valeur ajoutée) f [tay-vay-ah] VAT

TV par câble f [tay-vay par kahbl] cable TV

U

ulcère m [OOlsair] ulcer

un* [AN] a; one

une* [OOn] a; one

unité f [ɔɔneetay] unit

urgence f [ɔɔrjoNss] emergency

urinoir m [ɔɔreenwahr] public
urinal

usage: l'usage des WC est
interdit pendant l'arrêt du train
en gare do not use the toilet
while the train is in a station

usage externe for external use

usine f [ɔɔzeen] factory

ustensiles de cuisine cooking
utensils

utile [ɔɔteel] useful

utilisateur m [ɔɔteeleezaturr] user

utiliser [ɔɔteeleezay] to use

utiliser avant ... use before ...

utilisez un stylo à bille et
appuyez fortement use a ball-
point pen and write firmly

V

va: il/elle va he/she/it goes
comment ça va? [komoN sa]
how are you?
il va bien [eel va b-yaN] he's
well
il va mal he's not well
le bleu me va bien blue suits
me

vacances fpl [vakoNss] holiday,
vacation

vacances annuelles annual
holiday

vaccin m [vaxaN] vaccination

vache f [vash] cow

vachement [vashmoN] bloody,
damn(ed)

vagin m [vajaN] vagina

vague f [vag] wave

vague de chaleur [duh shalurr]
heatwave

vais: je vais [vay] I go

vaisselle f [vess-el] crockery
faire la vaisselle to do the
washing up

valable [val-abl] valid

valable jusqu'au ... valid until ...

validez [valeeday] validate

valise f [valeez] suitcase

vallée f [valay] valley

valoir [valwahr] to be worth

varappe f [varap] rock climbing

variable [varee-abl] changeable

varicelle f [vareessel]
chickenpox

vase m [vahz] vase

vas: tu vas [va] you go

vas-y [va-zee] go on

vaut: il vaut [vo] it is worth

véhicule m [vay-eekɔɔl] vehicle

vélo m [vaylo] bicycle
faire du vélo to cycle

vélomoteur m [-moturr] moped

vendanges fpl [voNdoNj] wine
harvest

vendangeur: on demande des
vendangeurs grape pickers
wanted

vendeur m, vendeuse f [voNdurr,
-urz] shop assistant;
salesman; saleswoman

vendre [voNdr] to sell
à vendre for sale

vendredi [voNdruhdee] Friday

vendu uniquement sur
ordonnance sold on
prescription only

venir [vuhneer] to come
venir de faire quelque chose to
have just done something
faire venir to send for
vent m [VON] wind
vente f [VONt] sale; selling rate
en vente ici available here
ventes hors taxes à bord duty
free sales aboard
vent fort strong wind
ventilateur m [VONteelaturr] fan
ventre m [VONtr] stomach
verglas m [vairgla] black ice
vérifier [vayreef-yay] to check
vérifiez votre monnaie check
your change
vernis à ongles m [vairnee a ONgl]
nail polish
verrai: je verrai [vairray] I will
see
verra: il/elle verra [vairra] he/
she/it will see
verras: tu verras [vairra] you will
see
verre m [vair] glass
verre à eau [o] tumbler
verre à vin [VAN] wineglass
verrez: vous verrez [vairray] you
will see
verrons: nous verrons [vairrON]
we will see
verront: ils/elles verront [vairrON]
they will see
verrou m [vairroo] bolt
verrouiller [vairoo-yay] to bolt; to
lock
vers m [vair] verse
vers towards; about
versement m [vairss-mON]

payment, deposit
verser [vairsay] to pay; to pour
version originale f [vairss-yON
oreejeenal] in the original
language
vert [vair] green
vessie f [vessee] bladder
veste f [vest] jacket
vestiaire m [vestee-air]
cloakroom; (US)
checkroom; changing room
vêtements mpl [vetmON] clothes
vêtements dames ladies'
fashions
vêtements enfants children's
wear
vêtements femmes ladies' wear
vêtements hommes menswear
vêtements messieurs menswear
vétérinaire m [vaytayreenair] vet
veuf m [vurf] widower
veuillez ... [vuh-ee-yay] please ...
veuillez établir votre chèque à
l'ordre de ... please make
cheques payable to ...
veuillez éteindre votre moteur
please switch off engine
veuillez fermer la porte please
close the door
veuillez libérer votre chambre
avant midi please vacate your
room by 12 noon
veuillez patienter please wait
veuillez patienter, nous traitons
votre demande please wait,
your request is being
processed
veulent: ils/elles veulent [vurl]
they want

veut: il/elle veut [vuh] he/she/it wants
cela **veut** dire … that means …
veuve f [vurv] widow
veux: je/tu veux [vuh] I/you want
vexer [vexay] offend
vidange f [veedONj] oil change
vide [veed] empty
vide-ordures m [-ord00r] garbage chute
vie f [vee] life
vieille [v-yay] old
vieille ville f [veel] old town
viendrai: je viendrai [v-yANdray] I will come
viendra: il/elle viendra [v-yANdra] he/she/it will come
viendras: tu viendras [v-yANdra] you will come
viendrez: vous viendrez [v-yANdray] you will come
viendrons: nous viendrons [v-yANdrON] we will come
viendront: ils/elles viendront [v-yANdrON] they will come
viennent: ils/elles viennent [v-yen] they come
viens: je/tu viens [v-yAN] I/you come
vient: il/elle vient [v-yAN] he/she/it comes
vieux, f vieille [v-yuh, v-yay] old
vignette f [veen-yet] road tax disc; postage label
vignettes montant au choix select postage labels to required value
vignoble m [veen-yobl] vineyard

vilebrequin m [veelbruhkAN] crankshaft
ville f [veel] town
en ville in town; to town
ville jumelée avec … twin town …
vingt [vAN] twenty
vins et spiritueux wine merchant
viol m [veeol] rape
violet [veeolay] purple
violon m [veeolON] violin
virage m [veerahj] bend
virage dangereux dangerous bend
virages sur … **km** bends for … km
virement m [veermON] transfer
vis f [vee] screw
visage m [veezahj] face
viseur m [veezurr] viewfinder
visite guidée f [veezeet geeday] guided tour
visiter [veezeetay] to visit
visitez … visit …
vite [veet] quick; quickly
vitesse f speed; gear
vitesse limitée à … speed limit …
vitre f [veetr] window
vitrine f [veetreen] shop window
vivant [veevON] alive
vivre [veevr] to live
VO (version originale) [vay-o] in the original language
vœux: meilleurs vœux [may-yurr vuh] best wishes
voici [vwa-see] here is; here are; here you are

voie f [vwa] platform; track; lane
par voie orale orally

voie ferrée railway

voie pour véhicules lents crawler lane

voilà [vwala] here is; here are; there you are
le voilà there he is

voile f [vwal] sail; sailing

voilier m [vwal-yay] sailing boat

voir [vwahr] to see

voisin m, voisine f [vwazAN, -zeen] neighbour

voiture f [vwatOOr] car; coach; carriage
en voiture by car

voiture de queue rear car

voiture de tête front car

voix f [vwa] voice

vol m flight; theft

volant m [volON] steering wheel

vol à voile [vwal] gliding

vol direct direct flight

voler [volay] to steal; to fly

volets mpl [volay] shutters

voleur m [volurr] thief

volley m [volay] volleyball

vols intérieurs mpl [vol zANtayree-urr] domestic flights

vols internationaux [zAntairnass-yono] international flights

vomir [vomeer] to be sick, to vomit

vont: ils/elles vont [vON] they go

vos* [vo] your

votre* [votr] your

vôtre*: le/la vôtre [luh/la vohtr] yours

à la vôtre! cheers!

vôtres*: les vôtres [lay vohtr] yours

voudraient: il/elles voudraient [voodray] they would like

voudrais: je/tu voudrais [voodray] I/you would like

voudrait: il/elle voudrait [voodray] he/she/it would like

voudriez: vous voudriez [voodree-ay] you would like

voudrions: nous voudrions [voodree-ON] we would like

voulez: que voulez-vous? [kuh voolay-voo] what do you want?

voulez-vous ...? do you want ...?

voulez-vous un reçu? do you want a receipt?

vouloir [voolwahr] to want

vouloir dire [deer] to mean

voulu [voolOO] wanted

vous* [voo] you; (to) you
vous désirez? can I help you?

vous êtes ici you are here

vouvoyer [voovwy-ay] to use the polite 'vous' form

voyage m [vwy-ahj] trip, journey

voyage d'affaires [dafair] business trip

voyage de noces [duh noss] honeymoon

voyage organisé [organeezay] package tour

voyager [vwy-ahjay] to travel

voyageur m [vwy-ahjurr] traveller

voyagiste m [vwy-ahjeest] tour operator

vrai [vray] true; real
  à vrai dire actually
vraiment [vraymON] really
vu [vOO] seen
vue f [vOO] view

W

wagon m [vagON] carriage
wagon-lit [-lee] sleeper,
  sleeping car
wagon-restaurant [-restorON]
  dining car
WC mpl [vay-say] toilet

Y

y [ee] there; it
  y a-t-il ...? [yateel] is there ...?;
  are there ...?
yeux mpl [yuh] eyes

Z

zéro [zayro] zero
zone bleue f [zon bluh]
  restricted parking area
zone piétonne [p-yayton]
  pedestrian precinct
zone piétonnière [p-yaytonair]
  pedestrian precinct

Menu Reader:

Food

abats [aba] offal

abricot [abreeko] apricot

agneau [an-yo] lamb

aiguillette de bœuf [ay-gwee-yet duh burf] slices of rump steak

ail [ī] garlic

ailloli [ī-olee] garlic mayonnaise

à la broche [ala brosh] roasted on a spit

à l'ail [alī] with garlic

à la jardinière [ala jardeen-yair] with assorted vegetables

à l'ancienne [aloNs-yen] traditional style

à la normande [ala normONd] in cream sauce

à la provençale [ala provONsahl] cooked in olive oil with tomatoes, garlic and herbs

alose [aloze] shad (fish)

amande [amoNd] almond

ananas [anana] pineapple

anchois [ONshwa] anchovies

andouillette [ONdoo-yet] small, spicy tripe sausage

anguille [ONgwee] eel

araignée de mer [aren-yay duh mair] spider crab

arête [aret] fishbone

artichaut [artee-sho] artichoke

asperge(s) [aspairj] asparagus

aspic de volaille [vol-ī] chicken in aspic

assaisonnement [assezonuhmoN] seasoning; dressing

assiette anglaise [ass-yet ONglez] selection of cold meats

aubergine aubergine, eggplant

au choix ... [o shwa] choice of ...

aux câpres [o kapr] in caper sauce

avocat [avoka] avocado

baba au rhum [o rum] rum baba

baguette stick of bread, French stick

banane [banan] banana

bananes flambées [banan floNbay] bananas flambéd in brandy

barbue [barbOO] brill (fish)

bâtard [batar] a half-size French stick (250g)

bavaroise [bavarwaz] light mousse

bavette à l'échalote [bavet a layshalot] grilled beef with shallots

béarnaise [bay-arnez] with béarnaise sauce (sauce made from eggs and butter)

beaufort [bofor] hard cheese from Savoie

bécasse [baykass] woodcock

béchamel [bayshamel] white sauce, béchamel sauce

beignet [ben-yay] fritter, doughnut

beignet aux pommes [o pom] apple fritter

betterave [betrahv] beetroot; (US) red beet

beurre [burr] butter

beurre d'anchois [dONshwa] anchovy paste

beurre d'estragon [destragoN] tarragon butter

beurre noir [nwahr] dark melted
butter

bien cuit [b-yan kwee] well done
(meat)

bifteck [beeftek] steak

bifteck de cheval [duh shuhval]
horsemeat steak

biscuit de Savoie [beess-kwee duh
savwa] sponge cake

bisque d'écrevisses [beesk
daykruhveess] freshwater
crayfish soup

bisque de homard [duh omar]
lobster bisque

bisque de langoustines
[loNgoosteen] saltwater
crayfish soup

blanquette de veau [bloNket duh
vo] veal stew

bleu [bluh] very rare; rare;
blue

bleu d'Auvergne [dovairn] blue
cheese from Auvergne

bœuf [burf] beef

bœuf à la ficelle [feesel] beef
cooked in stock

bœuf bourguignon [boor-geen-
yoN] beef cooked in red wine

bœuf en daube [oN dohb] beef
casserole

bœuf miroton [meerotoN] boiled
beef with onions

bœuf mode [mod] beef stew
with carrots

boisson [bwassoN] drink

bolet [bolay] boletus (mushroom)

bouchée à la reine [booshay ala
ren] vol au vent

boudin [boodAN] black pudding

boudin blanc [bloN] white
pudding

boudin noir [nwahr] black
pudding

bouillabaisse [booyabess] spicy
fish soup from the Midi

bouilli [boo-yee] boiled

bouillon [booyoN] stock

bouillon de légumes [duh
laygoom] vegetable stock

bouillon de poule [pool] chicken
stock

boulette [boolet] meatball

bouquet rose [bookay roz]
prawns

boutargue [bootarg] smoked
fish roe

braisé [brezay] braised

brandade de morue [broNdad duh
moroo] cod and potatoes,
mashed

brioche [bree-osh] round bun

brochet [broshay] pike

brochette [broshet] kebab

brugnon [broon-yoN] nectarine

cabillaud [kabee-yo] cod

cacahuètes [kaka-wet] peanuts

caille [kī] quail

cake fruit cake

cal(a)mar squid

canapé [kanapay] small open
sandwich, canapé

canard [kanar] duck

canard à l'orange [loroNj] duck
in orange sauce

canard aux cerises [o suhreez]
duck with cherries

canard aux navets [o navay]

duck with turnips

canard laqué [lakay] Chinese
roast duck, Peking duck

canard rôti [rotee] roast duck

caneton [kantON] duckling

cantal [kONtal] hard cheese
from Auvergne

câpres [kapr] capers

carbonnade [karbonad]
charcoal-grilled beef

cardon [kardON] cardoon,
vegetable similar to celery

cari [karee] curry

carotte [karot] carrot

carottes râpées [rapay] grated
carrots (with vinaigrette)

carottes Vichy carrots in butter
and parsley

carpe [karp] carp

carré d'agneau [karray dan-yo]
rack of lamb

carrelet [karlay] plaice

carte [kart] menu

carvi [karvee] caraway

casse-croûte [kass-kroot]
sandwich; snack

cassis [kasseess] blackcurrant

cassoulet [kassoolay] casserole
with pork, sausages and
beans

céleri (en branches) [selree (ON
brONsh)] celery

céleri rave [rahv] celeriac

céleri rémoulade [raymoolad]
celeriac in mayonnaise and
mustard dressing

cèpe [sep] cepe (mushroom)

cerise [suhreez] cherry

cerises à l'eau de vie [lo duh vee]

cherries in brandy

cervelas [sairvuhla] saveloy
(highly seasoned sausage
made from brains)

cervelle [sairvel] brains

chabichou [shabeeshoo] goats'
and cows' milk cheese

champignon [shONpeen-yON]
mushroom

champignons de Paris [duh
paree] white button
mushrooms

champignons à la grecque [grek]
mushrooms in olive oil,
tomatoes and herbs

chanterelle chanterelle
(mushroom)

charlotte dessert consisting of
layers of fruit, cream and
biscuits

chasselas [shassla] white grape

châtaigne [shateñ] sweet
chestnut

chausson aux pommes [shohsON
o pom] apple turnover

cheval [shuhval] horse

chèvre [shevr] goats' milk
cheese

chevreuil [shevruh-ee] venison

chicorée [sheekoray] endive,
chicory

chicorée frisée [freezay] curly
lettuce

chiffonnade d'oseille [sheefonad
dozay] sorrel cooked in
butter

chips [sheeps] crisps, potato
chips

chocolatine [shokolateen]

chocolate puff pastry

chou [shoo] cabbage

chou à la crème cream puff

choucroute [shookroot] sauerkraut with sausages and smoked ham

chou-fleur [shooflurr] cauliflower

chou-fleur au gratin [o gratAN] cauliflower cheese

chou rouge [shoo rooj] red cabbage

choux de Bruxelles [duh broo-sel] Brussels sprouts

ciboulette [seeboolet] chives

cigarette [seegaret] kind of finger biscuit (eg to serve with ice cream)

citron [seetrON] lemon

citron vert [vair] lime

civet de lièvre [seevay duh lee-evr] jugged hare

clafoutis [klafootee] batter pudding with fruit

cochon de lait [koshON duh lay] sucking pig

cocktail de crevettes [kruhvet] prawn cocktail

cœur [kurr] heart

cœur d'artichaut [darteesho] artichoke heart

coing [kwAN] quince

colin [kolAN] hake

compote [kONpot] stewed fruit

compris [kONpree] included

comté [kONtay] hard cheese from the Jura area

concombre [kONkONbr] cucumber

confit de canard [kONfit duh kanar] duck preserve

confit d'oie [kONfee dwa] goose preserve

confiture [kONfeetoor] jam

confiture d'orange [dorONj] marmalade

congre [kONgr] conger eel

consommé [kONsommay] clear soup made from meat or chicken

consultez aussi l'ardoise other suggestions on the slate

consultez notre carte des desserts have a look at our dessert menu

coq au vin [kok o VAN] chicken in red wine

coque [kok] cockle

coquelet [koklay] young cockerel, poult

coquilles Saint-Jacques [kokee sAN jak] scallops

côte de porc [koht duh por] pork chop

côtelette [kotlet] chop

côtelette de porc [duh por] pork chop

cotriade bretonne [kotree-ad bruhton] fish soup from Brittany

coulis [koolee] creamy sauce or soup

coulis de framboises [duh frONbwahz] raspberry sauce

coulis de langoustines [lONgoosteen] saltwater crayfish sauce

coulommiers [koolom-yay] rich

medium-soft cheese

coupe [koop] ice cream dessert

coupe Danemark [danmark]
vanilla ice cream with hot
chocolate sauce

coupe des îles [day zeel] vanilla
ice cream with syrup, fruit
and whipped cream

courgette courgette, zucchini

court-bouillon [koor-booyON]
stock for poaching fish or
meat

couscous [kooskooss] semolina
(usually served with meat,
vegetables and hot spicy
sauce)

couscous royal [rwy-al]
couscous with meat

couvert [koovair] cover charge

crabe [krab] crab

crème [krem] cream; creamy
sauce or dessert

crème à la vanille [vanee] vanilla
custard

crème anglaise [ONglez] custard

crème brûlée à la cassonade
[brOOlay ala kassonad] custard
covered with brown sugar
and 'grilled'

crème Chantilly [shONtee-yee]
whipped cream

crème d'asperges [daspairj]
cream of asparagus soup

crème de bolets [duh bolay]
cream of mushroom soup

crème de marrons [marON]
chestnut purée

crème de volaille [vol-ī] cream
of chicken soup

crème d'huîtres [weetr] cream of
oyster soup

crème fouettée [foo-etay]
whipped cream

crème pâtissière [pateessee-air]
confectioner's custard

crème renversée [rONvairsay]
custard dessert in a mould

crème vichyssoise [veeshee-swaz]
cold potato and leek soup

crêpe [krep] pancake

crêpe à la béchamel [bayshamel]
pancake with béchamel
sauce

crêpe à la chantilly [shONtee-yee]
pancake with whipped
cream

crêpe à la crème de marrons
[krem de marON] pancake with
chestnut purée

crêpe à l'œuf [al-uhf] pancake
with a fried egg

crêpe au chocolat [o shokola]
pancake with chocolate
sauce

crêpe au fromage [fromahj]
cheese pancake

crêpe au jambon [jONbON] ham
pancake

crêpe au sucre [sOOkr] pancake
with sugar

crêpe au thon [tON] tuna
pancake

crêpe de froment [duh fromON]
wholemeal flour pancake

crêpes Suzette pancakes
flambéd with orange sauce

crépinette [kraypeenet] sausage
patty wrapped in fat

cresson [kressON] cress

crevette [kruhvet] prawn

crevette grise [greez] shrimp

crevette rose [roz] prawn

croque-madame [krok madam] toasted cheese sandwich with ham and eggs

croque-monsieur [krok muhss-yuh] toasted cheese sandwich with ham

crottin de Chavignol [krotAN duh shaveen-yol] small goats' cheese

crottin de chèvre chaud [shevr sho] small goats' cheese served hot

croûte au fromage [kroot o fromahj] toasted cheese

croûte forestière [forest-yair] mushrooms on toast

crudités [krOOdeetay] selection of salads or chopped raw vegetables

crustacés [krOOstassay] shellfish

cuit cooked

cuisses de grenouille [kweess duh gruhnoo-yuh] frogs' legs

cuissot de chevreuil [kweeso duh shevruh-ee] haunch of venison

darne de saumon grillée [darn duh somON gree-yay] grilled salmon steak

dartois [dartwa] pastry with jam

datte [dat] date

daurade [dorad] gilthead (fish)

dinde [dANd] turkey

échalote [ayshalot] shallot

écrevisse [aykruhveess] freshwater crayfish

écrevisses à la nage [nahj] freshwater crayfish in wine and vegetable sauce

émincé de veau [aymANsay duh vo] finely cut veal in cream sauce

emporter: à emporter [ONportay] to take away; (US) to go

endive [ONdeev] chicory, endive

endives au jambon [o jONbON] chicory with ham baked in the oven

endives braisées [brezay] braised chicory

entrecôte [ONtr-koht] rib steak

entrecôte au poivre [o pwahvr] steak fried with black peppercorns

entrecôte maître d'hôtel [metr dotel] steak with butter and parsley

entrée [ONtray] first course

entremets [ONtr-may] dessert

épaule d'agneau farcie [aypol dan-yo farsee] stuffed shoulder of lamb

éperlan [aypairlON] smelt (fish)

épice [aypeess] spice

épinards [aypeenar] spinach

épinards à la crème spinach with cream

épinards en branches [ON brONsh] leaf spinach

escalope à la crème escalope in cream sauce

escalope de dinde à la crème et

aux champignons [duh dANd]
turkey cutlet with cream
and mushrooms
escalope de veau milanaise [duh
vo meelanez] veal escalope
with tomato sauce
escalope de veau normande
[normOND] veal escalope in
cream sauce
escalope panée [panay] breaded
veal escalope
escargots [eskargo] snails
escargots de Bourgogne à la
douzaine dozen Burgundy
snails
espadon [espadON] swordfish
estouffade de bœuf [estoofad duh
burf] beef casserole
estragon [estragON] tarragon

faisan [fezzON] pheasant
fait maison [fay mezzON]
homemade
farci [farsee] stuffed
farine [fareen] flour
faux filet sauce béarnaise [fo
feelay] fillet steak with
béarnaise sauce
fenouil [fenoo-yuh] fennel
fèves [fev] broad beans
ficelle [feessel] French stick
thinner than a baguette
figue [feeg] fig
figue de barbarie prickly pear
filet [feelay] fillet
filet de bœuf Rossini [duh burf]
fillet of beef with foie gras
filet de canard au poivre vert
[duh kanar o pwahvr vair] duck

breast with green pepper
sauce
filet de perche [pairsh] perch
fillet
financière [feenONss-yair] rich
sauce (served with
sweetbread, dumplings etc)
fines herbes [feen zairb] herbs
flageolets [flajolay] flageolets,
small green beans
flambé [flONbay] flambé
flan [flON] custard tart; crème
caramel; egg custard
flétan [flaytON] halibut
foie [fwa] liver
foie de veau [duh vo] veal liver
foie gras [gra] duck or goose
liver preserve
foies de volaille [vol-ī] chicken
livers
fondant au chocolat [fONdON o
shokola] chocolate fondant;
kind of brownie
fonds d'artichaut [fON darteesho]
artichoke hearts
fondue [fONdoo] Swiss dish of
cheese melted in white wine
fondue bourguignonne [boor-
geen-yon] meat fondue
(cooked in oil)
fondue savoyarde [savvy-ard]
cheese fondue
forêt noire [foray nwahr] Black
Forest gateau
fraise [frez] strawberry
fraise des bois [day bwa] wild
strawberry
framboise [frONbwahz]
raspberry

frangipane [froNjeepan] almond pastry

frisée [freezay] curly lettuce

frisée aux lardons [o lardON] curly lettuce with bacon

frit [free] deep fried

frites [freet] chips, French fries

fromage [fromahj] cheese

fromage blanc [blON] cream cheese

fromage de chèvre [duh shevr] goats' cheese

fruité [frweetay] fruity

fruits [frwee] fruit

fruits de mer [duh mair] seafood

fumé [fOOmay] smoked

galantine [galONteen] cold meat in aspic

galette [galet] round flat cake; wholemeal pancake

garni [garnee] with French fries or rice and/or vegetables

gâteau au fromage [o fromahj] cheesecake

gaufre [gohfr] wafer; waffle

gaufrette [gohfret] wafer

gelée [juhlay] jelly
en gelée [ON] in aspic

génisse [jayneess] heifer

génoise [jaynwahz] sponge cake

gésier [jayzee-ay] gizzard

gibelotte de lapin [jeeblot duh lapAN] rabbit stewed in white wine

gibier [jeeb-yay] game

gigot d'agneau [jeego dan-yo] leg of lamb

gigue de chevreuil [jeeg duh shuhvruh-ee] haunch of venison

girolle [jee-rol] chanterelle (mushroom)

glace [glass] ice cream; ice

goujon [goojON] gudgeon (fish)

grand veneur [grON vuhnurr] sauce for game

gras-double [gra-doobl] tripe

gratin [gratAN] baked cheese dish
au gratin [o] baked in a milk, cream and cheese sauce

gratin dauphinois [dofeen-wa] potato gratin with grated cheese

gratin de carottes [duh karot] carrots au gratin

gratin de langoustines [lONgoosteen] saltwater crayfish au gratin

gratin de queues d'écrevisses [kuh daykruhveess] freshwater crayfish au gratin

gratinée [grateenay] baked onion soup

grenade [gruhnad] pomegranate

grillade [gree-yad] grilled meat

grillé [gree-yay] grilled

grive [greev] thrush

grondin [grONdAN] gurnard (fish)

groseille blanche [grossay blONsh] white currant

groseille rouge [rooj] red currant

gruyère [grwee-yair] hard Swiss cheese

hachis parmentier [ashee parmONtee-ay] shepherd's pie

hareng mariné [arON mareenay] marinated herring

haricot de mouton [areeko duh mootON] mutton stew with beans

haricots [areeko] green beans; beans

haricots blancs [blON] haricot beans

haricots verts [vair] green beans

herbes [airb] herbs

herbes de Provence [duh provONss] herbs from Provence

homard [omar] lobster

homard à l'américaine [lamaireeken] lobster with tomato and white wine sauce

huile de soja [weel duh soja] soya oil

huile de tournesol [toornuhsol] sunflower oil

huile d'olive [doleev] olive oil

huître [weetr] oyster

île flottante [eel flotONt] floating islands (meringue on top of custard)

jambon [jONbON] ham

jambon au madère [o madair] ham in Madeira wine

jambon de Bayonne [duh ba-yon] smoked and cured ham

jardinière de légumes [jardeen-yair duh laygOOm] mixed vegetables

jarret de veau [jarray duh vo] shin of veal

julienne (de légumes) [jOOlee-en duh laygOOm] soup with chopped vegetables

julienne type of white fish

kugelhof [kOOgelhohf] cake from Alsace

laitue [lettOO] lettuce

langouste [lONgoost] crayfish

langoustine [lONgoosteen] saltwater crayfish; scampi

langue de bœuf [lON-g duh burf] ox tongue

langue de chat [sha] kind of finger biscuit (served with ice cream etc)

lapereau [lapero] young rabbit

lapin [lapAN] rabbit

lapin à la Lorraine rabbit in mushroom and cream sauce

lapin à la moutarde [mootard] rabbit in mustard sauce

lapin chasseur [shassurr] rabbit in white wine and herbs

lapin de garenne [garren] wild rabbit

lard [lar] bacon

lardons [lardON] small cubes of bacon

laurier [loree-ay] bay leaf

léger [layjay] light

légumes [laygOOm] vegetables

lentilles [lONteel] lentils

lièvre [lee-evr] hare

limande [leemONd] dab, lemon sole

livarot [leevaro] strong, soft

cheese from the north of France

longe [lONj] loin

lotte [lot] burbot

loup au fenouil [loo o fuhnoo-yuh] bass with fennel

macaron [makarON] macaroon

macaroni au gratin [o gratAN] macaroni cheese

macédoine de légumes [massaydwan duh laygOOm] mixed vegetables with mayonnaise

mâche [mash] lamb's lettuce

magret de canard [magray duh kanar] duck breast

mangue [mON-g] mango

maquereau au vin blanc [makro o vAN blON] mackerel in white wine sauce

marcassin [marcassAN] young wild boar

marchand de vin [marshON duh van] in red wine sauce

mariné [mareenay] marinated

marron [marrON] chestnut

menthe [mONt] mint

menu [muhnOO] set menu

menu du jour [dOO joor] today's menu

menu gastronomique [gastronomeek] gourmet menu

merlan au vin blanc [mairlON o vAN blON] whiting in white wine

mérou [mayroo] grouper

miel [mee-el] honey

millefeuille [meel-fuh-ee] cream slice

mont-blanc [mON-blON] chestnut sweet topped with whipped cream

morilles [moree] morels (mushroom)

morue [morOO] cod

mouclade [mooklad] mussels in creamy sauce with saffron, turmeric and white wine

moules [mool] mussels

moules à la poulette [poolet] mussels in rich white wine sauce

moules marinière [mareen-yair] mussels in white wine

mousse au chocolat [o shokola] chocolate mousse

mousse au jambon [jONbON] light ham pâté

mousse de foie [duh fwa] light liver pâté

moutarde [mootard] mustard

mouton [mootON] mutton

mulet [mOOlay] mullet

munster [mANstair] strong cheese from eastern France

mûre [mOOr] blackberry

muscade [mOOskad] nutmeg

myrtille [meertee] bilberry

nature [natOOr] plain

navarin [navarAN] mutton stew with vegetables

navet [navay] turnip

nèfle [nefl] medlar

noisette [nwazet] hazelnut

noisette d'agneau [dan-yo]

small, round lamb steak

noix [nwa] walnut, nut

nouilles [noo-yuh] noodles

œuf [urf] egg

œuf à la coque [kok] boiled egg

œuf cocotte à la tomate [kokot ala tomat] egg cooked with tomato in the oven

œuf dur [d∞r] hard boiled egg

œuf en gelée [ON juhlay] egg in aspic

œuf mayonnaise egg mayonnaise

œuf mollet [molay] soft boiled egg

œuf poché [poshay] poached egg

œufs à la neige [uh ala nej] floating islands (meringue on top of custard)

œufs au lait [o lay] egg custard

œufs au vin [VAN] eggs poached in red wine

œufs brouillés [broo-yay] scrambled eggs

œufs en meurette [ON murret] poached eggs in wine sauce

œuf sur le plat [urf s∞r luh pla] fried egg

oie [wa] goose

oignon [onyON] onion

olive [oleev] olive

omelette au fromage [fromahj] cheese omelette

omelette au jambon [jONbON] ham omelette

omelette au naturel [nat∞rel] plain omelette

omelette aux champignons [o shONpeen-yON] mushroom omelette

omelette aux fines herbes [feen zairb] omelette with herbs

omelette nature [nat∞r] plain omelette

omelette paysanne [pay-eezan] omelette with potatoes and bacon

opéra [opayra] plain chocolate and coffee gateau

orange givrée [geevray] orange sorbet served in a scooped out orange

oseille [ohzay] sorrel

oursin [∞rsAN] sea urchin

pain [pAN] bread

pain au chocolat [o shokola] type of pastry with chocolate filling

pain au lait [lay] kind of sweet bun

pain aux noix [nwa] walnut bread

pain aux raisins [o rezzAN] kind of brioche with custard and sultanas

pain bagnat [ban-ya] tuna salad sandwich in wholemeal bread roll (from the French Riviera)

pain blanc [blON] white bread

pain complet [kONplay] wholemeal bread

pain de campagne [kONpañ] farmhouse bread/loaf

pain de mie [mee] sliced white bread

pain de seigle [segl] rye bread

pain de son [SON] bran bread

pain viennois [vee-enwa] Vienna loaf

palette de porc [palet duh por] pork shoulder

palourde [paloord] clam

pamplemousse [pONpl-mooss] grapefruit

panaché ... [panashay] mixed ...

panade [panad] bread soup

pané [panay] breaded

papillote: en papillote [ON papee-yot] baked in foil or paper

parfait glacé [parfay glassay] frozen sweet

pastèque [pastek] water melon

pâte d'amandes [paht damONd] marzipan

pâté de canard [duh kanar] duck pâté

pâté de foie de volaille [fwa duh volī] chicken liver pâté

pâte feuilletée [paht fuh-ee-etay] puff pastry

pâtes [paht] pasta

pâtisserie [pateesree] cake; cake shop

pâtisserie maison [mezzON] home made gateau

paupiettes de veau [pohp-yet duh vo] rolled-up stuffed slice of veal

pavé de rumsteak [pavay duh] thick piece of steak

pêche [pesh] peach

pêche Melba peach melba

perdreau [pairdro] young partridge

perdrix [pairdree] partridge

persil [pairsee] parsley

petit beurre [puhtee burr] petit beurre biscuit

petite friture [puhteet freetOOr] whitebait

petit gâteau biscuit

petit pain [pAN] roll

petits pois [puhtee pwa] peas

petits fours [foor] decorated small cakes and biscuits

petit suisse [sweess] light cream cheese

pieds de cochon/porc [p-yay duh koshON/por] pigs' trotters

pigeon [peejON] pigeon

pigeonneau [peejono] young pigeon

pignatelle [peen-yatel] small cheese fritter

pilaf rice dish with meat, pilaf

pilaf de mouton [duh mootON] rice dish with mutton

pintade [pANtad] guinea fowl

pipérade [peepayrad] Basque dish with egg and tomatoes

pissaladière [peessaladee-yair] Provençal dish similar to pizza

pissenlit [peess-ON-lee] dandelion

pistache [peestash] pistachio

pizza quatre saisons [katr sezzON] four seasons pizza

plat de résistance [pla duh rayseestONss] main course

plat du jour [pla dOO joor] dish of

the day

plateau de fromages [plato duh fromahj] cheese board

plateau de fruits de mer [duh frwee duh mair] seafood platter

plat principal [pla pRANseepal] main course

pochouse [poshooz] fish casserole with white wine

point: à point [pwAN] medium

poire [pwahr] pear

poireau [pwahro] leek

poire belle-Hélène [bel aylen] pear in chocolate sauce

pois chiches [pwa sheesh] chickpeas

poisson [pwassON] fish

poivre [pwahvr] pepper (seasoning)

poivron [pwahvrON] pepper (vegetable)

poivron farci [farsee] stuffed pepper

pomme [pom] apple

pomme au four [o foor] jacket potato

pomme bonne femme [bon fam] baked apple

pomme de terre [duh tair] potato

pommes alumettes [pom alOOmet] French fries

pommes dauphine [dofeen] potato fritters

pommes de terre à l'anglaise [pom duh tair a lONglez] boiled potatoes

pommes (de terre) en robe de

chambre [ON rob duh shONbr] jacket potatoes

pommes (de terre) en robe des champs [ON rob day shON] jacket potatoes

pommes (de terre) sautées [sotay] fried potatoes

pommes frites [freet] chips, French fries

pommes paille [pī] finely cut chips, French fries

pommes vapeur [vapurr] boiled potatoes

porc [por] pork

potage [potahj] soup

potage bilibi [beeleebee] fish and oyster soup

potage Crécy [kraysee] carrot and rice soup

potage cressonnière [kressonee-yair] watercress soup

potage parmentier [parmONt-yay] leek and potato soup

potage printanier [pRANtan-yay] fine vegetable soup

potage Saint-Germain [SAN jairmAN] split pea soup

potage velouté [vuhlootay] creamy soup

pot-au-feu [potofuh] beef and vegetable stew

potée [potay] vegetable and meat hotpot

potiron [poteerON] pumpkin

poularde [poolard] fattened chicken

poule [pool] chicken

poule au pot [o po] chicken and vegetable stew

poule au riz [o ree] chicken with rice

poulet [poolay] chicken

poulet à l'estragon [lestragON] chicken in tarragon sauce

poulet basquaise [baskez] chicken with ham, tomatoes and peppers

poulet chasseur [shassurr] chicken with mushrooms and white wine

poulet créole [kray-ol] chicken in white sauce served with rice

poulet grillé [gree-yay] grilled chicken

poulet rôti [ro-tee] roast chicken

poulpe [poolp] octopus

praire [prair] clam

provençale [provONsal] with tomatoes, garlic and herbs

prune [prOOn] plum

pruneau [prOOno] prune

pudding plum pudding

purée [pOOray] mashed potatoes

purée de marrons [duh marrON] chestnut purée

purée de pommes de terre [pom duh tair] mashed potatoes

quatre-quarts [katr-kar] similar to Madeira cake

quenelle [kuhnel] dumpling, generally made with chicken or pike

queue de bœuf [kuh duh burf] oxtail

quiche lorraine quiche with bacon

râble de chevreuil [rabl duh shuhvruh-ee] saddle of venison

râble de lièvre [duh lee-evr] saddle of hare

raclette [raklet] Swiss dish of melted cheese with boiled potatoes and cold meat

radis [radee] radish

ragoût [ragoo] stew

raie [ray] skate

raie au beurre noir [o burr nwahr] skate fried in butter

raifort [rayfor] horseradish

raisin [rezzAN] grape(s)

râpé [rapay] grated

rascasse [raskass] scorpion fish

ratatouille [ratatoo-yuh] dish of stewed peppers, courgettes/ zucchinis, aubergines/ eggplants and tomatoes

ravigote [raveegot] dressing with herbs and shallots

reblochon [ruhbloshON] strong cheese from Savoie

reine-claude [ren-klohd] greengage

religieuse au chocolat/au café [ruhleejurz o shokola/o kafay] chocolate/coffee iced cream puff

rémoulade [ray-moolad] mayonnaise dressing with mustard and herbs

rigotte [reegot] small goat
cheese from the Lyons area

rillettes [ree-yet] potted pork
and goose meat

rillettes de saumon frais et fumé
[duh somON fray ay foomay]
fresh and smoked salmon
paté

ris de veau [ree duh vo] veal
sweetbread

rissole [reessol] meat pie

riz [ree] rice

riz à l'impératrice [lANpayratrees]
sweet rice dish

riz pilaf spicy rice with meat or
seafood

rognon [rON-yON] kidney

rognons au madère [rON-yON zo
madair] kidneys in Madeira
wine

romarin [romarAN] rosemary

roquefort [rokfor] blue ewes'
milk cheese from the south
of France

rosette de Lyon [rozet duh lee-ON]
dry salami-type sausage

rôti de porc [rotee duh por] roast
pork

rouget [roo-jay] mullet

rouille [roo-yuh] spicy sauce to
go with bouillabaisse

sabayon [saba-yON] dessert
made from egg yolks and
Marsala wine

sablé [sablay] shortbread

saignant [sen-yON] rare

saint-honoré [SANt-onoray] cake
with cream and choux

pastry decoration

saint-marcellin [SAN-marsuh-lAN]
goats' cheese

salade [sa-lad] salad; lettuce

salade aux noix [o nwa] green
salad with walnuts

salade composée [kompozay]
mixed salad

salade de gésiers [jayzee-ay]
green salad with gizzards

salade de tomates [tomat]
tomato salad

salade niçoise [neess-wahz]
salad with olives, tomatoes,
anchovies and hard boiled
eggs

salade russe [rOOss] diced
vegetables in mayonnaise

salade verte [vairt] green salad

salmis [salmee] game stew

salsifis [salseefee] oyster plant,
salsify

sandwich au fromage
[sONdweech o fromahj] cheese
sandwich

sandwich au jambon [jONbON]
ham sandwich

sandwich au saucisson
[soseesON] salami sandwich

sandwich aux rillettes [ree-yet]
pâté sandwich

sandwich crudités salad
sandwich

sandwich thon/mayonnaise [tON]
tuna/mayonnaise sandwich

sanglier [sON-glee-yay] wild boar

sauce aurore [o-ror] white sauce
with tomato purée

sauce aux câpres [o kapr] white

sauce with capers

sauce béarnaise [bay-ar-nez] sauce made from egg yolks, lemon juice or vinegar, butter and herbs

sauce béchamel [bayshamel] white sauce

sauce blanche [bloNsh] white sauce

sauce grand veneur [groN vuhnurr] sauce for game

sauce gribiche [greebeesh] dressing with hard boiled eggs, capers and herbs

sauce hollandaise [oloNdez] rich sauce made with eggs, butter and vinegar, served with fish

sauce madère [madair] Madeira sauce

sauce matelote [matlot] wine sauce

sauce Mornay [mornay] béchamel sauce with cheese

sauce mousseline [moossleen] hollandaise sauce with cream

sauce poulette [poolet] sauce with mushrooms, egg yolks and wine

sauce ravigote [raveegot] dressing with shallots and herbs

sauce rémoulade [ray-moolad] dressing made from mayonnaise, mustard and herbs

sauce suprême [sooprem] creamy sauce

sauce tartare mayonnaise with herbs, gherkins and capers

sauce veloutée [vuhlootay] white sauce with egg yolks and cream

sauce vinot [veeno] wine sauce

saucisse [sosseess] sausage

saucisse de Francfort [duh froNkfor] frankfurter

saucisse de Strasbourg [strazboorg] beef sausage

saucisson [sosseessoN] salami

saumon [somoN] salmon

saumon à l'oseille [lozay] salmon with sorrel

saumon fumé [somoN foomay] smoked salmon

sauté de dindonneau [dANdonno] sauté of turkey poult

savarin [savarAN] crown-shaped rum baba

seiche [sesh] cuttlefish

sel salt

selle d'agneau [sel dan-yo] saddle of lamb

selon arrivage depending on availability

service (non) compris service (not) included

sole bonne femme [bon fam] sole in white wine and mushrooms

sole meunière [muhn-yair] sole dipped in flour and fried in butter

soufflé au chocolat [o shokola] chocolate soufflé

soufflé au fromage [fromahj] cheese soufflé

soufflé au jambon [jONbON] ham soufflé

soupe [soop] thick soup

soupe à l'ail [lï] garlic soup

soupe à la tomate [tomat] tomato soup

soupe à l'oignon [lonyON] onion soup

soupe à l'oseille [lozay] sorrel soup

soupe au pistou [o peestoo] thick vegetable soup with basil

soupe aux choux [shoo] cabbage soup

soupe aux moules [o mool] mussel soup

soupe aux poireaux et pommes de terre [pwaro ay pom duh tair] leek and potato soup

soupe de légumes [laygoom] vegetable soup

soupe de poisson [pwassON] fish soup

steak au poivre [o pwahvr] pepper steak

steak frites [freet] steak and chips/French fries

steak haché [ashay] minced meat

steak sauce au poivre [o pwahvr] steak with pepper sauce

steak sauce au roquefort [rokfor] steak with roquefort cheese sauce

steak tartare raw minced beef with a raw egg

sucre [sookr] sugar

suprême de volaille [sooprem duh volï] chicken in cream sauce

surgelés [soorjuhlay] frozen food

surprise du chef [soorpreez doo shef] chef's surprise (gateau)

tajine [tajeen] North African stew of mutton or chicken, vegetables and prunes cooked in an earthenware dish

tanche [tONsh] tench (fish)

tartare tartar(e); raw

tarte [tart] tart; pie

tarte au citron meringuée [o seetrON muhrANgay] lemon meringue pie

tarte aux fraises [o frez] strawberry tart/pie

tarte aux myrtilles [meertee] bilberry tart

tarte aux poireaux [pwahro] leek flan

tarte aux pommes [pom] apple tart/pie

tarte frangipane [frONjeepan] almond cream tart/pie

tartelette [tartuh-let] small tart/pie

tarte Tatin [tatAN] baked apple dish

tartine [tarteen] buttered slice of bread

tendrons de veau [tONdrON duh vo] veal breast

terrine [terreen] rougher type of pâté

terrine du chef [doo shef] pâté maison, chef's special pâté

tête de veau [tet duh vo] calf's head

thon [tON] tuna fish

thon Mirabeau [meerabo] tuna cooked in eggs and milk

thym [tAN] thyme

tomate [tomat] tomato

tomme de Savoie [tom duh savwa] white cheese from Savoie

tourte [toort] pie

tourteau [toorto] kind of crab

tous nos plats sont garnis all our dishes are served with vegetables

tripes [treep] tripe

tripes à la mode de Caen [duh kON] tripe in spicy vegetable sauce

truffe [trOOf] truffle

truite au bleu [trweet o bluh] poached trout

truite meunière [muhn-yair] trout coated in flour and fried in butter

vacherin [vashrAN] strong, soft cheese from the Jura area

vacherin glacé [glassay] ice cream meringue

veau [vo] veal

velouté d'asperges [vuhlootay daspairj] cream of asparagus soup

velouté de tomates [tomat] cream of tomato soup

velouté de volaille [volī] cream of chicken soup

velouté d'huîtres [dweetr] cream of oyster soup

vermicelle [vairmeesel] very fine pasta used in soups

viande [vee-ONd] meat

viande hachée [ashay] minced meat

vichyssoise [veesheeswahz] cold vegetable soup

vinaigre [veenegr] vinegar

volaille [volī] poultry

yaourt [ya-oort] yogurt

Menu Reader:

Drink

---

alcool [alkool] alcohol

AOC (Appellation d'Origine Contrôlée) guarantee of the quality of a wine

Banyuls® [banyoolss] a sweet apéritif wine

bière [bee-air] beer

bière (à la) pression [press-yON] draught beer

bière (blonde) lager

bière brune [brOOn] bitter; dark beer

bière rousse [rooss] relatively sweet, fairly dark beer

blanc [blON] white wine; white

blanc de blancs [duh blON] white wine from white grapes

blanquette de Limoux [blONket duh leemoo] sparkling white wine from Languedoc

boisson [bwassON] drink

Bourgogne [boor-goñ] wine from the Burgundy area

Brouilly [broo-yee] red wine from the Beaujolais area

brut [brOOt] very dry

café [kafay] espresso, very strong black coffee

café au lait [o lay] white coffee

café crème [krem] white coffee

café glacé [glassay] iced coffee

café soluble [solOObl] instant coffee

café viennois [vee-enwa] coffee with whipped cream

calvados apple brandy from Normandy

camomille [kamomee] camomile tea

capiteux [kapeetuh] heady

carte des vins [kart day vAN] wine list

Chablis [shablee] dry white wine from Burgundy

chambré [shONbray] at room temperature

champagne [shONpañ] champagne

champagnisé [shONpan-yeezay] sparkling

Chartreuse [shartrurz] herb liqueur

Château-Margaux [shato margo] red wine from the Bordeaux area

Châteauneuf-du-Pape [shatonurf dOO pap] red wine from the Rhône valley

chocolat chaud [shokola sho] hot chocolate

chocolat glacé [glassay] iced chocolate drink

cidre [seedr] cider

cidre bouché [booshay] cider in bottle with a cork

cidre doux [doo] sweet cider

51® (cinquante-et-un) [sankONtay-AN] a brand of pastis

citron pressé [seetrON pressay] fresh lemon juice

cognac [kONyak] brandy

crème [krem] white coffee

crème de cassis [duh kasseess] blackcurrant liqueur

cru [krOO] raw; vintage

cru classé high quality wine

décaféiné [daykafay-eenay] decaffeinated

délimité de qualité supérieure superior quality wine

demi [duhmee] small draught beer; quarter of a litre of beer

demi-sec [duhmee-sek] medium dry

diabolo menthe/fraise etc [d-yabolo moNt/frez] mint/ strawberry etc cordial with lemonade

digestif [deejesteef] liqueur

eau [o] water

eau de vie [duh vee] spirit made from fruit

eau minérale [meenayral] mineral water

eau minérale gazeuse [gazurz] sparkling mineral water

Fendant [foNdoN] Swiss dry white wine

fine [feen] fine brandy, liqueur brandy

Fleurie [flurree] red wine from Beaujolais

frappé [frapay] well chilled, on ice

gazeux [gazurz] fizzy

Gewurztraminer [guh-wOOrztrameeanair] dry white wine from Alsace

gin-tonic gin and tonic

Gini® a kind of bitter lemon

glaçon [glassoN] ice cube

grand crème [groN krem] large white coffee

grand cru [krOO] fine vintage

Graves [grahv] red wine from the Bordeaux area

infusion [aNfOOz-yoN] herb tea

jus [jOO] juice

jus de pommes [duh pom] apple juice

jus d'orange [doroNj] orange juice

kir white wine with blackcurrant liqueur

kir royal champagne with blackcurrant liqueur

kirsch cherry brandy

lait [lay] milk

lait fraise/grenadine [frez/ gruhnadeen] milk with strawberry/grenadine cordial

limonade [leemonad] lemonade

Mâcon [makoN] wine from Burgundy

marc [mar] clear spirit distilled from grapes

Médoc [maydok] red wine from the Bordeaux area

menthe à l'eau [moNt a lo] mint cordial

méthode champenoise made in the same way as champagne

Meursault [murrso] wine from Burgundy

millésime [meelay-zeem] vintage

mousseux [moossuh] sparkling

Muscadet [m∞skaday] dry
  white wine from the Nantes
  area
muscat [m∞ska] sweet white
  wine

Noilly-Prat® [nwa-yee pra] an
  apéritif wine similar to Dry
  Martini
Nuits-Saint-Georges [nwee SAN
  jorj] red wine from
  Burgundy

orange pressée [orONj pressay]
  fresh orange juice

panaché [panashay] shandy
Passe-Tout-Grain [pass too grAN]
  red wine from Burgundy
pastis [pasteess] aniseed-
  flavoured alcoholic drink
Pernod® [pairno] a brand of
  pastis
pétillant [paytee-ON] sparkling
porto port
Pouilly-Fuissé [poo-yee-fweessay]
  dry white wine from
  Burgundy
premier cru [pruhm-yay cr∞]
  vintage wine
pression [press-yON] draught
  beer, draught

rhum [rom] rum
Rivesaltes® [reevsalt] a sweet
  apéritif wine
Ricard® [reekar] a brand of
  pastis
rosé [rozzay] rosé wine
rouge [rooj] red

Saint-Amour [sANtamoor] red
  wine from Beaujolais
Saint-Emilion [sAN-taymeelee-yON]
  red wine from the Bordeaux
  area
Sauternes [sotairn] fruity white
  wine from the Bordeaux
  area
Schweppes® tonic water
scotch scotch whisky
sec [sek] dry; neat
servir frais serve cool
sirop [seero] cordial

thé [tay] tea
thé à la menthe [mONt] mint tea
thé au lait [o lay] tea with milk
thé citron [seetrON] lemon tea
thé nature [nat∞r] tea without
  milk
tilleul [tee-yurl] lime-flower tea

VDQS (Vin Délimité de Qualité
  Supérieure) a category of
  wine between vin de table
  and AOC
verveine [vairven] verbena tea
Viandox® [vee-ONdox] beef
  stock, similar to Oxo®
vin [VAN] wine
vin blanc [blON] white wine
vin de pays [duh payee] regional
  wine
vin de table [duh tahbl] table
  wine
vin rosé [rozzay] rosé wine
vin rouge [rooj] red wine

Yvorne [eevorn] Swiss dry white
  wine